EAST–WEST PASSAGE

Also by Michael Edwardes:

A HISTORY OF INDIA (Thames & Hudson)
ASIA IN THE EUROPEAN AGE (Thames & Hudson)
BATTLES OF THE INDIAN MUTINY (Batsford)
THE LAST YEARS OF BRITISH INDIA (Cassell)
HIGH NOON OF EMPIRE (Eyre & Spottiswoode)
THE WEST IN ASIA 1850–1914 (Batsford)
BRITISH INDIA: A SURVEY OF THE NATURE AND EFFECTS OF ALIEN
RULE (SIDGWICK & JACKSON)
GLORIOUS SAHIBS: THE ROMANTIC AS EMPIRE-BUILDER (Eyre &
Spottiswoode)
PLASSEY: THE FOUNDING OF AN EMPIRE (Hamish Hamilton)
EVERYDAY LIFE IN EARLY INDIA (Batsford)
BOUND TO EXILE: THE VICTORIANS IN INDIA (Sidgwick & Jackson)
INDIAN TEMPLES AND PALACES (Hamlyn)
KING OF THE WORLD: THE LIFE AND TIMES OF SHAH ALAM,
EMPEROR OF HINDUSTAN (Secker & Warburg)

Michael Edwardes

EAST-WEST PASSAGE

The Travel of Ideas, Arts and Inventions between Asia and the Western World

TAPLINGER PUBLISHING COMPANY
NEW YORK

First Published in the United States in 1971 by
TAPLINGER PUBLISHING CO., INC.
New York, New York

Copyright © Michael Edwardes 1971

International Standard Book Number 0-8008-2355-9

Library of Congress Catalog Card Number 79-137663 1-24-77

Printed in Great Britain

CONTENTS

ILLUSTRATIONS

ACKNOWLEDGEMENTS

Archives Nationales, Paris, 16; Ashmolean Museum, Oxford, 24; Bibliothèque Publique et Universitaire, Geneva, 12; British Museum, London, 1, 7, 9, 13, 15, 21, 37, 47; Cassell & Co. Ltd, London, 31; Christ Church College, Oxford, 11; Country Life Ltd, London, 44; Edwardes Archive, London, 2, 4, 5, 6, 8, 17, 20, 27, 29, 32, 34, 38, 39, 40, 41, 45, 46, 49, 50, 52, 53, 54; Dr Desmond Flower, London, 28; Freer Gallery, Washington D.C., 26; Foreign and Commonwealth Office (India Office Library), London, 51; Mansell Collection, London, 14; Armand A. Mick, Vacaville, California, and Museum of the History of Science, Oxford, 22; National Film Archive, London, 36, 42; National Gallery, London, 25; National Tourist Organization of Greece, 3; Österreichische Nationalbibliothek, Vienna, 10; Radio Times Hulton Picture Library, London, 33; Royal Institute of British Architects (Drawings Collection), London, 43; Staatliche Museen, Berlin, 23; Tate Gallery, London, 35; Thames and Hudson Ltd, London, 48; United States Playing-Card Company, Cincinnati, 18, 19; Victoria and Albert Museum, London, 30.

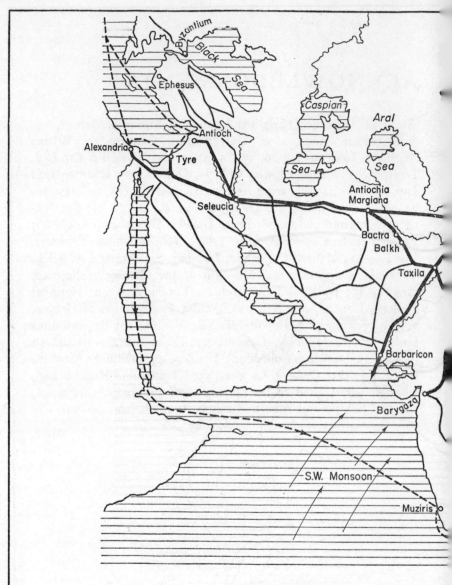

Byzantium
Black Sea
Caspian Sea
Aral Sea
Ephesus
Antioch
Alexandria
Tyre
Seleucia
Antiochia Margiana
Bactra
Balkh
Taxila
Barbaricon
Barygaza
S.W. Monsoon
Muziris

EASTERN TRADE ROUTES
at the time of the Roman Empire

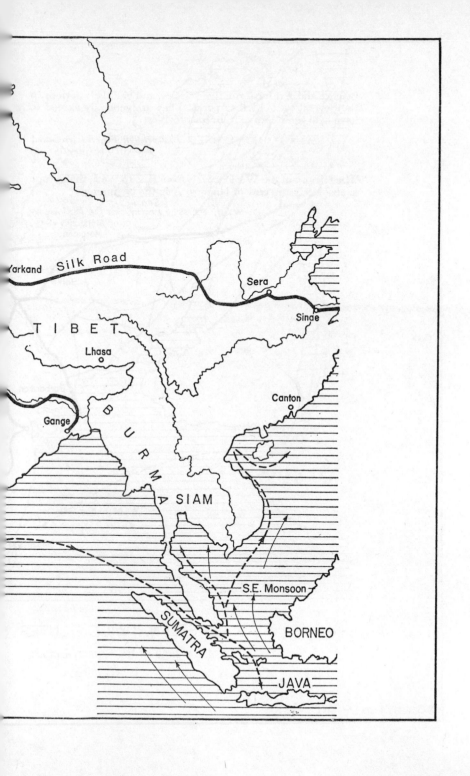

Science and Art have run their circles, and had their periods in the Several Parts of the World. They are generally agreed to have held their course from East to West.

SIR WILLIAM TEMPLE, *Essay upon the Ancient and Modern Learning* (1690)

The History of the World travels from East to West, for Europe is absolutely the end of History, Asia the beginning.

G. W. F. HEGEL, *Lectures in the Philosophy of History* (1832)

Preface

This book is an attempt to show something of the debt the peoples of the world owe to each others' civilizations and cultures. Many of the ideas, arts and inventions borrowed by one civilization from another have, over the years, become so well assimilated that they are now taken for granted as part of a *national* heritage. Yet, at some time in the near or remote past, they have made the long and often mysterious journey from one end of the world to the other. It is the story of these unrecognized debts, not the more obvious examples of cultural exchange, which I hope will give readers a taste of the surprise and excitement of discovery.

This book's main purpose is to demonstrate what kinds of things the West took from the East, what it did with them, and what it gave the East in return. It does not attempt to deal in any detail with the understanding of alien civilizations; oriental scholarship, as such, is touched upon only where it illuminates some particular episode in cultural history. The emphasis is placed not, for example, upon the progress of academic research in comparative linguistics, but upon the effects of language—in the form of literature—on novelists and poets; and the effects of art not on art historians but on painters and craftsmen. A similar attitude is taken towards inventions, and they are dealt with in terms not so much of their contribution to the development of technology— though this is of tremendous importance—as of how they influenced the lives of ordinary people. The technique of printing, for example, is seen as a revolutionary weapon, spreading literacy and education and opening the door to popular democracy—a *social* judgement, not a scientific one. Historians of science may well deplore this treatment, but this book is not for specialists in the various subjects that it deals with—though they may find some slight widening of their horizons if they are prepared to overlook its shortcomings in their own fields and read it for what it is—a general introduction to a vast subject, whose ramifications run through every level of human activity.

There are many problems facing the writer of this kind of book, especially as it is a pioneer work—for, to the best of my knowledge, this is the first book ever to treat the subject as a whole. Its range is as wide as the human mind, but its length is only 211 pages. To achieve in a brief volume a coherent, and interesting, view of nearly three thousand years of cultural exchange between Asia and the Western world has called for ruthless and nearly always agonizing discrimination. What is missing will be only too obvious to specialists. To them, I offer no apologies. I have read their books with care and often with profit. Indeed, the present work could not have been written without the authors, living and dead, of the thousands of books and articles in learned journals used in its preparation. A selection of the most valuable is given in the bibliography.

The problem of selection—of, frankly, what to leave out—was the major one, but there was also the problem of words and their meanings. Take *East* and *West*, for example, words used extensively throughout the text. What do they mean? In the modern world, they have come to be used in a special ideological sense. In this book, however, *East* and *West* are used in their old-fashioned and unpolitical sense. The East begins at the Bosphorus, and the Western world consists of the whole of Europe and, in the later parts of the book, North America.

The reader, too, may find he has his problems. However cosmopolitan we believe ourselves to be, deep in our unconscious minds lurk ancient prejudices. Some of these are racial, others national. Many are implanted at the most impressionable time of our lives, by apparently inoffensive school textbooks. I cannot help the reader with these problems before he has read the following pages. Afterwards, if I have succeeded at all, some of them at least should have disappeared.

Introduction

We always come back to the same questions. Who was talking about gear-wheels in 1st century B.C. Bactria? Did the Roman-Syrian merchant Chhin Lun, who visited China in A.D. 226, happen to take an active interest in cartography? Could a copy of a tractate of al-Haitham's on optics have reached Canton or Hangchow during his lifetime? What drawings of textile machinery could have been found in the baggage of Polo or Pegolotti?

JOSEPH NEEDHAM, *Science and Civilisation in China* (vol. I, 1954)

The Meeting of East and West

Today, the interchange of ideas and techniques is a simple process. Mass communications have destroyed barriers between minds. Accessibility often means no more than a journey to the nearest library, the cost of a subscription to a learned journal, or even the careful reading of a daily newspaper. The question, however, of how specific ideas and detailed techniques were transmitted in the past—and particularly in the remote past—is not so simple, and yet the answer, if there is a satisfactory one, is of considerable interest. The body of this book is concerned with the interaction of separate cultures in times where there is at least some historical certainty. But what of the period before this? Was there ever, for example, a time when there existed a universal culture, a continuity of East and West? Was there, perhaps, some common root of civilization, a centre from which it diffused throughout the world?

Not long ago, this question was the subject of great controversy among archaeologists and anthropologists. There were some who maintained—with a wealth of inductive detail—that all civilization radiated outwards from ancient Egypt; others, on just as much 'evidence', were able to derive Chinese culture from Mesopotamian origins. Such extremist views have very few supporters today, but this does not mean that cultures were entirely *self*-evolving. Parallel development in isolated cultures is, of course, to be expected; there is little doubt that in such conditions similar needs produce similar solutions, and primitive circumstances—both human and material—impose similar limitations on what is possible. But there are certain technical inventions (and even natural products, such as wheat) that can only have originated in one centre and been diffused outwards. These inventions are the most ancient and the most basic. The earliest civilizations of Mesopotamia are now believed to have been the source of such fundamental things as the wheel, the plough and weaving. Ancient Egypt supplied the swape, or counter-balanced bailing-bucket. From somewhere in the Fertile Crescent came the rotary quern. It

3

seems unlikely that any of these were separately—and independently—invented.

A glance at any world map reveals the closeness of the great river-valley civilizations of antiquity—the Nile, the Euphrates and the Indus. Only one stands out in isolation: the Yellow River, remote behind the immense barriers of the Himalayas and the harsh plateau of Tibet. Yet scholars, in recent years, have established the existence of a cultural continuity between China and Europe in the Bronze Age. This continuity is indicated by certain types of swords, tubes and buttons probably used to decorate harnesses, and a number of other items found at Hallstatt in Austria, in southern Russia and in China. All these were *purposeful*, and some of them were instruments of significant change—like the socketed celt, or hollow bronze axe fitted with a wooden handle, which was used to clear forests for agriculture. The purpose of some objects is still unknown. The bird-chariot, consisting of a bronze or pottery bird mounted on wheels, has been found in Egypt, China and Europe. Scholars have not yet come to any valid conclusion as to whether the bird-chariot was a toy or some sort of cult object, but there seems little doubt that it is an example of cultural diffusion from one end of the ancient world to the other. The difficulty of the route over the Himalayas restricted, though it did not wholly prohibit, the flow of ideas and techniques via northern India, but there appears to have been comparative facility of communication across the length of the Eurasian steppe.

It also seems reasonable that similar primitive societies should have produced similar ritual practices and similar mythologies. Rituals concerned with death ceremonies and sacrifices display a cultural pattern from the Aegean to China and South-East Asia. Fertility ceremonies—particularly those concerned with ploughing —have very close similarities. In all probability, much of this stems from the similarity of the means available to satisfy a widespread, similar need, rather than from diffusion from any single centre.

The growing sophistication of mankind, the development of skills of the mind and of the hand, increased the probability of independent technical invention. Where an invention appeared in two places simultaneously, or apparently independently, the problem of priority—of who thought of it first—has been exercising the minds of historians of science and technology in recent years. Their research has produced considerable, and continuing, revision of priorities. The problems of fixing these and of establishing at least the feasibility of the transmission of some particular technique, though formidable, are surpassed by the problems set by the actual movement of ideas. Certainly, there appears to be a general law concerning the travel of ideas. On the evidence available it is apparent that complete idea-systems do not travel—presumably because they are the product of a particular cultural milieu, in which they have specific ethnic relevances which do not exist elsewhere. Fragments, only, tend to be transmitted; there are many examples in this book. Yet there is, for example, an undeniable resemblance between Greek pneumatic medicine, Indian medicine, and Chinese physiological concepts, which points to a common origin. Astrological systems from Babylon, also, travelled to India and to China. These and other examples of the movement of complete, or almost complete, idea-systems are, however, the exception. On the whole, the travel of ideas was on a much smaller scale than that of techniques. Of the latter, the most important example is the transmission of technological inventions from China to Europe; something of this is told in the chapter entitled 'The Face and State of Things'. And yet, whereas inventions can be said to have poured into Europe in an almost continuous stream throughout the first thirteen hundred years of our era, very few Chinese *ideas*, scientific or aesthetic, made the long and difficult journey. The same applied in the reverse direction—for, until the arrival of the Jesuits at the beginning of the seventeenth century, China remained isolated from European ideas, in spite of the ease of communication between East and West during the preceding period.

This raises the whole dangerous question of the conditions necessary for the transmission and acceptance of ideas and techniques—dangerous because, though much thinking has been, and is being, done on the subject, the area of speculation remains vast. Nevertheless, the current state of research does permit certain general theories on the acceptance of ideas and techniques by one culture from another. Their actual movement, too, presents problems, but one thing at least is sure—the direction of that movement was primarily from East to West; until the nineteenth century, Europe had little to contribute to Asian (and, in particular, to Chinese) science and technology.

5

The *means* of transmission is fundamental to the movement of an idea or technique. The development of overland trade routes and the later expansion of maritime activity established communication between the West and Asia. These routes, though frequently interrupted, were never totally broken. Along them travelled not only trade goods but merchants, ambassadors and soldiers. The migrations of barbarian tribes—of Alans and Goths and various steppe peoples—which contributed to the fall of the Roman empire also provided carriers. So did the Mongols in the thirteenth century. It is undeniably established that, in Classical times and after, the conditions for transmission did exist. But though, generally speaking, we know from literary sources the names of certain individuals who *could* have carried ideas or techniques on their travels, the record is principally one of anonymous transmission, and is likely to remain so.

If the conditions favourable to transmission actually existed, what of the conditions favourable to acceptance of the idea or technique transmitted? All societies in the past were, in one sense, isolated—by language and the scripts used to express it, as well as by theologies and the idea-systems emerging from them. Chinese society was further isolated by distance. Where the great river-valley cultures of the ancient world interacted and continued to interact because of their proximity, China early developed a culture pattern distinctly her own. The separateness of Chinese civilization is perhaps best symbolized by its continued use of pictographic writing: that is, drawings conventionalized and stylized, but at one time representing the object referred to. Other scripts—cuneiform and hieroglyph, for example—developed into syllabic alphabets. The Chinese did not.

Perhaps the greater barrier to the acceptance of ideas was the difference in men's views of the nature of the universe. Even if medieval Europe had known of the Chinese concept of the universe as an empty space in which floated the planets and the stars, it could not have accepted it. European theology made the belief that the world was the centre of the universe into an act of faith and it was only with the growth of scientific scepticism that this belief began to be queried.

There was also a barrier—and one much more difficult of definition—to the diffusion of certain items of practical utility, even though these might have no theological implications. To recognize the practical value of inventions, there is no need for ideological analysis, merely a need for common sense. Because of this, inventions were more likely to travel, and more likely to be accepted by other cultures. Yet there are curious exceptions. These include watertight compartmenting in ships, paper money and the use of coal. All were known to medieval Europeans, but none of them fitted a need consciously felt at the time. The non-acceptance of the repeating or 'magazine' crossbow is even more peculiar, for all civilizations have always been anxious to expand military technology. It seems impossible that Europe was not aware of the existence of the repeating crossbow—which had been mass-produced in China from the second century onwards, and possibly even earlier—yet it was not accepted or even imitated.

Just as specific techniques were transmitted, so the *suggestion* that a particular technique might exist also took effect. A hint that someone, somewhere, had solved some particular problem in a particular way might stimulate others to try it—though, in doing so, they might produce a different solution. An example of this is the windmill, which probably originated in either Syria or Persia. At the time of the Mongol penetration of Europe, the sails of the Eastern windmill were mounted horizontally. But the first European windmills appeared some time in the fourteenth century, with the sails vertically mounted. It seems reasonable that the *idea* of a windmill was transmitted, perhaps by some returning Crusader, but that European millwrights solved it in their own way. There are many other examples, both in East and West, which support the view that responses to a suggestion—as distinct from a detailed idea—were dependent on the technical experience of the society involved.

Enveloped in such a vast cloud of uncertainties, the reader may well ask what proof exists for assuming that this or that idea or technique *was* derived from outside a particular culture, instead of being developed by some evolutionary process within it. From, roughly, the beginning of the seventeenth century onwards—the period, that is, of growing European political domination in Asia, and of Europe's parallel exploration of Asian cultures—there is ample proof. For the period before this, there is also satisfactory evidence of the mediatory role played by the Arabs in the retransmission of Greek science—with Arab improvements—to medieval Europe. But for the major, and indeed fundamental, legacy of Chinese technological inventions upon which the foundations of modern Europe were laid, conclusive evidence is frequently lacking. It is here that the question of priority is of paramount importance. Fortunately, there is firm evidence of use in China which precedes, sometimes by centuries, the appearance of such inventions elsewhere.

The debt the West owes to the East, and what little it has been able to repay, is the subject of the following pages. For a variety of reasons, the debt is largely unrecognized even today. In the past, there were a few men who observed something of its magnitude. 'Science and art,' wrote one of them, the English essayist Sir William Temple, in 1690, 'have run their circles, and had their periods in the several parts of the world. They are generally agreed to have held their course from East to West.' In the years that followed, Europe's political domination of Asia as well as cultural nationalism in both East and West eroded that agreement. Its reinstatement today would be an important contribution to international understanding.

I

Realms of Gold

And king Solomon made a navy of ships. . . . And Hiram sent in the navy his servants, shipmen that had knowledge of the sea . . . And they came to Ophir, and fetched from thence gold.

I Kings, ix, 26–8

The Seres [Chinese] are famous for the wool of their forests. They remove the down from leaves with the help of water, and then women have the double task of unravelling and weaving. It is thanks to these complicated operations in far-off lands that the Roman matron is able to appear in public in transparent garments.

PLINY, *Historia Naturalis*

From Distant Ophir

The dialogue between East and West opened and was continued in the language of trade. From the very earliest times, merchants had met at some convenient place to barter their wares or exchange them for gold. Three great trade routes existed. There was the sea route, difficult and roundabout, which followed the coasts of Persia and Arabia to Aden, then up the Red Sea to Suez. From there the cargoes from the East—gorgeous birds, fine horses, delicate and fragile cottons, ivory, jewels, gold and silver, exotic luxuries designed to appeal to the sophisticated rich of the great Western cities—were sent on, to Egypt perhaps, or to Tyre and Sidon. Indian ships, some of them very large, carried these wares for the first part of the journey, as far as the Persian Gulf. Whenever possible, they clung to the shore, but when forced out to sea they used, as Noah did, shore-sighting birds to guide them to land again.

Overland, cargoes travelled through the passes of north-western India to Balkh and onwards, either by the Oxus to the Caspian Sea and then to the Euxine, or all the way by land to Antioch. Probably the oldest route from India to the West, however, ran from the mouth of the Indus to the Euphrates, then on to Antioch and the ports of the Levant. Contact between the Indus valley and the Euphrates was of long standing. The cuneiform inscriptions of the Hittite kings of Mitanni, belonging to the fourteenth or fifteenth century B.C., refer to these monarchs by Aryan names and speak of their worshipping gods similar to those of the Aryan peoples who overran the Indus valley civilizations in the second millennium. The obelisk of the Assyrian conqueror Shalmaneser III, which dates from 860 B.C., shows Indian elephants which must have come in caravans by the long and dangerous route over mountains and deserts, harassed by hostile tribes. But profit drove the merchants on, often to Balkh, where the roads from India, China and the West met and cargoes could go on by land, or on great rafts down the Oxus.

Great trading emporia flourished at Balkh, Palmyra and Aden, where the apes and peacocks of India, the spices and perfumes of southern Arabia, were warehoused, and where the inhabitants formed a kaleidoscopic medley of merchants and agents. Trade, which was never direct, had to be filtered through the bargaining of countless middlemen. The Phoenicians—a nation of shop-keepers—sent a great fleet eastwards every three years to ship cargo at Ophir, which was probably an entrepôt at the mouth of the Persian Gulf. Though its location is arguable, its name became synonymous with gold.

The civilizations of East and West had a nodding acquaintance, little more. While building up their civilization, the Greeks were essentially a parochial people. Their world was Greece and the coasts of the Mediterranean Sea. Their desire to increase their knowledge was unlimited, but their initiative was small. They acquired their information about other parts of the world as they did their commodities, through mediators. It was not until tales of the wealth and wonders of India reached them that they began to develop that aggressive curiosity which was to lead them into Asia.

The encouragement for the Greeks to push through the iron curtain of intermediaries, to move from second-hand knowledge to direct observation, came from the Persians. Between 559 and 440 B.C. the Achamenid dynasty created and sustained a vast empire. The dominions of Cyrus the Great (559–530) stretched from the Aegean over the plateau of Iran to the River Jaxartes in Central Asia. His son added Egypt and the Greek North African colonies, while Darius (521–486 B.C.) conquered much of north-western India.

Darius constructed an empire of organized tolerance. Highly centralized in the matter of power, it was diffuse in cases of local administration. Great highways held the variegated parts together and linked their trade. Along the sea coasts, many harbours were built, new vessels were launched, and a ship canal linking the Nile with the Red Sea—begun by the Pharaoh Necho early in the sixth century B.C.—was completed. Darius established a fixed standard for coinage, and banks developed a system of credit. Trade expanded. New products appeared in the markets of Greece and northern India, in Egypt, and even on the margins of civilization in northern Europe. Some were luxury goods: frankincense and myrrh from Arabia, drugs and glassware from Egypt, pepper and strange scented barks from southern India, Greek wine and oil, amber and furs from the north. But there were also rice and the domestic fowl, and even the horses of Greece could now grow strong on the lucerne of the Ferghana.

This was only a difference of quantity, the commercialization of what had once been the exotic. Yet the mind, or rather the imagination, was fed too. There were some accounts of genuine explorations, such as that made by Skylax, who was sent by Darius in about the year 510 B.C. to discover where the Indus flowed into the sea, and who, after two and a half years of adventurous voyaging, reached a point near modern Suez. Such stories, however, had lesser currency than the tales of travellers. Not all the marvels these related were accepted uncritically, but none was totally disbelieved, and most survived to activate the imagination of later ages. There was no real questioning of wonders which concerned wealth—above all, gold. In India, so Herodotus, the Greek historian of the fifth century B.C., told his readers, there were giant ants which, burrowing in the ground, brought up gold, and chased away anyone who dared approach. That tale survived until as late as the sixteenth century.

A combination of curiosity and cupidity broke the shell of the Greek world and sent traders, mercenaries, scholars, craftsmen and conquerors into the wild and marvellous places in search of wonders and profit. Under Darius, the horizons had been pushed to new and intriguing limits. As they marched to the margins of the expanding earth, the Greeks took with them the narrow, yet to them all-satisfying, spirit of their civilization. And their gods marched with them.

In the Shadow of Olympus

Though there were many Greeks living within the confines of the empire of Darius, they were comfortably isolated by the tolerance of the rulers. Remaining conscious of the superiority of their civilization, they were hardly in a position to embark on a civilizing mission, even if they had wanted to. The hellenization of Asia had to await the coming of a hellenized conqueror.

For a hundred and fifty years after the death of Darius there was a slow and irregular decline in the fortunes of his empire. Its future was menaced not only by the external threat of the bellicose Greek city-states, but by internal dissensions which permitted the governors of provinces to rebel against the central authority and make themselves autonomous—the traditional scenario of decaying empires.

During this period of decline, aggression, and preparation, there was very little restriction upon the movement of ideas. Who were the merchants in this intellectual barter—traders, perhaps, with an interest in metaphysics, or merely solitary philosophers curious enough to make a journey to northern India? No one knows, but in some of the works of Plato—that philosopher who was a synonym for the Greek mind—there is evidence of Indian ideas. In the *Republic* (in 'The Vision of Er the Pamphilian') are stated the Hindu doctrines of *karma*, the transmigration of souls—'each soul returning to a second life and receiving the one agreeable to his desire'—while the concept of *maya*, 'the illusion of the senses', is clearly outlined in Book VII, 'The Myth of the Cave'.

It was partly intellectual curiosity, partly a sense of destiny and partly a desire to carry Hellenic civilization to the outer margins of the known world that inspired Alexander of Macedon to attempt the conquest of the Persian empire. In 334 B.C. he crossed the Hellespont on the first stage towards realizing his ambition to become 'Lord of the Four Quarters of the World'.

The army of Alexander was accompanied by historians and geographers from whose investigations the ancient world's

14

knowledge—particularly of India—was to be vastly increased. Much of this information was accurate, but much was fantasy. Nearchus, who with Alexander explored the Indus, reported in great detail what he saw. He described the clothes worn by Indians and recorded that it was difficult to decide whether their dress was made of a cotton which was 'of a brighter white colour than any found elsewhere' or whether 'the darkness of the Indian complexion makes their apparel look so much whiter'. But he also reported that there were said to be people who slept in their own ears, and others who had no mouths but were 'gentle by nature and live round the sources of the Ganges and sustain themselves by means of vapours'.

Colonization cannot eliminate hearsay, but it can diminish it. Wherever his armies moved Alexander planted military colonies, each of them a microcosm of the Greek homeland. These were to be the pillars of his new empire. But he was allowed no time for consolidation, no time to see the substance of his dream of a world empire in which the civilizations of East and West would meet and blend. In 323 B.C., at the age of thirty-three, he died suddenly at Babylon. His death unchained the conflicting ambitions of his successors, those satraps in whom he had invested the task of governing the provinces of his empire. Between them, they tore the empire to pieces.

But they also made a significant contribution to the hellenization of the East. They did not have Alexander's dreams. They inherited instead the administrative and economic problems he had not lived long enough to solve. As a result, they introduced into their dominions the only system they knew, and to service it attracted Greek administrators. They also induced philosophers, scholars, teachers, poets, engineers, lawyers, physicians, even actors, to add a top layer of Greek civilization to the palimpsest of oriental cultures they found in their kingdoms. This was both a nostalgic necessity and a pragmatic defence against the seductions of oriental monarchism. Such a development was only possible where the successors of Alexander had managed to maintain their conquests without opposition. Elsewhere, things were somewhat different.

By 315 B.C., though considerable numbers of Greek colonists remained at various settlements throughout the Punjab, Greek *rule* there was at an end. When news of Alexander's death reached the Punjab, there had been a rising of the native population inspired by one Chandragupta, who, according to tradition, had earlier fled from the kingdom of Magadha—in what today is the Indian state of Bihar—after an abortive attempt to overthrow the ruling king. It was said that he had then met Alexander in the Punjab and tried unsuccessfully to persuade him to attack Magadha. From his own base in the Punjab, however, Chandragupta marched against Magadha and, in 322 B.C., occupied its capital, Pataliputra, and founded the Maurya dynasty. Seventeen years later, when the most powerful of Alexander's successors, Seleucus, tried to reconquer the Indian satrapy, Chandragupta was strong enough to force an agreement. Relations between the first Maurya emperor and Alexander's successors became close and friendly. Chandragupta married a daughter of Seleucus, and his successor, Bindusara, carried on a correspondence with him, asking, in one surviving fragment, for a sample of Greek wine, some raisins, and 'a sophist'. Seleucus replied that, while he sent the wine with much pleasure, he regretted that it was not considered good manners among the Greeks 'to trade in philosophers'.

An ambassador sent by Seleucus to Chandragupta has left the only complete account of the court and administration of the first Maurya emperor. This man, Megasthenes, was the first Greek to penetrate the heart of India, and his observations were remarkably acute and detailed. Of Greek *influence*, there is little trace. The customs of the Maurya court were Persian, as was the provincial organization. Chandragupta lived, like Darius, in great seclusion, surrounded by an Amazon guard which seems to have been composed of Greek girls bought as young children. A guard of dependent foreigners was a fairly obvious precaution against assassination.

The first two Maurya emperors were Hindus, but the third embraced the doctrines of Buddhism. When Asoka assumed the dominions which had been established by Chandragupta and extended by Bindusara, there was little to distinguish him from any other Hindu ruler. But in 261 B.C., intent on enlarging his inheritance, he decided to conquer Kalinga, the last independent state on the Bay of Bengal. The campaign was won at the cost of considerable suffering to the conquered. Shortly afterwards, horrified at the misery of war, Asoka was converted to Buddhism, that gentle faith which had been propounded by Gautama three centuries earlier. With the enthusiasm of the convert, Asoka made the compassion of the Buddha the basis of his government.

As something new to the majority of the people, Buddhism had to be demonstrably different from the Hindu world that surrounded it. The Hindus gave their gods human shape, so the Buddhists chose to create symbols for their godhead. The Buddha himself had always disclaimed divinity, and Asoka therefore had him represented only by symbols and ciphers. The wheel, the symbol of the doctrine, the Bodhi-tree, the symbol of enlightenment—these became the visual synonyms of the Buddha. His footprints, representing the passing, rather than the presence, of God, served the Buddha's followers as a reminder of him. Anxious to share his discovery of a new faith, Asoka even sent ambassadors to other countries to spread the gospel.

Asoka's conversion was not the mere formal acceptance of a new religion, and had none of the empty symbolism of 'defender of the faith'. But his genuine belief in the rightness of the Buddha's teachings was reinforced by the social and political advantages they offered. To Asoka, Buddhism was not really a religion at all; it was a pattern for social behaviour. Here, in fact, he was following the precepts of the founder. Gautama had wished to move away from the aridities of Hinduism and its need to approach the gods through such mediators as the priests, who had refined Hindu doctrine into a mysterious and arcane theology accessible only through them. Seeking an instrument with which to break the power of the priests, and of the rulers whose ideological support they were, Gautama chose to open a way to God through the actions of ordinary people. He was really a political thinker but, as politics were inextricably entwined with the religion of Hinduism, he was compelled to give his politics a religious framework. He had no alternative, for no other framework existed. Gautama took some of the beliefs of Hinduism and embedded them in what can only be described as a theology of equality. All men were equal in what they could attain, all started from the same level in their quest for God. It was a republican faith, a faith of individualism, but one which demanded—as later did Christianity—an active awareness of the condition of one's fellow men. This, Asoka realized, was just what was needed for his new empire, in which a new class structure was emerging. The new merchant class and the new leisure class, concentrated in new towns, found themselves without standing in the old Hindu caste structure. So they were willing to accept the religion of the emperor, as a symbol of their status.

Meanwhile, outside the Asokan empire, the successors of Alexander still ruled. But who these successors were—and who were *their* successors—is still a subject for disagreement amongst historians. One thing at least is certain: the Greeks or the hellenized Macedonians who picked up the pieces of Alexander's empire were compelled to come to terms with the Asia they ruled. The majority of their subjects were non-Greeks, and their coinage therefore became bilingual. Trade, of course, continued, interrupted only by armed incursions, palace revolutions and the deaths of kings.

The death of Asoka in 232 B.C. was followed by growing anarchy in northern India which offered a standing invitation to invaders from the north-west and, in particular, from Bactria, which made itself independent of the Seleucids in about 208. Historians are still arguing over a hellenized king named Demetrius, who seems to have conquered parts of India in about 180, and who struck coinage bearing both Greek and Kharoshti characters His are the earliest such coins which have survived.

Menander, who followed Demetrius, inspires less confusion, for both Greek and Indian references to him survive. Before he died, between 150 and 145, he had extended his dominions as far as the old Maurya capital of Pataliputra. On his coinage, Menander assumed the insignia of Asoka. This was the wheel, which was not only a Buddhist symbol, but a symbol of the sun and the cosmos, and therefore that of the *chakravartin*, or universal emperor. Menander's use of it was a deliberate statement, at least for his Indian subjects, that he had succeeded to the empire of Asoka. That his claim was accepted, at least by Buddhists, is clear from the evidence of the *Milindapanha* ('The Questions of Milinda', *Milinda* being an Indian form of *Menander*), and from the fact that at his death his body was burned and the ashes distributed to the cities of his empire where they were interred under *stupas*, mounds of brick, in the Buddhist manner. As a foreigner, Menander had no place in the Hindu caste system. It seems most unlikely that he became a Buddhist, but, with Buddhism, he could create outside the Hindu system a position backed by all the prestige of Asoka and could use Asoka's religion as an instrument with which to assert himself against a reviving Hinduism. Through Buddhism, he sought to acquire the identity of the universal emperor. Menander used Buddhism politically, as an exercise in public relations; he wanted not to transform it, merely to utilize it. To him, the Buddha was not a person, whereas the Greek goddess Athena was. But, being a conqueror and not particularly sure of his dominion, he kept his Greek and Indian sides separate.

Throughout the period—a period empty of historical certainty— merchants went on with their business and the ebb and flow of trade continued. Caravans arrived, even from distant China, and wares were exchanged at the emporia of Central Asia. Trade is a peculiarly well-armoured human activity. Somehow, in the centre of what appears to be enveloping chaos, business goes on, the caravans move through peaceful pockets of country, the urge for profit supplants the fear of death. Anarchy in the ancient world was never the fission of complete collapse. Cities survived behind the thickets of their walls, and vast tracts of country knew nothing of the march of conquerors.

The world of the historian is a synopsis of happenings which reduces the gaps between events and packs them together in abrasive contact. But, all the while, great changes were taking place in the interstices. The Greeks in Asia were becoming asianized. The Greeks in India, cut off from the pattern of hellenism elsewhere, became indianized from roughly the first century B.C., and in the end drowned in the great sea of India. Some Greeks undoubtedly became Buddhists, perhaps because to them the doctrines of Buddhism had something of the Greek ideal about them. But of the Greeks of whom we have records—and they number only five—three were certainly not Buddhist. One was Heliodorus, whose column still stands at Besnagar. Its inscription begins:

> *This Garuda pillar of Vasudeva, the god of gods,*
> *Was erected by Heliodorus, a Bhagavata—*
> *The son of Dion and an inhabitant of Taxila . . .*

All this attests, as do other references, to the fact that the Greeks in India were becoming naturalized. Before they vanished completely, however, the Greeks in India gave their greatest gift, and, because those who remained Greek longest were those embedded in a Buddhist world, it was to Buddhism that they gave it. This was the art of making a man into a god and a god look like the ideal of man.

In the west and north Buddhism had become, as with Asoka in the east, an instrument of state. It had offered the Greeks a doorway into the world of India, for it was a faith without exclusiveness, egalitarian and welcoming of converts. Hinduism, on the other hand, sought to exclude—though it, too, had its intellectual appeal and was by no means as rigid as some commentators would make it seem. A Hindu revival had begun in the heart of Aryavartha, in those parts of Asoka's dominions where the religion of the emperor and of the new classes had shaken but not destroyed the old Hindu social order. There the Brahmins, who had been displaced from power, began to regain it during the chaos that followed the fall of the Mauryas. The wave of revival spread across northern India, and carried with it the Hindu gods, familiar, recognizable, and real in their stylized human form.

In the second century B.C., out of the wilds of Central Asia, came the nomadic hordes who were to brush aside the hellenized kings. The Greek rulers of the Punjab were defeated by the Sakas (or Scythians), and Menander himself was killed in battle with them.

The nomadic hordes conquered a civilized land. To maintain their conquest they had to become respectable, to adopt a recognized mode of behaviour and an acceptable religion. As foreigners, they could only view the resurgence of exclusive Hinduism as a threat to their dominion, so they looked towards the Buddhism of their new country and found in it a belief that could be converted into a religion. In Gautama Buddha, behind his symbols, they saw the materials of a saviour.

Man has always yearned to make God man, an ideal man, a superman perhaps, but bearing man's own lineaments none the less. The new Buddhists felt an urgent need for a representational saviour, a figure personifying compassion and, above all, accessibility. Consciously or unconsciously, they had to choose the form in which the personified Buddha would appear. The Hindu gods, stylized though they were, were recognizably Indian. The Buddha had to be different. The desire for an image grew up in a hellenized atmosphere where the sculptors could take the Greek ideal for their model, and so—commissioned perhaps by some Indian Buddhist —they took the image of the god Apollo and indianized it. The result of their work was not the face of a saviour nor the rapt expression of a great redeemer, but the suave, beautiful, disdainful features of some oriental Apollo. It was, however, the meeting of a need with the only form available to satisfy it. After that there was no going back to symbols—the Buddha had irrevocably taken human form.

The sequence of events in this period of history is by no means established with any certainty, and widely differing dates—all backed by logical and convincing arguments—are given for the same occurrence. The development of the Buddha in human form is a case in point. The first Saka king of whom we have records was Maues, whose conquest of Gandhara probably took place about 70 B.C. On the reverse side—the god's side—of his coins there appears the image of a seated figure. Early numismatists believed this figure to be that of Maues himself, but it now seems certain that it is an image of the Buddha. Furthermore, it probably represents not the Buddha himself but a statue of the Buddha.

Having conquered Gandhara, Maues must have felt it necessary to reassure his new subjects that he would protect their religion. Nothing could have been a clearer statement of his goodwill than the striking of a coin which honoured their Buddha. But the gesture would have been meaningless had the Buddha image not already attained wide currency. The statue form must have been well established before Maues ever arrived, and it could not have been well established unless many sculptures had already been made and set up in many places.

The migrations of Apollo, god of the Greeks and Romans, now transformed into a representation of the Buddha, were by no means over. He was to march, in the baggage of merchants, soldiers and scholars, along the caravan routes of the ancient world as far as China, and through Korea to Japan. Across the seas, too, Buddhist missionaries and traders took with them the image of their god. From India, the Buddha moved throughout the countries of South-East Asia, giving reason and purpose to men who sought new ways of salvation, and the sanction of the supernal to the ambitions of kings. During the journey, many of the Greek conventions disappeared, and the Buddha image became naturalized in the hands of sculptors who knew nothing of the human relevance of Hellenic art. The Greek face—portraying not a saviour withdrawn in bliss, but a man-god, extrovert, athletic, warm and active with youth—was to be submerged and finally lost for ever behind the closed eyelids and the smile, at once knowing and compassionate, of the Asian Buddha. Yet something remained of the Greek idiom to inform the sculptor's hand, and to irritate and intrigue art historians of a later world. In the draping of a robe or the curl of the hair, the rather effeminate Buddha of sixth-century China claims with the princely figure from the Cambodia of the Khmers a common ancestor in the sun god of the Greeks.

This, then, the image which travelled many leagues from Olympus to the realms of gold, which gave reality—and, therefore, strength—to an intangible faith, was the first great landmark in the East–West passage.

The Silk Road and the Monsoon Wind

The expansion of the Greek world through the conquests of Alexander the Great had as its primary purpose and natural consequence the acquisition of wealth by both the conquerors and the merchants for whom Alexander created a special place in his new empire. But the disintegration of that empire after his death led to the division not only of the conquests themselves, but also of the trade of the separate parts. Monopolies rigidly exercised by the successors of Alexander restricted enterprise in the interests of dynastic ambition. Where Alexander had hoped to encourage economic expansion by releasing the hoarded treasures of Susa and Persepolis and simultaneously spreading the Alexandrian peace over the trade routes, his satraps, fighting amongst themselves, were unable either to expand trade or to protect it. One consequence was that the commerce of the post-Alexandrian world fell into the hands of middlemen.

The prices of goods to the consumer fluctuated considerably, depending upon the greed of the middleman, and upon the depredations of the tax-gatherer and of the brigands and pirates who preyed upon some of the trade routes. Wars encouraged all these, disorganizing long-distance commerce and, by increasing the rapacity of kings, inhibiting the accumulation of wealth amongst the mercantile classes. But a new empire was in the making. Wherever the Roman legions set their foot, they were followed by merchants who profited from the security maintained by the *pax Romana*. Under its protection, commerce was to boom upon a scale comparable only with that of the early nineteenth century. The Roman businessman, or at least his agents, penetrated to Ireland and the shores of the Baltic, traded in the bazaars of India and met Chinese merchants along the caravan routes which stretched to farthest Asia.

A few years before Gaius Gracchus passed the legislation which laid the foundations of Roman commerce, later extended by Julius Caesar and built upon by Augustus, the Chinese emperor Han

Wu-ti had sent an emissary, one Chang Ch'ien, to the Far West. In 138 B.C., Chang Ch'ien set out on one of the most remarkable explorations of antiquity. In making his two-thousand-mile journey across deserts, oases and high passes, he broke through a cordon of nomad barbarians into a civilization which still retained the form of its hellenic mould. With Chang's arrival in Bactria, two civilizations, the Greek and the Chinese, touched for the first time. Chang Ch'ien's mission had been intended primarily to win allies against the Huns, whom Wu-ti wanted to subdue as part of his plan for expanding Chinese rule throughout upper Asia. Wu-ti hoped that another nomad people, the Yueh-chi, who had been driven out of their homelands by the Huns, would turn against them from the west. But when Chang Ch'ien finally reached the Yueh-chi—after having spent ten years as a prisoner of the Huns— he found that they were otherwise occupied, having turned in 130 B.C. to the conquest of the Greek kingdom of Bactria, one of the successor-states of the Alexandrian empire. Chang Ch'ien returned to China in 126 with a great deal of practical information about the things he had seen with his own eyes or had heard about from traders and travellers. He also carried back with him to China a varied collection of plants and other natural products, among them the grape-vine and lucerne grass.

Chang Ch'ien's mission was followed by others, their aim partly diplomatic, partly mercantile. All carried with them gifts of silk, for Chang had reported that the secrets of its production were unknown in the West. Soon the commerce in silk was to give its name to the routes followed by the ambassadors. But Wu-ti still sought to expand Chinese sovereignty across Central Asia and in 104–100 B.C. he conquered the area of the Ferghana, where there was a famous breed of horse said to sweat blood. When the king of the Ferghana refused to send stallions to China for breeding, a force of sixty thousand men set off to teach him a lesson and take the stallions by force. This Chinese expedition in search of horses from the West touched the farthest eastward point reached by Alexander the Great.

Though the Chinese were unable to retain control of the Silk Road for any length of time, it was in the interests of those who dominated its parts to keep trade flowing with as little interruption as possible. Certainly, the demand for raw silk and silk garments was continuous and expanding. The peace and security later brought to Rome by Augustus increased the wealth and the numbers of the leisured class. They wanted—and, because they had the money to pay for it, they were supplied with—every luxury the East could offer, from silk and jewels to aromatic spices. Unfortunately, Rome had little to offer in return except gold, but, like the dollar and the pound today, the Roman *aureus* was the international currency of its time, famous for purity and sure of acceptance everywhere.

There were, however, some items from the provinces of Rome which travelled along the trade routes in the other direction as far as India and China. One such was the *theriac*, a preparation originally conceived to counteract the effect of animal poisons. In the mind of Mithridates, king of Pontus (*c*. 120–63 B.C.) this blossomed into the idea of a universal antidote. From this time onwards, the search for such an elixir became one of the great preoccupations of physicians and philosophers. The number of ingredients used in compounding *theriaca* varied fantastically: Pliny mentions six hundred, and even the great Graeco–Roman physician Galen had a recipe for this dubious medicine, which, centuries later, was to be rediscovered by the Arabs along with so much of the Greek science lost to Europe after the fall of Rome. False gems of glass, and the mysteriously named 'night-shining jewel'—probably a fluorospar which glows when heated—were accepted as exotic novelties by the Chinese. These magical objects were a particular speciality of the Syrians, who also exported asbestos cloth and other fabrics, one of which, *byssus*, came to be surrounded with fabulous tales. It seems to have been made either of cotton or of a mixture of linen and cotton. But because the word *byssus* was also applied to the threads produced by certain marine molluscs, which could be dried and woven, stories of creatures part animal, part plant, soon grew up to compound confusion with myth. The Chinese at one time believed that *byssus* was woven from the fleece of 'water sheep', and a similar theory was to have an extremely long life in both East and West. The tale of a lamb growing on a stalk, like a plant, was still being picked up by the great European travellers in fourteenth-century Asia, and was perpetuated even into the sixteenth century and beyond. Only in modern times has the composition of *byssus* cloth been discovered.

25

Of all the exchanges between Rome and China, perhaps the most unusual were jugglers and acrobats, who again came mainly from Roman Syria. The Chinese were fascinated by the mechanics of juggling, and it was as a result of their observation of human dexterity that the automatons which so intrigued China's emperors were constructed. The place of jugglers and acrobats in the history of technology is perhaps more important than scholars have so far admitted.

Skins and cinnamon bark are also known to have been traded, and Pliny mentions a specially fine type of iron which may well have come from the highly developed metal industry of China. But the principal commerce was in Chinese silk. This trade was so profitable for the middleman nations that they were prepared to go to any lengths to preserve it and to prevent Chinese ambassadors from making direct contact with Rome. They did not want to risk the Romans finding out just how high a profit their merchants were making. No Chinese, merchant or ambassador, is known actually to have reached Rome, although at least one did make the attempt, in the first century A.D.

Though it was possible to leave the Silk Road at any one of a number of places and complete the journey by sea, the main centre for processing the silk was in Syria and the natural route was overland. Ultimately, with the decline of Roman power, the sea routes were to be closed to European shipping when control of the Red Sea fell into the hands of Abyssinians and Arabs. Roman merchants found themselves forced to buy Indian and Chinese goods either from these new masters or from the Persians, who now dominated the overland routes from the East to Syria and Armenia. The Byzantine emperor Justinian (527–65) tried first to break the Persian monopoly. Failing in this, he attempted to negotiate new maximum prices—and the Persians refused to sell at all. Wars followed, but in 552 the eggs of the silkworm moth *Bombyx mori*, hidden in a hollow bamboo, were brought to Justinian. These, with the mulberry leaf, were to transfer the monopoly of silk from China to Byzantium, with great political consequences.

So much for the Silk Road. The sea route, by the beginning of the Christian era, had become unsafe through the weak and extravagant rule of the later Ptolemaic kings of Egypt. But the peace of Augustus, the 'immense majesty of Roman peace', as Pliny calls it, brought a new vitality to the antique world. Order and purpose emerged out of war and confusion. Augustus emptied the seas of pirates and filled them with the fleets of traders. The sailors who sailed to the eastern seas were usually Greek or Egyptian, and it was one such who made the sensational discovery of the existence of the monsoon winds.

When this discovery was made is open to controversy. Some historians believe it to have been about A.D. 45, others as early as 85 B.C. It seems probable that the Arabs, in whose hands lay most of the commerce with India before the end of the first century A.D., knew and used the monsoon winds, but that they had managed to keep any knowledge of them from the few Graeco–Egyptian captains, even when rumours reached the West. The West's discovery of the winds is attributed to a sea captain, 'Hippalos'—though whether or not he was a real person is not clear. But the first known reference to the *use* of these winds is in an anonymous pamphlet, *The Periplus of the Erythraean Sea* (that is, the Indian Ocean, Persian Gulf and Red Sea). This was written in about A.D. 70 by a merchant whose home was on the Red Sea and who had sailed to India and back across open water, instead of hugging the coast as ships had done in the past. The effect on Rome's trade of the discovery of the monsoon winds was considerable. A ship could now leave Egypt in July and, blown by the south-west monsoon, arrive in India by the end of September. After disposing of their cargo, the merchants could then load up with oriental luxuries and set sail again in November, in time to be blown back by the north-east monsoon. The return journey could now easily be made within a year.

Trade in luxuries vastly increased and, apart from a few periods of forced economy, continued at a very high level. It was well organized and well protected. For a while, a Roman fleet was even stationed in the Red Sea. Naval expeditions were sent against Arab raiders. The emperor Trajan (98–117) had the Nile–Red Sea canal cleaned out, and his successor, Hadrian, built a new road to the Red Sea across level country and placed garrisons and reservoirs at convenient distances along it.

The expansion of trade widened geographical knowledge. The author of the *Periplus* knew of nothing farther east than the mouth

27

of the Ganges in western India, but by the time of the great geographer Ptolemy (c. 90–168) a few merchants from the West had journeyed as far as China. This does not mean that Ptolemy's knowledge was more than vague and confused. His sources were the reports of illiterate seamen who misunderstood the names of the ports they had visited and were incapable of plotting distances accurately. Ptolemy admits to calculating from the average day's run of a ship. He contrived some startling distortions in the coastline of India, and believed that the coast of China bent southwards to meet that of Africa. But just as Western sailors and merchants were extending their travels to the edge of the Pacific and it seemed as if the scope of geographical knowledge was to be vastly increased, the Roman empire itself came under attack at its very centre. Rome was about to be assailed from both inside and out, by civil wars and powerful foreign enemies, by the slack rule of weak princes, and by more subtle invaders from the Orient.

The very success of Roman trade had been chipping away at the foundations of the empire. It was a commerce not of necessity—of dealings in barley and cheese, in meat and oil—but of conspicuous waste. The new empire of Augustus saw the old noble families fall into decay and a new aristocracy, almost a professional class in the modern sense, emerge. The new men of consequence became businessmen and, within the technical limitations of the time, industrialists too. Tin and lead, coral and the fine glass of the Lebanon and Alexandria travelled along the trade routes as far as China. So, in small quantities, did fine wines to India—and their fragrance is still extolled in the poetry of southern India. Exquisitely wrought silver vessels, singing boys, and fair-skinned girls for the harems of the kings of western India were exported too.

But because these were the luxuries of the few, the trade involved was small. It was quite a different matter in the case of goods shipped in to Rome and the provinces of the empire. Aromatic spices were much in demand by the rich. A fashionable extravagance was the use of vast quantities of sweet-smelling frankincense, cinnamon and spikenard at funerals. On the pyre of Poppaea in A.D. 66 the emperor Nero burnt more spices and aromatic oils than Arabia produced in a year. The principal trading ports of western India were Barygaza, in the west, and Muziris, on the coast of Malabar to the south. The former was dangerous with shoals and huge tides which at one moment would flow out, leaving ships stranded, and then flow back—in the words of the author of the *Periplus*—with a roar 'like an advancing army'. From Barygaza went ivory, silk, cotton, rice and ghee and spices. At Muziris, merchants bought pearls and small beryls from the famous mines of Cranganore. For pearls there was a tremendous demand. According to Pliny, the fashionable women of Rome even wore shoes covered with pearls. 'It is not enough to wear pearls,' he said, 'but they must tread upon them and walk with them underfoot as well.'

But the Romans placed the greatest value on *Piper nigrum*, the berry of a vine-like shrub extensively cultivated in South India. It was a favourite luxury, adding flavour to the diet of the rich, and it fetched a fantastically high price, even though vast quantities were exported through Muziris and other ports. Pepper was to remain highly prized for centuries. When Alaric the Goth sacked Rome in 410 part of the ransom he demanded was three thousand pounds of pepper; and it was the desire to wrest control of the pepper trade from the Turks that sent Vasco da Gama around Africa to India in the fifteenth century.

Rome's foreign trade, by both land and sea, built up a serious adverse balance of payments. This was mainly due to a lack of goods—either in sufficient quantity or in sufficient demand—to exchange for the pepper, the pearls and the fine silks of the East. Instead, Rome had to pay in gold and silver. The elder Pliny (23–79) had much to say about the drain of bullion into the pockets of Eastern kings and merchants. In his *Historia Naturalis*, written in the seventies of the first century, he declared that something in the region of one hundred million sesterces (about five million pounds sterling or twelve million dollars at today's reckoning, but in value many times that amount) went to India every year, a tremendous drain of precious metal from Rome. 'So dearly,' he wrote, 'do we pay for our luxuries and our women.'

But something remains today of this money spent on the frivolities of a leisured class. Indian merchants, profiting from trade with the West, gave donations towards the building of Buddhist and Hindu monuments. At Karlé, not far from present-day Bombay, for example, merchant-donors and their wives stand for ever, sculptured in stone, on the screen that is the entrance to a Buddhist cathedral hacked out of the living rock.

This indirect patronage by Rome of India's architects and sculptors had a more direct counterpart in the influence of Roman art upon that of the Kushans, another tribal branch of the Yueh-chi with whom the Chinese emperor Wu-ti had sought an alliance against the Huns. The Kushans became the rulers of most of north-west India towards the end of the first century. In direct contact with Rome, they became highly romanified. They imitated and restruck Roman coins. They encouraged the expansion of Buddhism and, in the sculpture of the Gandhara 'school', adapted Roman forms—themselves a legacy of Greece. Corinthian columns can be found in friezes depicting the life of the Buddha, as can semi-human creatures like the centaur, triton and hippocamp. Under the Kushans, the suave Apollo-face of the Buddha statue gradually changed into the frozen mask so typical of that period of Roman sculpture which art historians call 'Late Antique'.

Roughly contemporary with Kanishka, the greatest of the Kushan kings (though historians cannot agree about his dates), was the Roman emperor Marcus Aurelius (161–80). While the Kushan sought to create a synthesis of many civilizations cemented by the worship of a saviour god, the Buddha, the Roman looked back to the hellenic base of Roman civilization, to the Stoic philosophers, and forward to a world order calm, reasonable and sure. But the gods of the East were massing against Rome, while the barbarian tribes scratched at the shell of the empire.

Barbarian pressure fell heavily upon the Han rulers in China, too. In fact, the history of the Chinese and Roman empires often ran on parallel lines. The zenith of Rome's expansion in Asia under Trajan had coincided with that of China's in Central Asia. Now, in the second century, the Roman empire was on the edge of its long defeat, and the empire of the Han was even nearer to collapse. In Rome, however—though the emperor was sadly aware of the decline in those Roman virtues which he believed gave cohesion to the empire, and though Rome, like China, had been weakened by wars and was to face a terrible plague which was to depopulate whole provinces—trade still flourished and the forces of the empire still seemed strong.

The continuing vitality of merchant enterprise can be seen in the arrival in China, in 166, of an embassy allegedly from Marcus Aurelius himself. The emperor's Parthian wars had caused a complete break in the overland trade with China; this was a serious blow to the silk merchants of Antioch and Alexandria, and it was probably they who sent the embassy, by the long sea route to China, pretending to come from the emperor of Rome. Certainly there is no mention of such an embassy in Western records, and from the Chinese documents it seems that the Chinese were sceptical of its official character. The ambassadors did not take jewels or other Western products as gifts, but only ivory, rhinoceros-horn and tortoiseshell—which they had probably bought on their journey, while passing through Annam. The enterprise of the silk merchants, however, did not result in a great new era of economic expansion, although the opening-up of direct communication between Rome and China might have been expected to produce an increase in commerce. Soon, with the decline of Roman power, the silk trade fell back into the hands of middlemen.

Curiously enough, the embassy of 166 may well have brought back with it information on the silkworm. Pausanius, who died in 180, gives in his *Description of Greece* the only approximately correct account of silk and silkworms in classical Western literature, just about the time when the 'ambassadors' must have returned from China. No one paid much attention. Indeed, even after the secrets of silk production were discovered in the time of Justinian nearly four hundred years later, the old myths persisted. They were still current in the twelfth century. The secret of silk was one of the best kept in all history, probably because people were unwilling to believe the simple truth.

It has been through the baggage of merchants and the packs of soldiers that many of the ideas and techniques of one civilization have been introduced to another. Between the Roman world and China little passed, because there was virtually no direct contact until both China and Rome were falling into anarchy. In the case of India the story was very different, for more or less constant communication with the West began in the time of Darius and did not end until the sack of Rome by the Goths, nearly a thousand years later. The Romans, however, thought that the East had little but luxuries to offer until, when the empire was shaking at the foundations, a frightened population turned to the oriental mysteries for assurance. This great ideological subversion was to help undermine the very fabric of Roman civilization.

The barbarian nomads felt the same unease as the population of the Roman empire. Some historians attribute the migrations of Alans, Goths and the peoples of the steppes to such physical factors as exhaustion of the soil and the expansion of deserts. But there were other factors, too. The barrier of the Great Wall of China prevented the Huns from migrating to the south-east and turned them westwards, pushing other nomads before them until they reached and overcame the walls of Rome. The effect of Roman and Chinese wars on the trade of the Silk Road also sent tribes off westward on a quest for safer lands. Trade was the catalyst not only of conquest but of chaos and defeat.

II

The Fertile Centuries

Search for learning, though it be as far away as China.

MUHAMMAD

The Egyptians . . . brought us foreign riches and wares wholly unknown to our people. Their coming always yielded us advantage and honour. In addition, the immeasurable tribute which they paid yearly was a source of strength and increase both to the royal and to private treasuries.

WILLIAM OF TYRE (c. 1130–90), On the War between the Franks and the Muslims of Egypt

Manna and dates, in argosy transferr'd
From Fez; and spiced dainties, every one,
From silken Samarcand to cedar'd Lebanon

JOHN KEATS, The Eve of St Agnes

The Funeral of the World

The reign of Marcus Aurelius, the stern philosopher, lay at the edge of that darkness into which Graeco–Roman civilization was to fall in the third century of our era. No emperor who followed—not even Diocletian or Constantine who, for a while, snatched the Roman empire into the light again—was to exercise the same power or enjoy the same prosperity as in the age before Marcus Aurelius. The Stoic emperor is the symbol of the divide between the Classical world and the medieval. After him, as the empire was ravished by civil strife and by the attacks of barbarian tribes, the beliefs that had created it died of a leukemia of the spirit. Some who ruled the empire after his death were shallow and weak, kings of the twilight, shadowy and insubstantial. Others, like Septimius Severus (193–211)—who militarized the administration of the empire and began to move new classes into indirect control of the fortunes of the state—temporarily imposed their own vision upon a dissolving world. From then on, the social climate became increasingly anti-intellectual and anti-urban. The Roman empire turned finally away from Hellas and looked to the East for a politics of order and authority and a religion of salvation. Septimius's own son, co-regent and eventual successor, Caracalla (198–217), in the midst of chaos and misery, dreamed of uniting the Persians and Romans, the two most warlike and cultured races of the world he knew, so that they might together stem the tide of barbarism. But this was just a dream. Romans and Persians continued to fight, and in 260 the Roman emperor Valerian died a slave of the Persian king Shapur I. Caracalla's romantic vision, even if it had been possible of fulfilment, could not have saved Rome from the barbarians, who had already penetrated the empire. The Roman army had become almost entirely an army of peasants —many of them from barbarian tribes settled inside the frontiers of the empire—officered by Germans and other semi-civilized peoples. The soldiers, emerging from the sea of misery which was rural life at this time, envied and hated the luxury, the order and arrogance of the towns, and the emperors of the third century deferred to the army. During the fighting between rival emperors and pretenders, it was always cities that were ravaged and plundered, with fatal results for administration and trade.

The city bourgeoisie, that thrifty and productive class, declined. The aristocracy of learning, too, became suspect. The economy suffered from debased coinage and lack of domestic markets—though the trade in luxuries, many of them from the East, still flourished. In this dark world men turned to the gods of darkness, the secret ones worshipped in darkness, mysterious Eastern saviours like Serapis and Isis and Cybele. These saviours were for the sophisticated. The soldiers preferred the more elemental Mithras. All these cults were concerned with immortality, with life after death. They were also extremely personal. Asian religions are almost always concerned with the individual, rarely with the group. Man's search for salvation is a search made alone, achieved and enjoyed alone. Christianity, as taught by Jesus, offered more than the other cults: it opened a way to immortality, as did all the others, but it was a way shared, a road travelled with companions. Christ preached a gospel similar to that of the Buddha: of responsibility for one's fellow men, of certain salvation, and of an escape from darkness into light. But, like Buddhism, the teaching of Jesus was too cold in its naked austerity. It needed—indeed, the times demanded—warmth, mystery, a magic ritual of forms.

As Christianity spread across the Oriental provinces of the Roman empire, Christian philosophers such as Origen (186–253) and Clement of Alexandria (d. c. 220) began to look to the East to polychrome the austere marble of Jesus's teaching, just as, later, the Christian emperors of Byzantium were to take from the East the chromatics for imperial Christian art. But Origen and Clement lived in Egypt, the former having been born there and the latter having fled from the persecution of Septimius Severus. In Alexandria, there were many Indians, and Hindu and Buddhist ideas were well known in learned circles. Clement describes with some accuracy the Hindu doctrine of transmigration of souls, and Origen, who incorporated this belief into his Christian apologetic, was later condemned for it as a heretic.

Though the influence of one set of religious ideas upon another is seldom amenable to precise definition, it is certain that the early

Christians in Alexandria were quick to absorb some Hindu and Buddhist ideas into their nascent religion. Asceticism, too, was to take an extravagant form in the territory around Thebes in Egypt, which became a favourite resort of Christian hermits and anchorites in the third and fourth centuries. This flight into the loneliness of the desert, where a man might examine his soul alone and in communication with the divine, coincided with the time when India's influence was at its height in Alexandrian literature. Tales of Indian ascetics are scattered about the books of the early Christian fathers.

The desire to withdraw from the secular life of the cities was reinforced by the persecutions of the emperors Decius and, later, Diocletian, when Christians in Rome hid their worship from the emperor's soldiers in caves and catacombs. It was, in fact, to Diocletian the persecutor as well as to Constantine that Christianity owed its ultimate triumph over the pagan gods. When Diocletian came to power in 284 he inherited an empire shaken and sick with chaos and violence. Hatred and envy formed the scaffolding of relations between the classes. Work was disorganized, commerce ruined by insecurity, the administration corrupt and demoralized. The Roman state had sunk almost into the barbarism of the majority of its citizens. Diocletian recognized that it would be impossible to revive the sophisticated mechanism of the Augustan state, which was too urban, too subtle, for the semi-civilized masses, so he and his successors chose to institutionalize and control the rude and violent methods of the third century, to legalize robbery and oppression in the interests of the salvation of the state. For the peasant masses, the old concept of the emperor as the first magistrate amongst Roman citizens lacked authority as well as glamour and mystery, so Diocletian turned instead to the pattern of oriental monarchy, to the sacred mystery of kingship and the identification of the emperor with God. Caligula and Nero, Domitian, Commodus and others had already tried and failed to establish such a doctrine, mainly because they had identified themselves with the god of one particular cult, and their claim had therefore been rejected by the worshippers of other gods. Diocletian, however, stressed only the supernatural character of his power.

When the turn of Constantine came, he identified himself with

37

the most dynamic and popular of the gods and, in doing so, laid the basis of a typical oriental despotism—force, compulsion and religion. The Christian Church by the beginning of the fourth century—offering as it did, love, compassion and the assurance of a better life after death—had grown enormously, for it did not offer only spiritual relief but also, through charity, some practical amelioration of the miseries of life. Diocletian had permitted Christians to be persecuted, but Constantine realized that church and state needed each other. The Edict of Milan of 313 gave Christianity the status—and freedom from persecution—of all the other religions of the empire. The next logical step was to adopt an imperial religion. Diocletian had already converted a constitutional empire into an Eastern monarchy. Now the emperor surrounded himself with the pomp and inaccessibility of Persian kings. He wore the diadem and the purple robe, and the act of audience became a ritual in some divine ceremonial. The public face of the emperor, a personification in stone and marble, was no longer the face of a man but the embodiment of a sacred institution. The rigid monumentality, the staring eye at once remote and all-observing, the unnatural colours of face and hair, were all there to express the supernatural, that ambience of the gods in which the emperor alone walked. This dehumanization of the office meant that the man who occupied it might die or be overthrown while the office itself remained immobile and eternal—an extension, in effect, of the hand of God.

The pattern of society, too, came to reflect the change in the nature of the monarchy. The old structure of the empire, in which movement among élites was not only permitted but encouraged, gave way to a system of rigid castes. Even the most dynamic individuals were not allowed to move. This restriction applied as much to the landlord as it did to the peasant, to the ship-owner as to the artisan. All became bound not only to their professions but even to their places of residence. Though there were differing levels and shades of bondage, all became slaves.

The servile state saps the creative instinct of man. It also proliferates corruption. If the state pursues a policy of organized robbery, cheating and bribery flourish in an attempt to avoid its effect. The mechanism of state exploitation is, itself, susceptible of exploitation. In Rome, great fortunes were made by skilful manipulation, and the castes of the empire were reduced to two—those who became steadily poorer and those who slowly enriched themselves at the expense of the state. The new rich strove to be men of culture, and the mosaic floors which are all that remain of their villas can still suggest something of their elegant and useless lives. But though their appearance was majestic, they were hollow men, whom the barbarian invaders, after a moment's admiration, were to sweep aside.

Constantine and his successors were deeply involved in the rapid diffusion of Christianity among the masses. They looked upon Christianity as the Maurya emperor Asoka had looked upon Buddhism: as an instrument |of state. The doctrine of both religions, of love and compassion towards one's fellow men, could be used to reduce conflict and impose a sort of moral discipline. But whereas Asoka achieved considerable success in his own lifetime—primarily because he had little to fear from external aggression—the Roman empire of the fourth century was in a very different condition. The empire was saved only in one sense, and only by turning its face to the East. Constantine moved his imperial capital to the new Rome of Constantinople, and the new empire was steadily orientalized until it was transformed into Byzantium. The pope and the emperor parted company. The vicegerent of the Christian god remained in Rome to confront the barbarians who were later to christianize the whole of Europe.

But links remained between emperor and pope. Neither could exercise lasting power without the sanction of the other. Christianity had been made a matter of politics, and politics demanded orthodoxy of opinion. This the early church had not, of course, possessed—a persecuted religion needs only faith to give it cohesion and strength, but when it becomes respectable, when it becomes accepted and powerful, it must be dogmatic. To establish a dogma, Constantine called an ecumenical council at the town of Nicaea in 325. His motive was simple. If Christianity was to be the support of the throne and the cement which would bind together the varied elements of a disintegrating empire, there must be no schism between the leaders of the church. The controversy that was then threatening to divide the Christian world was concerned with the personality of Christ Himself and the nature of His relationship with God the Father. Essentially, the conflict was between the idea of a multiplicity of gods, such as had flourished in the pagan past of the Graeco–Roman world, and the monotheism of the Jews. To the Jews the concept of one god had the authority and reality of historical experience. That their Jehovah had become more than the god of the Jews did not make him any less personal. But to men brought up in the atmosphere of hellenism, a single, all-embracing God was a highly sophisticated philosophical concept. Those thinkers who drew their inspiration from the Jewish origins of Christianity saw Jesus as a man who had become the mouthpiece of God. But those who remembered the gods and heroes of the Greek and Roman pantheon saw Jesus as the 'divine man'. He was not of flesh and blood but had merely occupied the human form for as long as was necessary to His revelation.

To settle this confusion, early theologians developed the doctrine of the *logos*—the Word which had created the world. 'God spoke and it was done.' The Word, they said, was 'made flesh', and was known amongst men as Jesus. This explanation failed to satisfy those who believed in the separate personality of the Redeemer, and it was for this reason that Arius, a priest of Alexandria, taught that Jesus had been created by God to act as His agent, to suffer and to change as a man. This teaching, however, implied that Jesus was not a direct manifestation of the substance of God, but, in effect, a secondary deity.

This not only struck at the concept of the one god; it threatened to interpolate a god of an inferior order between the Supreme Being and the emperor of Rome. The emperor called the Council of Nicaea to reassert the doctrine of the indivisibility of the godhead; Arius was condemned as a heretic, and the Nicene Creed formulated articles of faith which were to prove permanent.

This did not mean that controversy concerning the nature of God and of the Son ended. When rigid dogma—whether it be Christian or Marxist—lies at the foundations of a state, there are always those who resent its interpreters. The new Christian empire was no exception. Pagan gods and certain of their festivals were quietly absorbed into the practices of popular Christianity, but the central belief in the nature of God Himself still aroused bitter argument.

The attacks upon the orthodoxy of Nicaea came, in the main,

from theologians of the East, schooled in that metaphysical curiosity which is typical of oriental religions. It was the West that became the principal defender of the Nicene Creed, though barbarians found the Arian heresy more to their taste, and thus added another element to the tension between themselves and the empire. In the East, religious activity had not been the sole prerogative of the Christians. In Persia, the religion of Zoroaster—in which deified Good and Evil existed in perpetual strife—was to have its influence on the development of Christianity. The system preached by Mani (executed *c*. 276), who wanted to create a universal religion, took the teachings of Zoroaster, Jesus and the Buddha as its base. Despite persecution, the Manichaean concept of the two natures, light and darkness, good and evil, warring inside man, spread both east and west. The teaching of Mani found its way along the Silk Road to China; through North Africa and into Italy. St Augustine, the greatest of the Latin Fathers of the Church, gave Mani his adherence before he was baptized as a Christian. The pagan underground, also, successfully rebelled against Christianity in the person of the emperor Julian (361–3). But it was a false return. The pagan deities were dying and were soon banished to the private sanctuaries of those who still paid homage to the gods of Greece and Rome. Christianity had taken too large a hold upon the population of the empire for the old gods to walk in public again.

But though the Christian god was winning all the battles, Rome itself continued to crumble. Even in the time of Constantine, the empire—though still nominally whole—had really divided into halves. When Rome was in peril, Constantinople, strategically placed near the trade routes, became the fortress of the empire. But the very choice of the new capital encouraged the collapse of the West. Constantinople drained to itself all the remaining strength of the dying colossus. In 395, the empire was finally divided between two emperors. The western part was already reeling under the ambitions of the barbarians both inside and out. In 410 the city of Rome itself fell to the Visigoth Alaric, though it was still prosperous enough to pay the ransom of three thousand pounds of pepper demanded by the conqueror. It is significant, too, that in the general destruction churches seem to have been spared. But Rome and all it stood for had fallen to the barbarians.

41

St Jerome declared: 'The human race is included in its ruins.' St Augustine compared the destruction of the city 'made with hands' to the city of God, 'eternal in heaven'. Sidonius Apollinaris, a provincial Roman of the late fifth century, looked back upon this and the subsequent invasions of the Vandals and Huns as 'the funeral of the world'. But it was only the funeral of *his* world. A new Europe was in the making, and, in the East, something of the legacy of Greece and Rome was preserved in the empire of Byzantium—to which Constantine's foresight gave over a thousand years of life, and whose most glorious emperor, Justinian, made the last vain attempt to revive the empire of Augustus.

The Triumph of the Son of God

The collapse of the Roman empire in the West was symbolized by the fall of the imperial city itself, but, for all the drama of the event, it is no more than a symbol. There had been a long sapping of the foundations of Roman polity. Though there were many potential successors waiting to grab the heritage of Rome, none were at first strong enough. The area of central and northern Europe was without political form; it existed as an anarchy of petty princes, of barbarian chiefs who had become kings and imposed a military tyranny upon a population romanified in varying degree. In a comparatively short time, however, many of the conquerors gave up part of their independence for the sake of alliance with others stronger than themselves. These alliances pyramided into large kingdoms—that of the Franks covering present-day France and the Netherlands; of the Visigoths, Spain; and the Ostrogoths, Italy. The rulers of these kingdoms came to profess the same religion as their subjects, but their art continued to use the vocabulary of their pagan past. The motifs of their gold and enamel ornaments showed that they still remained bound to the Asian heartland out of which the barbarian migrations had exploded into Europe.

But significant changes were at hand. The Merovingian rulers of the Franks realized—as had Constantine in Rome—the need for a partnership of church and state. Soon the Frankish dominions were increased by Charles Martel (an illegitimate son of Pepin II) who, though nominally only Mayor of the Palace, became the real ruler of the kingdom (715–41). Martel's son, in turn, disposed of the Merovingian king. The Carolingian dynasty was established and its second ruler, Charlemagne (768–814), conquered northern Italy, became suzerain of the Papal State and, in his own view, the logical successor of Constantine the Great. This was certainly true of his political ideas. His conception of the role of church and state, of pope and emperor, was essentially Byzantine. Priests were there to pray, kings to rule. The existence of an eastern emperor, the legitimate successor of Constantine, did, of course, present a problem. But Charlemagne made no claim to usurp his title; he merely wanted recognition as coregent, as ruler in effect of a revived western Roman empire. The next step was taken out of Charlemagne's hands. On Christmas Day 800, while Charlemagne knelt at Mass in St Peter's in Rome, Pope Leo III suddenly placed a golden crown upon his head and acclaimed him emperor of the Romans.

Charlemagne resented the pope's action. He made it clear in public that, had he known of the pope's intentions, he would have prevented the coronation. Fortunately, there was no Byzantine emperor at the time—as the throne had been seized by a woman—but Charlemagne still sought an arrangement with the eastern empire. He finally achieved it in the reign of the emperor Michael I. But delay in arriving at a legal settlement, important as that was in a particularly formalistic age, did not hamper Charlemagne's plans. These were concerned, above all, with the revival of culture and civilization which had been submerged in the anarchy that followed the fall of Rome. The central figure in the colossal task of salvage was the Northumbrian monk Alcuin (c. 735–804). One of his first preoccupations was to achieve a decent standard of education among the Frankish clergy, on whom would depend the dissemination of knowledge. The Latin tongue was therefore revived as the common language of scholarship, and this naturally led to the development of a uniform script for its expression. To the Carolingian minuscule the West owes not only its alphabet but the vast majority of the Latin classics, nearly all of which came down to us through Carolingian copies.

The empire of Charlemagne did not long survive his death. It had only existed because of the genius and dynamism of Charlemagne himself, who united the self-interest of the clergy, the great land-owners and the warrior lords in the greater self-interest of his own ambition. When that was removed, the parts reasserted their independence. The confines of the empire, too, were threatened from without. In 843, the Norsemen devastated parts of northern France, and just over forty years later were only just prevented by a massive bribe from sacking Paris; in 846 the Saracens looted St Peter's in Rome; the Hungarians penetrated into Bavaria. For a second time, the empire of the west seemed to be falling apart. The century that followed has been called 'the century of iron'. It was certainly a dark age, more truly black than the Dark Ages of old-fashioned history books.

Fortunately, some light still shone. Charlemagne had insisted upon the establishment of schools in every monastery and cathedral. It was in these that civilization was carefully kept afloat in a sea of semi-barbarism. The monasteries in particular preserved the new art of manuscript illumination. It was only proper that this should be so, for it was in the monastic *scriptoria*—founded originally for the copying of texts—that a new pictorial art had been created. The imperial art of Charlemagne was that of Byzantium, but it reflected the cold light of northern Europe more than the warm sun of the East. Its austerity was an austerity of climate, both material and intellectual. The illuminated book, however, was not a manifestation of imperial art; it owed little to kings, and much to bishops and abbots. It was an art, not of public propaganda, but of private belief. It therefore had no need either to overawe the ignorant or to come down to their level.

The art of the illuminated book had many ancestors, and, consequently, a wealth of symbolism on which to draw. The very variety which is apparent in the treatment of sacred subjects was of paramount importance, for it demonstrated that the word of God need not be expressed in the language of appearance; that there was, in effect, no orthodox representation of the divine from which the artist would deviate only into heresy. Because, too, the illuminated book was designed for the use of an intellectual minority, the artist was permitted a much wider area of exploration in his search for expression. Abstract forms, motifs derived from the art of the barbarian goldsmith, a display of calm geometry or of explosive and intense emotionalism—none of these would be rejected by the men for whom this art was created. The illuminations of this period were once thought by art-historians to be crude, clumsy, and unsophisticated, because they did not represent the real. But they were never intended to do so. They were not imitations of life but expressions of the supernal.

In the anarchy of the 'century of iron', there were really two separate Christianities: that of the peasants, and that of the monks. These two religions were *aware* of each other, and there was communication between them, but, in a very real sense, they did

not mix. To the monks, the illuminated book was a sacred talisman, enshrining the word of God and so preserving it. The moment
security came again to the countryside and the need for proselytizing and propaganda returned, the sacred was forced to use lay-
man's language and adapt itself, in time, to the lineaments of the
real. This journey towards reality was a journey of liberation.
Western Christianity severed itself from the weight of Byzantinism,
moved God out of the darkness into the daylight, and established
a dialogue between Him and man.

In one way this liberation was a return to the Graeco–Roman
past. It had been the Greeks who brought the gods out into the
open. The deities of the East lived isolated in their sanctuaries,
their divinity enriched by the shadows. But the Greeks united
the temple with the market-place, the gods with the people. Above
all, they established a communion between the human and the
divine. The images of the gods stood outside the temple. The
temple itself, filled with light, was an extension of the real world.
The dramatic rejection of this by Christianity was to be epitomized
in the great church of the Sancta Sophia in Byzantium. The first
Christian churches had reflected the beginnings of the religion.
The basilica was a place of worship perpetuating the secrecy
which had been necessary to avoid discovery by pagan oppressors
of the faith. Once again, the gods were worshipped in darkness, in
the heart of the sanctuary. The early Christian basilica was simply
a pagan temple turned outside in. Sancta Sophia, however, was
much more than that. When the emperor Justinian saw what he
had caused to be built, he exclaimed, 'I have conquered thee,
O Solomon'—meaning that he had created a finer building than
the temple at Jerusalem. He was interested in producing not an
impressive successor to the Roman temple but, as André Malraux
has put it, an architecture appropriate to mystery.

Like the basilicas, Sancta Sophia has no façade. It is a gigantic
crypt raised high above the ground. Its ancestor is not the acropolis
but the catacomb. Unadorned, the Sancta Sophia would have
been without mystery. But its architects had taken from the East,
in which they were nurtured, the cupola, the concept of space lost
in shadow. It was in that space that the symbols of God were
placed. These symbols were not earthbound, approached through
a row of pillars, but floating in the air, inaccessible and remote.

To the Byzantines, God *was* inaccessible and remote. To establish the difference *in essence* between the pagan gods and the Christian god, sculpture was abandoned for mosaic, realism for the supernatural. The Byzantine mosaic is an affirmation of the disincarnation of God. This 'otherworldliness' was reinforced by the use of 'unnatural' colours, a commonplace in representations of Eastern gods. The Christian images also displayed a rigid frontality, like that of the gods of Palmyra, their eyes fixed on some distant perspective of the divine.

The mosaic, and the use made of it by the Byzantine emperors, was by no means the only style of Christian art. But it was the imperial art of the Byzantine state, and it was an instrument of propaganda as well as a weapon in the war against heresy. Theologians were not the only ones to argue about the relationship of the Son to the Father. Ordinary people tended to isolate Jesus and make him the hero of a magical saga. The Christ of the Byzantine mosaic is not the *man* Jesus, but an aspect of the indivisible God. What was human was driven out of sacred art. God *was* Love, but it was not a human love, for it did not contain that element of pity which, like pain and emotion, is strictly a human attribute. The God that is depicted in the mosaics is an oriental deity; even the Virgin and Child have as little relation to reality as the gods of the Hindus.

It is fundamental to any understanding of the nature of sacred art to recognize that the artist did not consider his creation as a 'work of art', a mere decoration. It was a medium for the expression of the divine. The artist produced his work not for connoisseurs and art-collectors but for worshippers. Nor did the worshipper react as an art critic. He was a believer in the validity of the message, not of the art of the messenger. It is only the modern world—the world begun by the Reformation—that has come to divorce the subject from the technique used to express it and to treat art as Art. To the men of the medieval world, a religious painting, mosaic or sculpture was an icon expressing the Truth.

In the West, Charlemagne accepted the Byzantine mosaic because it *was* imperial. But neither the form nor the theology behind it could survive the anarchy that followed his death. When peace came again to Europe, not only a new theology was required; a new art was needed to express it. The device of declaring a

'Truce of God' between warring princes established a new and revolutionary doctrine—'one Christian who slays another Christian sheds the Blood of Christ'. This declared a new relationship between man and God: that the worshipper shared something of the nature of the divine. The eleventh century witnessed a sudden outburst of religious enthusiasm. Western Christendom became intoxicated with God. Sacred art, stumbling out of the monastery into the life of the people, began to respond to their need for a God whose nature they could understand. This breaking-down of the old barriers between God and man was first reflected in the architectural embellishments of that theatre of God, the church. It can best be seen in the use of the tympanum—the panel between the arch and the top of the door—under which the worshipper passes into the sanctuary. In the sculptured reliefs of the tympanum, twelfth-century religious architects brought God out of the darkness into the light of day and His image took its place *on the outside of the church*. This symbolized the revulsion against oriental mystery. God walked once again amongst men, became part of the world of His own creation. This development reflected, too, the triumph of Jesus, the once incarnate Son, over the remote figure of God the Father. Stage by stage, from the awe-inspiring figure of the great abbey-church of Moissac, through the merciful divinity of Reims, the process of humanization continued until the sacred scene could be rendered without blasphemy in a world resembling the world of men. The golden background of the mosaic gives way to hills and rivers or the interior of a church. God inhabits, though He is never part of, the landscape of the living.

This was still to come. It was to be the creation of artists released from anonymity, the painters and sculptors of the Renaissance. But the beginnings are to be found in such portals as that of Moissac.

What were the reasons for what was, in effect, a re-evaluation of the nature and purpose of religion? Like all historical change, it resulted from a variety of social causes. The new technology of agriculture may have been one. During the ninth and tenth centuries, the heavy mouldboard plough displaced the old scratch plough that had originated in the East, where soil is light and dry. The damp, heavy earth of northern Europe could not be turned with

THE TRIUMPH OF THE SON OF GOD

it. The coming of a heavier plough coincided with the introduction of efficient animal harnesses from China. The new plough helped to create a new social unit, for it needed strong animals to pull it, and such animals were too costly for individuals to own. So small communities evolved. Agricultural productivity increased and so did the population.

The population explosion of the eleventh century burst the seams of the old social order. New institutions, new hierarchies, new disciplines, were needed to control it. Both church and state, at first caught unprepared, acquired new vitality and aggressiveness. The reforming monks of the Abbey of Cluny in Burgundy became spiritual colonizers, and their Houses spread throughout the West. The Norman invaders of France took institutions with them as well as arms on their subsequent conquests. The Normans and the Cluniacs, in an alliance of faith and force, created a new order to fit the pace of an expanding economy and a growing population. Under Cluniac inspiration, Christendom began to stretch outward into the lands held by the Muslims in Spain and Portugal, and to the still pagan areas of eastern Europe, building monasteries and castles. It was a colonizing movement. Where the barons went, the monks of the new missionary orders that were springing up went too. The Cistercians, for example, were great agricultural exploiters, to whom waste land was anathema. Their colonial communities in time became thriving towns, out of which another new social order was to emerge. But the eleventh century was still the age of feudal imperialism. Europe was on the edge of the Crusades and it was also at the gate of the age of discovery. The Arabs, driven on by *their* faith, had not only conquered the Mediterranean world but become the saviours of Greek science. They were ready and waiting to transmit its legacy back to a West that had almost forgotten it had ever existed.

Ancient Wisdom and Foreign Riches

In the West the Roman empire had been faced with—and later yielded to—the pressure of nomad barbarians. To the East the threat had come from the highly civilized Persians, but the new Rome of Byzantium had contrived to preserve its independence.

In the seventh century, however, Persia itself was conquered by nomads, who were to change the face of western Asia and North Africa, and, less directly, that of Western Christendom as well. These nomads were the Arabs, restless and warlike, inhabiting a harsh and arid land. All that they had needed to set them off on the conquest of the two tired civilizations in the north was a leader and a faith. The prophet Muhammad supplied them with both. Regarding Jesus and the Hebrew prophets as his predecessors, he preached a pure faith, an old revelation cleaned and refurbished. But he injected moral ideas of a kind which was revolutionary, at least to Arab tribesmen. His vision extended beyond the tribe to the whole of mankind. Muhammad taught the duty of forgiveness, not revenge, and promised the reward of heaven to those martyred for the faith. The new religion came to be called Islam (surrender), and its believers Muslims (self-surrenderers). By 629, Islam was knocking at the gates of the Byzantine empire, and after Muhammad's death in 632 the Arab conquerors began to occupy the outlying provinces of that empire. The Persian dominions, tattered by anarchy, were taken in 649.

The tide of conquest continued to flow. The old Latin and Christian civilization soon disappeared from North Africa, and by 711 Islam was poised to cross the Mediterranean and proceed to the conquest of Spain. Twenty-one years later only the generalship of Charles Martel prevented the Arabs from conquering France. Martel's grandson the emperor Charlemagne, however, was to exchange ambassadors with the Caliph Harun ar Rashid and receive from him, it is said, a splendid tent, a water clock, an elephant, and the keys of the Holy Sepulchre. These presents were symbolic of the change that had come over the Arabs since they emerged out of the desert. In fact, the empire of Harun ar Rashid was far more civilized than that of Charlemagne, as a result, perhaps, of the barbarian Arabs' desire for the learning of the peoples they conquered. The Prophet had said: 'Search for Learning, though it be as far away as China.'

The cultural acquisitiveness of the Arabs had much material to work on. In Persia, they found themselves heirs to the Greek scientific tradition. To the east, they were in contact with the Chinese; to the south, with the Hindus. The Arabs were to become the great mediators between Europe and Asia. They transmitted Chinese technology, Hindu mathematics, and the ancient wisdom of the Greeks to the Latin West, which knew nothing of the first two and had, to all intents and purposes, forgotten the third. The Arabs also inherited the splendours and luxuries of the empire of Persia. This can be seen particularly in the richly decorated textiles, with Sassanian motifs, that were later treated with special respect in Christendom, where nothing remotely resembling them could be found. Popes and saints were wrapped in these gorgeous cloths for burial—sent on their way to heaven supported by embroidered words lauding the princes of Islam or reiterating the credo of Muhammad.

The principal seat of learning in western Asia which had fallen to the Arab conquerors was the city of Jundishapur in south-west Persia. There, exiled Greek scholars and Christian heretics had met Syrian, Persian and Hindu men of learning, and created a scientific syncretism which the Arab conquerors were to inherit and diffuse.

It is almost impossible to exaggerate the importance of the Islamic contribution to science and technology in the West. Between the eighth and twelfth centuries, the followers of Muhammad held in their hands the knowledge of East and West, of the antique and the contemporary worlds. The diffusion of this knowledge owed most, if not all, to the Arabic language. The Prophet himself had said that all believers must know the language of the Koran, the holy book of Islam, and the Islamic conquerors made Arabic the international language not only of the Faith but of the knowledge they themselves had inherited. From Jundishapur and, later, Baghdad, this learning spread to Cairo in the ninth and tenth centuries, and from Cairo to Spain in the eleventh.

Through the court of Córdoba, something of the Classical world was soon to be given back to Europe. But even more important than this was the transmission of the numerals the Arabs had adapted from those of the Hindus.

It is difficult today to conceive what it must have been like before the nine digits and the zero became not only an essential tool of scientific experiment but part of everyday life. Yet these numerals have only been in general use for about four hundred years. Before then, the crude notation which the Roman conquests had imposed was the most widely used in Europe. People calculated on their fingers, and even the most learned mathematicians show in their once famous textbooks that their mathematics were very elementary indeed. Some scholars have suggested that it was Boethius (c. 480–524) who introduced numerals into Europe, but the book on which this suggestion is based is probably spurious. The Venerable Bede, writing some two hundred years later, does not mention them at all. It is known, however, that in c. 773 an Indian savant took an astronomical work to Baghdad and that this was immediately translated into Arabic. Hindu numerals may have reached the Mediterranean by this means, or they may have been transmitted by traders. In any case, the Islamic conquerors carried Hindu numerals as far as Spain, where Gerbert of Aurillac, who revived the abacus, the counting-frame of the Romans— and who, as Sylvester II, was one of the most remarkable popes in history—may have learned something of them, though he did not know the use of zero. But the times were not quite ripe for the new mathematics, although the same currents that were to revolutionize sacred art were also preparing the way for a new attitude to the sciences. A number of writers mention Hindu numerals, among them Leonardo Fibonacci of Pisa, the most noteworthy mathematical genius of the Middle Ages, who in 1202 published his *Liber Abaci*, where Hindu numerals are explained and demonstrated. But their use spread very slowly and did not become general until the early sixteenth century. The great outburst of technological invention which followed could hardly have taken place without them.

The transmission of Hindu numerals by the Arabs was the transmission of something new—which probably accounts for their slow acceptance in Europe. But works of Greek science and medicine, which the Arabs had preserved and in many cases improved upon, were to be welcomed enthusiastically by the intelligentsia of a newly awakened Europe. In fact, the 'lost' works of Classical antiquity were to exercise such a fascination on European scholars that, when translations were made out of Arabic into Latin, it was almost always the works of the great Greek writers that were chosen. This may have been because the names of the famous authors of antiquity had survived, and because there also existed a desire to revive a purely European past. Whatever the explanation, European curiosity did not extend to the works of those Islamic writers who concerned themselves with Indian and Chinese science. A parallel to this intellectual myopia in Europe can be found in Asia, in the failure of the Chinese to take Greek scientific classics from the Arabs, though it seems likely there was at least one translation of Galen into Chinese before the tenth century. Even so, Greek medicine had no discernible influence on that of China.

The Arabs owed much of their early knowledge of Greek science and medicine to the scholars of Jundishapur, who had translated into Syriac—the language which, after the fifth century, replaced Greek in the learned circles of western Asia—many important works. In about 750, on the rise of the Abbasid caliphs of Baghdad, there began the great period of translations from Syriac into Arabic. Perhaps the greatest attention was given to works of medicine. In the ninth century one translator, Hunayn ibn Ishak (809–77) rendered the entire works of Galen into Arabic, a colossal undertaking which had the most profound effect, not only throughout the Islamic world, but also in Europe. It was Hunayn who virtually created Galen's supreme position in the medicine of the Middle Ages. He is also believed to have translated some of the works of Aristotle, and the Greek Old Testament, while others rendered into Arabic the *Materia Medica* of Dioscorides and works on astronomy, mathematics and philosophy. Islamic scholars were able to improve on much of the legacy of Greek science. They began to move science out of the realm of speculation into that of experiment. They were observers, practical men rather than thinkers, and they excelled in such practical fields as optics. But in medicine, their urge to experiment was inhibited by the fact that their faith vetoed the dissection either of human bodies or of living animals. Instead, they carefully classified and systematized diagnosis and treatment.

Greek science had been translated from Greek into Syriac or Hebrew, then into Arabic. Now, from Arabic it was rendered into Latin and thus reintroduced to Europe. During the lifetime of Constantine the African—the translator of Galen who, in 1070, began his work at Salerno—Christian Europe began to make inroads into the world of Islam. Its first successes were in Spain and Sicily, and it was from these two places that the legacy of Islam flowed like a refreshing river into the parched mind of medieval Europe.

In Spain, Toledo fell in 1085 to Alfonso VI, King of León, who, though nominally a Christian, was really a product of Islamic civilization. Indeed, he regarded himself as 'emperor of the two religions'. Toledo retained the intellectual supremacy it had held under Islamic rule, and its schools began to attract scholars from all over Europe, including such men as Adelard of Bath, Hermann of Carinthia, and his pupil Rudolf of Bruges. Latin students came to admire the monuments of an Islamic civilization and stayed to translate the Greek classics. The scholars they found already there—who were, often through the Spanish tongue, to be intermediaries between them and the Arabic versions of the classics— were mainly Jews, who played much the same role in twelfth-century Toledo as Christian heretics had played in Jundishapur and Baghdad three centuries before. Toledo was to have its own Hunayn in Gerard of Cremona who, between 1167 and his death twenty years later, produced nearly eighty translations of authors ranging from Galen to Aristotle.

It is worth noting that many classical works did in fact still exist in the original Greek. The Byzantine empire still nourished the Greek tradition; Greek was the official language of church and state, of learning and literature. But even at the height of Roman power the Greek authors had rarely been translated into Latin, the language which a reviving Europe was later to adopt as its common tongue. Europe in the barbarian centuries knew virtually nothing of Greek and the Greek classics were therefore forced to take a devious linguistic route—from Greek into Syriac or Hebrew, then into Arabic, and finally (often via Spanish) into Latin. This long journey did, however, ensure that the Latin

West gained access not only to the classics of antiquity but also to the intervening experiments and conclusions of Islamic scholars. Arabic scientific terms—such as *almanac, zenith* and *nadir, alcohol* and *alkali*—filtered in to become a permanent part of the language of science. The word *algebra* was introduced into Europe in 1145 through Robert of Chester's Latin translation of the work of the great Arab mathematician al-Khwarizmi, whose name was soon converted into *algorismus* and became a synonym for the new arithmetic using Hindu–Arabic numerals.

The tide of Arabic learning rolled out of Spain into southern France, to centres such as Narbonne, Béziers, Toulouse, Montpellier and Marseilles. But the influence of Toledo was by no means exhausted. In Spain, Islamic learning was to find its greatest Christian patron in Alfonso X, called *el Sabio* ('the Wise'), who ruled Castille and León from 1252 to 1284. Under his immediate supervision a vast number of works, many compiled from Arabic sources, was undertaken. He himself, in his *Crónica general*, devoted two chapters to a strange life of Muhammad. His studies included the famous 'Alfonsine Tables', which consisted of astronomical observations based on the meridian of Toledo and which were used throughout Europe for some centuries. He also compiled a treatise on precious stones and a work on games. Among these was chess, and it is in Spain that the first European reference to this game can be found. It occurs in the will of a member of the family of the Counts of Barcelona, dating from about 1008. But the first actual description of the game in a European language is that of Alfonso the Wise. Chess, though originated by the Hindus, became one of the most characteristic of the legacies of Islam, for it exemplified the kind of mental exercise so dear to the Islamic scholar and so lacking in medieval Europe.

Alfonso the Wise was also responsible for one of the greatest collections of medieval poetry, the *Cantigas de Santa María*, complete with musical settings. The form of the poems is one peculiar to Muslim Spain, and its influence was to spread across the Pyrenees to become the framework of the love lyrics of the troubadours, whose name may well derive from the Arabic word *tarrata*, which means 'to make music'. The wandering minstrels took not only the form but sometimes the content of Arab tales and fables—themselves originating in Persia or India. The settings and the musical notation used in the *Cantigas* also display Islamic forms. Even the instruments for which they were scored were Moorish in design. Some Moorish instruments passed into common European use—the guitar, for example, despite its universal popularity today, is still looked on as a characteristically Spanish instrument. The very word *guitar* comes from the Arabic *gitara*, as does *lute* from *al'-ud*. Arabic instruments, like Arabic literary forms, were popularized by the minstrels who travelled from court to court. Through them, many Arab words became embedded in the languages of Europe.

Naturally, under such a patron as Alfonso, Toledo continued to be a centre for translations from the Arabic. The twelfth century was its golden age, but the glitter of discovery still lingered on in the thirteenth. Through Spanish sources, the philosophy and natural science of Aristotle and his Arabic commentators were transmitted in the form which was to revolutionize European thought. Out of Spain came Euclid, the new algebra, treatises on optics and perspective.

But there was also another gateway through which the ancient wisdom of the classical world made its way into Europe. This was the Norman kingdom of southern Italy and Sicily, which had come under Islamic rule in 878. In the eleventh century, when Muslim power in the western Mediterranean was on the wane, the Normans—insatiably ambitious—were quick to take advantage of it. They finally conquered Sicily in 1091, and the island soon settled down under its Norman king, Roger I, whose army was almost entirely composed of Muslim Saracens and whose administration was part Muslim, part Byzantine. Under Roger II (1130–54) this improbable yet harmonious amalgam of East and West, spare north and luxurious south, was to result in such architecture as the Capella Palatina at Palermo. Latin and Byzantine ground-plans were merged; the chapel has both a main aisle and a central space; in the main aisle, classical pillars support Islamic pointed arches; Byzantine mosaics decorate the walls and the vault of the cupola; the ceiling is covered with geometrical designs edged with inscriptions in *kufic*, the stylized form of Arabic script. The building is alive with the colours of the Byzantine and Islamic East.

Roger II and his successors encouraged translations direct from Greek—still known in Sicily, which had once been part of the

Byzantine empire—into Latin. He encouraged Muslim weavers, whose work profoundly influenced the design of later Italian textiles. And on a gold coin of his reign, 'Arabic' numerals appear for the first time in Europe (1138).

The last flowering of this unique Sicilian–Arabic culture was to take place under Roger's grandson, Frederick II Hohenstaufen (1212–50), who was also Holy Roman emperor. He inherited from his Norman predecessors a deep love of Eastern learning and luxury. His mind was wide and catholic. He was fascinated by the ways of birds, wrote a famous work of falconry, imported Muslim falconers, and carried out extensive scientific experiments. He had questions compiled and sent to Muslim scholars in Spain and Egypt, on such matters as science, and Aristotelian philosophy. He wanted to know why, when partly covered with water, oars and lances appeared to be bent; and what caused the illusion of floating specks before the eyes of people suffering from cataract. Following the example of his predecessors, Frederick gave his patronage to the great medical school at Salerno, near Naples. In fact he decreed that no physician should practise in his dominions without a licence from the Salerno masters. The medical theories of Salerno enjoyed an immense reputation throughout Europe. The school itself had been founded at some time in the tenth century, but it was the versions of Galen and other scholars translated from Arabic by Constantine which developed the school's activity and consequently its fame.

Frederick's principal interest, however, was in zoology, and he kept a menagerie of elephants, leopards, camels and other animals sent to him by friendly Muslim rulers. He encouraged translations by his favourite, Michael Scot (d. 1235), who had studied at Toledo and who rendered into Latin the entire biological and zoological works of Aristotle. Dante alludes, in the *Inferno*, to Michael Scot's fame as a magician, and in the folklore of his birthplace, Scotland, he is remembered as the 'wondrous wizard'. In fact, Scot was no necromancer, but his was an age of incredulity and superstition. In the popular mind, great learning lay near to the edge of mystery and the revelations of Arab science assumed an aura of magic. In a very real sense they deserved it, for they transformed the face, and the substance, of European thought.

Through the gates of Spain and Sicily came many things which took no root in Europe or which were compelled to wait for the development of other techniques before they became acceptable. One such was the art of paper-making, which began its journey from China, arrived in Samarkand in the eighth century, in Cairo about 900, and in Spain about 1150. The first references to European-made paper come from Italy, around 1268, and France about the same time. When printing followed paper from China in the fifteenth century, the two together were to complete the transformation of Europe which had been begun in the twelfth and thirteenth centuries through the mediation of Islam.

Intellectual transmissions, as distinct from technological inventions and the appurtenances of a higher standard of living, came almost entirely through mediating cultures. At the same time, Europe was meeting the Muslim East face to face in that fantastic series of encounters known collectively as the Crusades. Fundamentally, the Crusades were Europe's first essay in colonization, in the search for profit, territorial, commercial and spiritual. The Cross was emblazoned on the shields of military adventurers who were in the Levant in order to extend not the frontiers of European knowledge but Christian dominion and the boundaries of their own wealth and power. They were transmitters none the less, although, in fact, the Muslim East by now had little more to offer in the way of learning. The only known scholarly work actually carried back to Europe by the Crusaders was an important medical treatise of al-Mujusi, translated by Stephen of Antioch in that city in 1127. But it was an exception. The activity of Arab thought had begun to decline; the great luminaries of Arab culture, the eminent philosophers and physicians, were dead.

It is, however, also true to say that the cultural standards of the Crusaders were low. The knights who poured into the Levant formed an army of occupation living in forbidding fortresses and armed camps. They *did* have contact with the people they ruled— the peasants and the artisans—but seldom with the intelligentsia. In that great anonymous narrative of the First Crusade the *Gesta Francorum*, completed about 1101, the Crusaders appear as knights of Christ and the Turks as barbarians and enemies of God. To the author, who knew nothing of the Orient, the Crusaders formed a miraculous army, surging out to rescue the Holy Places from the defiling fingers of the heathen. But the author spoke only for himself and a few others, reflecting that 'passion for God' which was often felt by the common people—which indeed, made the Crusades possible—rather than the cupidity of most of their leaders.

When the Crusaders settled down, however, and were able to observe the superior material culture of the people they now ruled, they sensibly immersed themselves in the pleasures and the luxuries of oriental life. As some element of stability came to the Latin kingdoms of the Levant, immigration from the West increased, trade and commerce flourished, peaceful—even happy— relations developed with the Muslim inhabitants, and a new tolerance grew up amongst the resident Christian population. But it was a conditional tolerance, expressing a European admiration of Asia which stopped at the point where actual power began. The later Crusaders had more than the Holy Places to fight for: they had the comforts of their new and vastly expanded affluence. Unfortunately for them, these were threatened not only by the heathen but by that destructive greed which is the engine of colonial expansion. In the later Crusades, what Edward Gibbon called 'the World's Debate' was blatantly manipulated for personal gain, not only by the knights themselves but by bankers and merchants who had made fortunes out of this great meeting of East and West.

Such activity naturally had its effect upon the technology of war. The Normans who formed the vanguard of the Crusaders had already been leaders in the European expertise of the time before they landed in Palestine. Their enemies, however, were expert in different types of warfare and new weapons and new techniques were needed to combat them. In particular, the Crusaders learned much from siege tactics developed in the East. The well-protected cities of the Levant had walls which could not be breached by the rather primitive devices of the Europeans. The art of sapping and mining—in an age before explosives— became one of considerable sophistication. Europeans learned the hard way about the use of incendiaries, which the Muslims had brought to a high peak of effectiveness. In the field of 'artillery' (which then consisted of machines for hurling stones), the mangonel, a large and sophisticated kind of catapult, was constantly being improved. In the case of more portable weapons, the crossbow—known in China in very early times—may have well been

59

transmitted by the Muslims. Certainly, there are no records of its existence in Europe before the Crusades. The wearing of chain mail, and cotton pads beneath armour, were of Crusading origin, as was the use of carrier-pigeons for sending messages. Though pigeons were used as carriers in Sicily before the Crusades, it was the military needs of the campaigns in the Levant that brought them into general use. Armorial devices on shields and pennants were used by the Mamluks, the one-time Turkish slaves who ruled Egypt from the thirteenth to the sixteenth centuries, to distinguish the various corps of their armies; the idea was taken over by the Crusaders with many of the symbols of Muslim heraldry, such as the double-headed eagle, which, starting life on Hittite monuments in remote antiquity, passed through the badge of the Seljuk sultans of Persia early in the twelfth century, to become the blazon of the Holy Roman emperors less than two hundred years later.

In military architecture, designed of course to withstand the new siege-engines, there was an interchange of techniques. The Crusaders took with them a substantial knowledge of military masonry, which they passed on to the Arabs. The citadel of Cairo, which still survives, was greatly influenced by the castles built by the Crusaders in Palestine. Christian prisoners probably laboured at its construction. But the Europeans borrowed from the Arabs machicolation—an arrangement of brackets, closely spaced, carrying a projecting parapet. Between the brackets were holes closed by trap-doors, through which boiling oil and other deterrents could be showered on attackers who tried to scale the walls. The first example of Arab machicolation, in Syria, dates from 729, and there is a machicolated gateway at Cairo which was constructed a century before the first example appears in Europe. This, at Château Gaillard, was built in 1184 by Richard Coeur de Lion. But the single invention which was to revolutionize military technology completely was still not known to the West, nor apparently to the Arabs. It was not until the Mongols swept across the Eurasian heartland in the middle of the thirteenth century that gunpowder was to reach Europe.

Though Arab origins can be traced in many details of military architecture, European buildings were not in general influenced by the experience of the Crusaders. But in the minor arts, in the *luxe privée* of the rich, Europe went through a period of arabesque taste comparable with the chinoiserie craze of the eighteenth century. Returning Crusaders brought back with them new fashions, new furnishings, new textiles. All were seized upon by those who could afford them and who were anxious to bring something of the comfort and luxury of the East into their homes.

Wealthy European households would now have over the bed a baldaquin, a canopy of brocade; the name comes from that of the cloth itself, in Italian *baldacco*, a corruption of Baghdad. Rich hangings and covers would be decorated with the *fleur-de-lis*, a heraldic motif adopted from the Arabs. Velvets, silks and brocade were at first imported from Egypt and Syria, although they were later imitated by Italian weavers. On the floor might be the special luxury of a carpet, a covering used for centuries in western and central Asia not only for floors but for hangings and sleeping-mats. Rugs and carpets, sometimes with smooth faces like tapestries, sometimes with loose threads knotted into the fabric to produce a 'pile' resembling velvet, were at first regarded in Europe more as treasures to be admired than as something to walk upon. Stained glass for windows became popular in both sacred and secular buildings after the Crusaders had become acquainted with the enamelled and tinted glass of Syria. These and many other luxuries were introduced into Europe during the period covered by the Crusades. There were jewels, for which Syria had been famous in Roman times; toilet articles and powders from Cairo. Mirrors of glass replaced those of polished steel; new colours and dyes banished the drabness of rich women's clothes. Among the new colours was lilac (from the Arabic *laylak*), as well as carmine and crimson, the Arabic words for the last two coming originally from Sanskrit. Soon, with the new vocabulary of texture and ornament, European craftsmen began to reproduce the wares of the Muslim East. In textiles and carpets, in metalware and ceramics, the Crusades brought a fertile and continuing legacy.

But there were also tastes other than those to which the fingers and the eye respond. While in the Levant, Crusaders discovered the perfumes, spices, sweetmeats and other exotic products of Arabia and India. The old fascination for rich flavourings, which had helped to destroy the economy of the Roman empire, now took hold of that empire's successors. The diet of northern Europe was quickly enlivened with pepper and other condiments. By the end of the twelfth century no banquet would have been thought complete without spiced dishes. The repertoire of the medieval cook was limited by the coarseness of ingredients, particularly in winter. Salted meats and dried fish offer little variety to the tongue. Spices turned this rough fare into something palatable. The prices of these delicious condiments, however, were high, and most baronial households kept their spices locked in a wardrobe to be doled out to the cook only in the amount required for some particular dish.

In the twelfth and thirteenth centuries most of the spice trade passed through Italy to the great fairs of France and Germany. Later, the Venetians sent their trading galleys direct to Flanders and to England. There was a profound ignorance of exactly where the spices that so titillated the palates of the rich came from, even among those who had actually visited the entrepôts of Egypt and Syria. The fables of the time—believed with all the superstitious awe of the Middle Ages—are best observed in the words of that mirror of knightly knowledge the Sieur de Joinville (*c.* 1224–1319), friend and biographer of St Louis of France. Joinville thought that spices came from the Earthly Paradise, whence they were blown into the Nile. There, he explained, 'before the river enters Egypt, people . . . cast their nets into the river at night, and when morning comes they find in their nets such goods as are sold by weight, and brought into the land, viz., ginger, rhubarb, wood of aloes and cinnamon'.

After spices, perhaps the most revolutionary import was sugar. Before the experience of the Crusades, Europeans used honey for sweetening. But the early Crusaders discovered fields of sugar-cane in Syria and other parts of the Islamic East. The introduction of sugar led to the making of soft drinks and all varieties of candies and sweetmeats, as well as of a whole new range of medicines.

The knightly sport of the tournament, in the modern view so particularly characteristic of the Middle Ages, was borrowed from the Muslim paladins. Though jousts of one sort or another had existed in Europe before the Crusades, the tournament as an aristocratic social event, and the institution of that chivalry which it seems to express, was developed on the plains of Syria. But it should not be thought that the Crusaders themselves were particularly chivalrous; this is an illusion fostered by those tales of heroes which still play so large a part in our view of the past. On the whole, the Crusaders were ruffians, gangsters out for loot and pleasure. But the military orders which emerged during the Crusades began to impose certain standards of moral discipline upon their members. In time, knightly bravery became associated with gentleness and courtesy to women. The tournament became an elaborate display of aristocratic manners, representative of a more refined society.

To claim all this as the result of contact with the civilization of the Muslim East may seem to go too far. But improvements in material culture create new rules, new patterns of behaviour, for those who benefit from them. The 'knightly' virtues took time to develop. Refinement and brutality coexisted, as they do to this day, but both were a consequence of the immense widening of horizons brought about by the Crusades.

Much of the effect of the meeting between East and West was confined to the upper and middle classes, who profited from it in one way or another. The common people, on whose religious enthusiasm the Crusades had been founded, felt few of the advantages, though great forces were released which would, in time, change their lot. But there were some general benefits— the public bath, for example. Rome, following the Greeks, had made public bathing an important part of everyday life, and successive emperors had enriched Rome and other cities with grandiose baths. These were, indeed, more than places to bathe. They had become places of amusement. The early Christian Fathers condemned public baths because of the licentiousness of the entertainment provided there. Public bathing had come to be associated with sin. But the Muslims developed a bathing system very like that of the earlier Romans, and the custom was spread throughout Europe by the Crusaders. Hospitals, too, received stimulus from the Crusades. A great many were founded throughout Europe in the late twelfth and thirteenth centuries, no longer under monkish supervision as before, and based on Islamic prototypes. In Paris, a hospital was founded by St Louis. Many of the new hospitals were built as lazar-houses for lepers—for among the gifts carried back to Europe by returning Crusaders was the terrible disease of leprosy.

One of the most seminal of the Arab legacies was to ornamentation and design. Through contact with Muslim civilization in Spain and Sicily, as well as through the trade in luxury goods which was a consequence of the Crusades, a number of decorative motifs entered the vocabulary of European art. A particular example occurs in the use of Arabic letters for purely decorative purposes. These, in their formal, geometrical abstraction, appealed so much to European artists that they were frequently introduced into the representation of sacred figures. Giotto's portrait of Christ, in 'The Raising of Lazarus', in the Arena, Padua, shows an early use of *kufic* script. Fra Angelico and Fra Lippo Lippi also used this kind of decoration constantly, without knowing that it was actually a form of writing. But those who developed *kufic* script into Gothic black-letter did so in the consciousness that they were taking one decorative script and creating another from it. Gothic architecture, too, contains a number of Muslim idioms, such as the pointed and the cusped arch. The contribution of the Islamic world to European culture was so vast that it is impossible yet to catalogue it. Even such objects as the simple rosary, used in the counting of prayers, were probably introduced into western Europe by the Crusaders. In many ways the meeting of East and West enriched the practice of the new Christianity as well as the pockets of the Italian merchants who controlled the sea trade with the Muslim East.

Trade between Europe and the Muslim cities of the Mediterranean did not originate with the Crusades, but its volume before then had been comparatively small. As Crusade followed Crusade, however, and as European colonization stretched out into the Muslim lands, the coastal towns of Italy recognized—and seized—the opportunity. Soon a regular system of shipping was developed, and shipping companies with headquarters at Venice, already pre-eminent in oriental commerce, and at Marseilles were formed by merchants—and by some of the military orders—to operate the system. Along Europe's internal trade routes, too, new towns began to cluster. The city, as such, was soon to reinstate itself in the position it had held in Roman times but had lost in the anarchy of a collapsing empire. Europe surged and bubbled with activity—military, political, religious, intellectual and commercial. The scale of the new commerce called for new methods of financing.

2 *Head of the Buddha. Cambodia,
   tenth–eleventh century* A.D.

*The transformations of Apollo
(pp. 14–22). Head of a Buddha in
Hellenized style. From Gandhara,
second–fourth century* A.D.

3 *Head of Apollo. From the Temple of
   Zeus, Olympia, fifth century* B.C.

4   *The characteristic Han horse* (pp. 24 and 90). *From a cave-tomb.*

5   *The Lamb of Tartary, growing on a stalk out of the ground* (p. 25).

Silver fountain made for Mangu Khan by Guillaume Boucher (p. 72). From the four spouts came, respectively, mare's milk, wine, honey liquor, and rice wine.

7   *A European system of counting, using the fingers.*

8   *The progress of numerals from India to Europe (p. 52). Top: Hindu, c. A.D. 500. Centre: Arabic, A.D. 970. Bottom: European, thirteenth century A.D.*

10   *An exercise in the abstract; God worshipped through geometry. A ninth-century illuminated initial (p. 45).*

INCIPIT LIB
SAPIENTIAE

ILIGITEIUS
tiam quiiudicatis
terram. senate
dedno inbonitate
etinsimpli citate
cordis quaerite.
illum . qnmmue
nitur abhis quinon
temptant illum.
Apparet autem
eis quifidem ha
bent in illum. per
uerfacenim cogita
tiones feparant ado . probata autem uirtus . cor
ripit infipientes . q nm inmaliuola anima nonin
troibit fapientia . nec habitabit incorpore sub
dito peccatis .

S es enim spr disciplinae effugiet ficium ea auferet
se a cogitationib; quaesunt sine intellectu . et cor
ripietur a superueniente iniquitate . Benignus é

The language of European
revival (p. 44). Latin
minuscule of the ninth century.

*11   An example of European borrowing from Arabic
military technology (pp. 59–60); a mangonel.*

12 *Luxuries from the East* (p. 61). *Charles VI of France surrounded by objects originating in the Muslim East.*

13 *Interior of a public bath in the Muslim East*
    (p. 63).

14 *The shoulder-band of Christ's robe is decorated*
    with Kufic script (p. 64).

15 *Reminders of home. Dutch merchants playing billiards at Deshima* (pp. 80 and 120).

16 *Letter from Arghun, Ilkhan of Persia, to Philippe le Bel, King of France* (pp. 74–5).

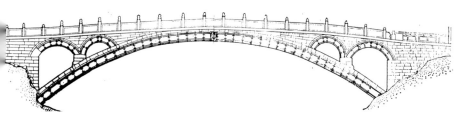

17 *The first segmental arch bridge, China*, A.D. *610*
(p. 85).

18/19 *Ancestors of the printed word; two of the earliest known European playing cards, c. 1440.*

20   *Chinese playing-card, c. 1400.*

21   *The earliest dated specimen of block printing in the world. China, c. A.D. 868 (pp. 89–93).*

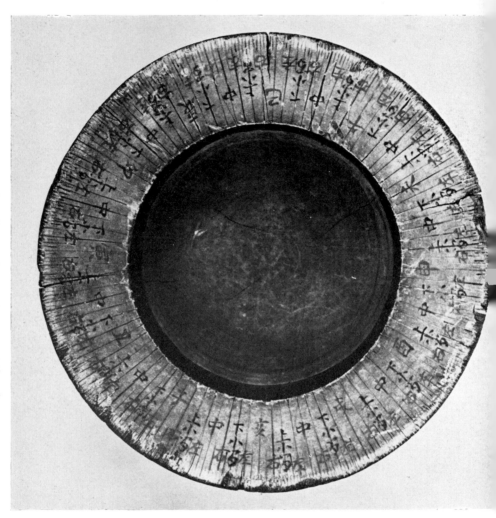

22   *A Chinese floating compass. The 'needle' was probably a wooden
turtle in which was embedded a piece of lodestone suspended on a
sharpened stick.*

23 *The magical background to navigational magnetism; a diviner of the Han period using a geomantic spoon.*

24 *The earliest accurate representation of an English sea-compass* (pp. 95–6).

25   *Chinese influences in a painting by Leonardo da Vinci.*

26   *Characteristically Chinese hills, by Kuo Hsi* (p. 89).

Bankers emerged at Genoa, Pisa and Siena with branches in the Levant and a system of credit and credit-notes to facilitate trans-actions; the military orders, too, notably the Templars, themselves became bankers. The investment of large funds called for some form of security. Monopolies were created in the new conquests and special privileges were assigned to merchants. Gold returned to the coinage of Europe, from which it had disappeared after the fall of Rome, when Venetian merchants in the Levant struck for themselves a gold coin, the *Byzantini Saracenati*, to be used for purchases in the hinterland. Until 1249—when Pope Innocent IV protested about it—these coins bore Arabic inscriptions and were dated according to Muslim years. In Europe, the first gold coins for internal use were minted by the Florentines in 1252.

The growth of trade brought with it a shift in the centres of power. The ambitions of merchants soon became as important—and as influential—as the ambitions of kings. In the Fourth Crusade of 1204, for example, the Venetians persuaded the knights, instead of attacking the infidel, to seize what was still the greatest city in Europe, Constantinople. The Arabs had brought to Europe the treasures of Greek learning; the capture of Constantinople spread throughout Europe some of the treasures of the Greek empire of Byzantium.

This disreputable affair reflected the true nature of the Crusades. They were, in spite of their ideological overtones, no more than the first wars of conquest and colonization. Europe reached out to Asia but, at that time, proved unable to hold on to it. The Mongols, however, were starting their journey across the Eurasian heartland and soon travellers from Europe were to reach the land of myth and legend which lay at the end of the Silk Road. The way to China was about to be opened.

III

The Augmentation of the Indies

In India are more than five thousand isles that men dwell in, good and great, without others that men dwell not in. And in ilk one of those isles are many cities and towns of mickle folk.

The Travels of Sir John Mandeville (c. 1371)

. . . he does smile his face into more lines than is in the new map, with the augmentation of the Indies.

SHAKESPEARE, *Twelfth Night* (1601)

This Discovery, when perfected, will lay open to us an *Empire of Learning*, hitherto only fabulously described; this will admit us to converse with the best and greatest of that Empire, that either are, or ever have been; this will Discover a new Indian Mine and Treasure, and make a new Trade to bring it hither.

ROBERT HOOKE, F.R.S., *Some Observations concerning the Character and Language of the Chinese* (1686)

The Opening Door

The twelfth century can truthfully be called the century of European revolt—revolt against the material and spiritual twilight that had followed the fall of Rome. But in the next century the revolt collapsed. Between the Renaissance of the twelfth century and the Renaissance that began in the fifteenth, most of Europe developed a cowardice of thought and action. The cause of this regression—and of that even more sensational revival of spirit and purpose which followed it—has been, and will continue to be, the subject of much learned argument. But to both, the Mongol conquests of the thirteenth century contributed a great deal. They struck a devastating blow at the hopes of the Christian powers of Europe, while at the same time supplying the means by which ideas and techniques could travel directly between East and West. In Europe it was to be a period of germination, of acclimatization to new ideas, the result of which was to be the birth of the modern world itself.

The Mongols, like the Huns before them, came from east of Lake Baikal in the heartland of Asia. They were nomads, exceptionally skilful horsemen, by religion Shamanists—worshippers of nature-spirits—but with a tolerant interest in other faiths. They were by no means primitive savages; only a highly organized and intelligent people could have moved and supplied huge armies across the length and breadth of Asia. Like the Arabs, they had minds quick to discover, evaluate and absorb the ideas and techniques of more civilized but flabbier people. From the Chinese they took their military engineering, from neighbouring tribes the art of writing. They produced in Genghiz Khan (1162–1227) a Napoleon of the steppes, prepared to adapt to his own ambitions the expertise of those he conquered. Mongol laws and orders were published in Uighur script. Most of his officials were Christians, and it seemed that through them Christianity was suddenly offered the most seductive opportunity of converting Asia to the teachings of Christ.

The Christians who served—and influenced—the Mongol rulers were Nestorians, men of the same persuasion as those through whom the Arabs had discovered Greek culture. The history of the Nestorians is one not only of tragedy, courage and endeavour, but of a civilizing mission of great potency. Among other things, they brought alphabetic writing to many Asian peoples.

The rise of evangelical Islam had driven the Nestorians farther and farther into Asia, where their conversion of such tribes as the Uighurs and the Keraits probably gave rise to the legend of the mysterious Prester John, the Christian king in Asia who was alleged to have written letters, in 1165 and 1177, to the Byzantine emperor Manuel and Pope Alexander III. These letters—forgeries by some Crusading propagandist—represented Prester John as ruling over seventy tributary kings and living in a palace in which, he wrote, 'the windows are of crystal. The tables on which our courtiers eat are of gold and some of amethyst. . . . The chamber in which Our Sublimity reposes is marvellously decorated with gold and stones of every kind. At our table thirty thousand men . . . are daily entertained.' The letter to the emperor also announced the Asian king's intention of subduing the enemies of Christ. To a crusading Europe, nothing could have been more welcome. The Pope even sent a reply—though nobody knows to whom it was delivered. But from this time forward, all Europe was convinced of the existence of a great Christian ruler somewhere in the heart of Asia. When news reached Europe of the conquests of Genghiz Khan, who after taking Peking in 1215 had turned westwards, it was believed that Prester John was on the move, intent on crushing Islam between East and West.

With Genghiz's successor Ogotai, however, Europe found itself involved in a drama of blood and ruin. The chronicler Matthew Paris wrote that, in 1240, 'a detestable nation of Satan, to wit the countless armies of the Tartars, broke loose from its mountain-environed home, and piercing the solid rocks [of the Caucasus] poured forth like devils'. The Mongols attacked both Islam and Christendom. Persia was almost overrun, and Mongol armies swept through Russia and poured into Poland, Hungary and even Germany, burning and killing with a terrifying and irresistible fury. 'No eye,' one Russian manuscript records, 'remained open to weep for the dead.' Only the death of Ogotai (1241), which forced the Mongol generals to return home to elect a new khan, saved Europe from yet another barbarian conquest.

The ferocity of the Mongol armies and the contemptuous way in which they had flung aside the Christian knights who had barred their way hardly seemed appropriate behaviour for an allegedly Christian king. But Europe still believed in Prester John and sent missions to find him. Ignorance of Central Asia was profound, though in fact the barrier which had descended between Europe and Asia after the barbarian invasions of the Roman empire was never total. The route along the old Silk Road had still to some extent remained open. It seems likely, for example, that trade between China and Byzantium continued, and the typically Chinese designs on a door at St Mark's, Venice, were probably copied from a Chinese figured textile. But for all practical purposes, the Silk Road *was* closed to travellers and to any extensive trade. Consequently, Europe created an illusory world inhabited by all the luxuries as well as the oddities of the medieval imagination— headless giants, one-legged men, and other similar marvels. The persistence of myth over reality, of wonder over sober truth, is one of the great certainties of history. Europe's view of an Asia peopled with monsters survived by many centuries the observations of travellers. East and West were approaching one another, but they did so in a darkness intensified by the fecund imagination of fabulists.

Missions dispatched by Pope and Crusader were sent not to observe marvels but to find allies against the enemies of Christ. The first of these missions was headed by an Italian friar, John of Plano Carpini, former companion of St Francis of Assisi. He was sent by Pope Innocent IV in 1245, when Christian Europe still believed itself menaced by the Mongols, and carried a letter 'to the king of the Tartar people' warning them to 'arrest their on-slaughts on Christendom through fear of Divine Wrath'. The mission did in fact reach the court of Khan Kuyuk at Karakorum in 1246, but the Khan informed Friar John that God had given him the lordship of the world and if the Pope wished his friendship he had better come in person. The short reign of Kuyuk (1246–8) did, however, see the rise of Nestorian advisers to positions of great influence. Mongol policy was to become pro-Christian and anti-Muslim. In 1251, Kuyuk's successor Manghu was elected.

At about the same time, Louis IX of France (St Louis) sent a Flemish monk, William of Rubruck, on a fact-finding mission. At the court of Karakorum, which he reached in 1254, William found the administration full of Nestorian Christians. He did not think very much of their moral character—but he was, of course, prejudiced by his hatred of the Nestorian heresy. While William does not seem to have believed that the Great Khan was Prester John, he was convinced that the dominions of that Christian king were near at hand.

At Karakorum, the envoy found a number of European Christians, including one 'Basil by name the son of an Englishman, who was born in Hungary'. How these Europeans happened to be at the Mongol court is not known, though it is probable that some of them had been captured during a Mongol attack on Hungary. Nor is there any evidence to suggest that they were responsible for transmitting specifically European ideas or mechanical principles to their captors. About one of these men something *is* known. His name was Guillaume Boucher, and he was a Parisian goldsmith and mechanic who served Kuyuk and Manghu between 1246 and 1259. Boucher is believed to have constructed a silver fountain for Manghu Khan, which, by the application of simple hydraulics, dispensed liquids of various sorts. This was not an exclusively European form of expertise as water-operated clocks and other automata had been constructed by the Chinese since the seventh century, and by the Byzantines certainly before 473. In the case of Manghu's fountain, Boucher was more craftsman than mechanic.

William of Rubruck gives only the most cursory information about this little community of Western Christians, but he did collect a vast amount of detail about the countries he passed through. He also learned that the Mongols were planning the complete conquest of Asia by two simultaneous offensives, to be commanded by two of Manghu's brothers: one to the east, against China, by Kublai, and the other to the west by Hulagu.

Hulagu opened his campaign against the caliphate of Baghdad in 1256. Though he himself was a pagan, his wife was a Nestorian Christian and so was his most trusted general, Kitboga. It seemed that a new Christian offensive had begun. In fact, one modern historian has called this the 'Mongol–Nestorian Crusade'. Certainly,

Hulagu showed the most violent animosity towards Islam. When he captured Baghdad in 1258, eight hundred thousand men, women and children were said to have been killed, and the proud mosques and palaces of the city were reduced to ashes. Only the Christians, gathered in their church, were spared. After this, Christians in the East began to hail Hulagu as a new Constantine, delivering them from five centuries of Muslim oppression. Soon, three Christian leaders—the King of Armenia, Count Bohemund of Antioch, and the Mongol general Kitboga—were riding together in triumph through the streets of Damascus. But again, the death of the Great Khan was to interrupt the flow of history. Manghu died in China in 1259. The unity of the Mongol leadership died with him and so did the Nestorian dream of a new Christian empire in the Near East. A dispute over the Mongol leadership was followed by Kitboga's defeat by the Mamluks of Egypt. This was the first time the Mongols had ever been beaten in battle. Islam revived, flexed its muscles, and set about the task of reconquest. Muslim civilization began to flower again, with Cairo as its new Baghdad.

Away to the east, Kublai Khan's conquest of China was continuing, though it was not complete until 1279. But Kublai himself had already been conquered by Chinese civilization. In two generations the Mongols had moved from semi-savagery to considerable sophistication. The Chinese discovered that their new ruler was not a barbarian intent on burning and killing but almost like one of themselves.

To the court of Kublai came Niccolo and Matteo Polo, two merchants from the city of Venice, that great profiteer of the Crusades. Venice—its warehouses and its merchants fat with the riches of the East—considered itself the finest, most powerful and most beautiful city in the world. But in 1269 the two Polos returned, after nine years' absence, with letters from Kublai Khan to the Pope and tales of great cities surpassing even Venice in their beauty and riches. That the Polos were able to make this long and difficult journey shows that the old Silk Road was open and controlled by one great unifying power. The conquests of Genghiz Khan and his successors were to make China better known to Europe than at any time before.

The letters carried by the elder Polos asked the Pope to send a hundred learned scholars, 'well schooled in the seven arts', but the Holy See did not grasp an opportunity that might have changed the course of history. Instead, when the Polos set off again for China, they were accompanied by Niccolo's son, Marco, who was to conjure up such a vision of Cathay—full of palaces and pavilions of dazzling splendour, of pearls and gold and precious stones— that it was to haunt the European imagination for centuries. In his own times, Marco Polo was thought to be a liar, but later men thought differently and strove to prove him right. Columbus, whose carefully annotated copy of Marco's travels still survives, set out to discover a route to that same Cathay and found a New World instead. The Portuguese, too, were to reach out their hands for the riches of Marco Polo's Asia.

On the caravan routes followed by the Polos could be seen not only travellers from the West, but also Mongol emissaries to the pope and the princes of Europe—for, oddly enough, where once Western missions had journeyed to Karakorum and been rebuffed by the Great Khan, now Mongol ambassadors went to the West suggesting military co-operation against the Mamluks of Egypt. The most interesting of these envoys was the Nestorian monk Rabban Sauma, who was probably a Chinese, though some authorities believe him to have been an Uighur born in China. In any case he was the first Chinese citizen that we know of to visit Europe.

In 1278 Rabban Sauma and a companion decided to make a pilgrimage to Jerusalem, but they never reached the Holy Land. The companion became Nestorian Patriarch in Tabriz, while Rabban Sauma was sent on to Europe as the envoy of the Ilkhan of Persia, Arghun, the grandson of Hulagu. Arghun was obsessed with the thought of crushing those Mamluks who had so humiliated the Mongol armies. His predecessor had gone so far as to send six emissaries to Edward I, King of England, who before he had ascended the throne had fought in Palestine, and through them had proposed an alliance with the Mongols. Arghun himself, in 1285, had proposed a joint campaign to Pope Honorius IV, but the proposition was ignored. The Ilkhan, however, was determined, and in 1287 Rabban Sauma was sent to Europe as ambassador. He also carried letters from his old companion the Patriarch to the pope.

The Mongol envoy passed through Constantinople, where he was welcomed by the Byzantine emperor Andronicos II. There Rabban Sauma seems to have spent most of his time seeing holy relics—such as the still moist tears of the Virgin Mary—with which the city abounded even after the plundering of the Fourth Crusade. In Rome, he found that Pope Honorius was dead, but was able to revere such objects as the hand of St Matthew and the foot of St Philip. Since there was no sign of the election of a new pope, Rabban Sauma went on to Paris. On his journey he stopped at Genoa, where the merchants were anxious for a Mongol alliance as a stimulus to their trade, which was declining as Venice increased her hold on the commerce of the East. In September 1287, Rabban Sauma reached Paris. In the palace of the Louvre, the young king, Philip the Fair, received the Mongol envoy with great respect and told him that, God willing, the French would fight side by side with the Mongols to capture Jerusalem. From Paris, Rabban Sauma went on to Bordeaux and there met the English king, Edward I.

Finally, Rabban Sauma returned to Rome, where there was now a new pope, and then began his journey home. He took with him Edward of England's sincere desire for an alliance, an emissary from Philip of France, letters from the pope in Rome, and some pieces of holy relics. Arghun seems to have been pleased with his envoy.

Believing that the ground for future co-operation had been prepared, in 1289 Arghun sent two more emissaries—one of whom was a Genoese—to the pope and to the French and English kings. The letters they carried were identical, and the one sent to Philip the Fair still survives. It is in the form of a roll, six and a half feet long and eleven inches wide, and is written in Uighur script. Impressed upon it is a seal of state in Chinese characters, given to the Mongol ruler of Persia by Kublai Khan. These seal impressions were, perhaps, the nearest approach to block-printing that Europe had then seen. The letter itself contained the news that Arghun intended to march on Jerusalem early in 1291. 'If you keep your word and send troops at the appointed date,' the Ilkhan wrote to the two kings, 'and if God favours us; when We have taken Jerusalem, We shall give it to you.'

But the expedition never set out. Arghun died in Persia on

10 March 1291, six days after the last remaining Crusader strong-hold in Palestine had fallen to the Mamluks. An English embassy which arrived in Arghun's capital in 1292 brought back nothing more than the present of a leopard for King Edward. In 1295, Arghun's successor became a Muslim, though this did not end Mongol attempts to form an alliance with the Christian West against the Mamluks. The last Mongol embassy reached England in 1307 but by then Edward too was dead. This was really the end. The Crusaders had been thrown out of Syria and, in the words of Edward Gibbon, 'a mournful and solitary silence prevailed along the coast which had so long resounded with the World's Debate'.

But though Christianity, both Western and Eastern, was in retreat in Asia by 1300, the Mongols had destroyed the cultural supremacy of Islam for ever. That unity of Muslim civilization which had once extended from Turkestan to Spain was broken. Under Mongol attack, Islam lost its tolerance and intellectual curiosity. Even the Arabic language retreated from its dominant position in the Muslim world. The intellectual leadership of the world was to pass to the West, but it could not have achieved its dominating role without the legacies from the East.

As long as the Mongol dynasty survived in China, travellers from the West still made their way there. The *pax Mongolica* protected merchant and missionary, and the road to Cathay was trodden by Europeans of all kinds with skills and crafts to sell. The quest for Prester John still exercised its pull. Friar John of Monte Corvino built a Christian church in the Chinese capital in 1299, and converted a prince whom he described as a scion 'of the family of Prester John of India'. But he had no success with the Mongol rulers themselves. The best known of Marco Polo's successors was Friar Odoric de Pordenone, who entered China through Canton—a city, he wrote, 'as big as three Venices . . . and all Italy hath not the amount of craft that this one city hath'. He returned to Italy in 1330 after thirteen years of travelling in Asia, and his narrative is full of careful observations made in the countries he visited. On a more practical plane, in 1340, one merchant wrote a handbook for other merchants, giving detailed instructions for the overland journey to China. It seemed that once again, as when Rome first touched China in the reign of

Marcus Aurelius, the door between East and West was opening wide. It was—and much profit in gold and ideas came through it—but soon it was to be slammed in the face of Europe by the resurgence of a purely Chinese nationalism. In 1294 Kublai Khan died. His successor was energetic and conscientious but, after his death in 1337, the Mongol dynasty rapidly degenerated, and in 1368 its last emperor fled from Peking. A native dynasty, the Ming, seized power.

The new dynasty, having overthrown foreign rule, turned against foreign merchants and the missionaries of foreign religions. Europe retreated. When the Chinese did move outwards once more, early in the fifteenth century, Chinese junks began to explore the southern seas even as far as the east coast of Africa. But just as Europe was also about to reach out again, the Chinese for some unknown reason stopped their maritime activity. What might have been the fate of Asia if, at the end of the century, the Portuguese had found the Indies dominated by Chinese sea power?

The inspirer of these Portuguese explorers, Prince Henry the Navigator (1394–1460), was something of an isolated figure, surrounded with visions. But he followed his visions in an intensely practical manner. All the maritime experts of the period were brought to Portugal—seamen, cartographers, builders of ships. Tiny Portuguese caravels moved farther and farther out into the great seas until, thirty-eight years after the death of the prince, Vasco da Gama set foot in India and Asia's European Age began. Da Gama, when asked by the ruler of Calicut what he had come for, replied, 'Christians and spices.' Thus he expressed, in the late fifteenth century, the same mixture of motives that had lain behind the Crusades.

In Europe, Islam was on the move again, this time with the armies of the Osmanli Turks. In 1453 they had washed over the walls of Constantinople, and the Christian world was now threatened by the rising tide. The Portuguese hoped to find allies in Asia against the Turks—for the legend of Prester John had lost none of its potency—and also hoped to break the Muslim monopoly of the spice trade.

From the viewpoint of today, the Portuguese adventure may seem the beginning of a new and splendid Europe, dynamic,

77

purposeful, flushed with enthusiasm. But this view is the imposition of philosophers and art-historians, so blinded by the glare of the Renaissance that they cannot see the anguish that lay behind it. The rediscovery of the Classical World, the vocabulary of paganism which painters and poets used to express themselves, the golden light which seems perpetually to illuminate the human landscape—all these have created the impression of a new world free from the terrors of darkness. This is by no means the truth. To those who lived in the fifteenth and sixteenth centuries, the world seemed in decline. Christendom, instead of expanding, was actually shrinking under the assaults of the heathen. When da Gama planted his foot upon the soil of India, the advance-guard of the Turks was at the gates of Vicenza. In fact, as the Portuguese advanced against Islam in the Indian Ocean, Christendom seemed to be on the retreat in Europe.

A close look at the age of discovery suggests that it was also an age of despair. The literature of the time was the literature of escape, the religion that of mysticism. The Dance of Death, that most popular symbolism, served as a constant reminder that prince and bishop, merchant and knight, must inevitably take death by the hand. Beside the vitality of the sculptor's portrayal of fresh and virile youth lay the symbols of death and putrefaction. There seemed little to hope for, and a glance at the profound melancholy of Michelangelo's figures on the Medici tombs reveals the resignation of the times. Conquest beyond the seas seemed of very little value. Busbecq, the Flemish diplomat and Habsburg ambassador to Turkey from 1556 to 1562, wrote: 'We set out to conquer worthless empires beyond the seas, and we are losing the heart of Europe.' But in the gloom of the sixteenth century, lights *were* being lit. Reaction against the clutch of despair was soon to give a new and tremendous vitality to the European mind. The Reformation, that great catalyst of change, was about to begin.

The lure of the old dream of Asia—of mountains of jewels and palaces of gold—reasserted itself, and the maritime nations of Europe were each to annex their Golconda. The Crusades had enriched the lives of those who could afford the luxuries of the East. The new era of European colonization was to do the same. But if the East had nothing more to contribute to science and technology in Europe, it had much to give to literature, art and philosophy.

The European settlers in Asia—like the Crusaders in the Levant—enjoyed the affluence of Eastern living. In Goa, the centre of Portuguese power in India, they created a magnificent city, 'Golden Goa', as it came to be called. The Portuguese, those skilful navigators of uncharted seas, very soon gave up the hard life of the pioneer. Slaves ministered to their needs. The streets were full of elegant *fidalgos*, and even the common soldiers could afford to masquerade as men of quality. 'You would say,' recorded one shrewd French observer at the beginning of the seventeenth century, 'they were lords with an income of ten thousand livres, such is their bravery, with their slaves behind them and a man carrying over them a big parasol.'

The riches of the Indies began to have their effect in Portugal too. An extravagant architecture—known as Manueline—blossomed with maritime symbols and strange trees displaying, as it were, both the means and the consequence of Portuguese expansion.

But Portuguese virility was being sapped. The chain of entrepôts which stretched to China was soon threatened by another European nation—Holland. Pride, idleness, wealth and vice had bitten deeply into the Portuguese in Asia and had disarmed them against the challenge. The future was with the Dutch—and later the English. But in China the Portuguese retained enough influence to frustrate Dutch attempts to open up commerce. After a change of dynasty in China in 1644, when the Ming fell to the Manchu (of Mongol origin), Holland was able to send an embassy to Peking. It reached the Chinese capital in 1665, but its only gain was permission to send another embassy in eight years' time. Elsewhere the Dutch were better off. Even when Japan closed its doors to the West in 1641, Holland was allowed to retain a precarious foothold.

The Dutch in turn were threatened by the English. They too were inspired by thoughts of the gorgeous East. Sir Francis Drake—who, in circumnavigating the globe, had reached the Spice Islands of the Java Sea in 1579—aroused the interest of the newly emerging merchant classes with tales of the wealth of the Indies. In September 1599, eighty merchants of the city of London met to establish the East India Company. In the first year of the new century they received a charter from Queen Elizabeth. The great adventure which was to end in British domination of India—and much more—had begun.

But the beginnings were small and without thought of dominion; in fact, the English were anxious to avoid acquiring territory. Their aim was the profit of commerce. The Dutch, however, were exercising sovereign power in the areas they had seized from the Portuguese and, as the century grew older, the English too became ambitious—though against the wishes of the merchants in London. The English in India began to acquire a new arrogance and show, to enjoy the comforts of oriental living, although they did not submerge themselves in the mainstream of Indian life. They had no contempt for Indian social customs. On the contrary, they adopted those which made life more comfortable and luxurious. But though they accepted Hindu superstitions, they knew nothing of Hindu philosophical ideas. They took Indian words into their vocabulary, but never learned the local languages, carrying out their business in the debased Portuguese which had become a sort of common tongue in the coastal settlements. The early European in India remained at heart very much what he had been in his own country.

In Europe, trade with the East began to add more to life than spices for the tables of the rich. Since the Crusades there had been a steady rise in the quality of living. Not, of course, amongst ordinary people; but the aristocracies of Europe and the growing merchant bourgeoisie grasped at the exotic works of the East to add lustre to their own social position. The possession of curious and beautiful objects, of the outward shows of wealth which were themselves wealth of another sort, became the index of status. This new world—extravagant and luxurious—was given artistic expression in the canvases of the great Dutch masters of still life. The fruits of the world in glorious profusion, surrounding elegantly chased silver, fine glass and Chinese porcelain, all seem a preview of the vast plunder which Europe was to carry back over the following centuries. But there was more than this to the European penetration of Asia. There were others besides merchants and adventurers, with larger and perhaps less attainable ambitions. Matteo Ricci, of the Society of Jesus, lived for ten years in Peking and died there in 1610. His dying words were directed towards the missionaries of his own creed, but they were as meaningful for others, too. 'I leave you,' he said, 'facing an open door.'

The Face and State of Things

The dying words of Matteo Ricci symbolized the end of the isolation of Asia—and particularly of China. In the coming centuries,
Europeans and Asians were to learn much about each other and,
in the process, to establish new areas of misunderstanding. The
impact of Europe on Asia was to have its creative consequences,
even though these might be overshadowed by the apparent
disintegration brought about by imperialism. Asia's own contribution to the new world which Europe and European ideas were to
dominate was immense, particularly in the field of technology.
But ironically, perhaps, when the Europeans themselves passed
through the open door into the civilizations of Asia, the contribution of Asia to Western technology was already virtually exhausted.
We know this, but the men of the new world—the philosophers
and the scientists—did not. They did not even know where the
foundations of their new world had come from, though they were
fully aware of their significance. Francis Bacon, that extraordinary
Englishman whose intellectual curiosity reflected the spirit of his
age, wrote in his book *Novum Organum*, published in 1620:

> It is well to observe the force and virtue and consequences of
> discoveries. These are to be nowhere seen more conspicuously
> than in those three which were unknown to the ancients, and of
> which the origin, though recent, is obscure and inglorious;
> namely, printing, gunpowder, and the magnet. For these three
> have changed the whole face and state of things throughout the
> world. . . .

Bacon's ignorance of the source of these inventions has been
perpetuated ever since by scholars and publicists unwilling to
sully Europe's incontrovertible claim to have created modern
science by admitting that it emerged from a legacy of science and
technology much of which was derived from Asia.

Francis Bacon's three determinants of the modern world were

all revolutionary in effect—gunpowder changed the basis of power from the muscle of man to the muzzle of the gun; printing, by democratizing knowledge, eroded the foundations of faith; the magnet, used in the compass, made it possible for Europe to expand until its fingers enclosed every corner of the world. There were many things from Asia which helped to shape the face and state of things in seventeenth-century Europe; this chapter describes some of them.

It was towards the end of the ninth century that charcoal, saltpetre and sulphur were first mixed together in China. By the year 1000, gunpowder was being used in simple bombs and grenades, but the explosive was not particularly destructive and it was treated more as a propellant. Early in the eleventh century, a kind of rocket was invented. Here, the Chinese made use of a natural tube of bamboo, which needed only to be filled with propellant and attached to an incendiary arrow. The point of transition from rocket to gun, to a stationary barrel hurling some form of projectile, is difficult to determine. Mention of destructive explosions does not appear in Chinese records until about 1230, and even then it is possible that they were the result of bombs hurled from catapults. The first mention of a metal-barrelled gun is in the West, about 1280.

The formula for gunpowder was most probably transmitted by the Mongols to the Arabs, though the Arabs were using incendiary materials during the Crusades and it is just possible that they had themselves developed a destructive explosive compound. However, the first Arab mention of saltpetre occurs towards the end of the thirteenth century, when it is called 'Chinese snow'. In any case, gunpowder became known in Europe a short time after it was used in warfare in China.

Their military exploitation of gunpowder did not save the Chinese from the Mongols, nor did it particularly affect the basis of Chinese society. But in Europe matters were very different. There artillery and, later, hand weapons of considerable destructive power helped to change the social order. The castle—that symbol of military–aristocratic feudalism—offered little protection against the new weapons. Armies were now to consist not of knights in heavy armour but of bombardiers and matchlockmen. With the collapse of feudalism—already partly undermined by the growth of the merchant classes, another product of the Crusades—there began a further development of cities, no longer strait-jacketed by the old feudal institutions. This was particularly evident in Italy, which profited most from material and cultural contacts with the East.

The commerce generated by the Crusades brought great wealth which soon produced independent merchant communities, societies based upon trade or upon the banking necessary for trade. The emergence of the bourgeoisie into positions of influence and power resulted in new attitudes and new values. More sophisticated state administrations turned to Roman law to provide their scaffolding, and the professional class needed to operate them was drawn almost entirely from amongst laymen.

The culture of these new communities was a secular culture, overwhelmingly concerned with the world of appearances. This does not, of course, mean that the men of the new world—the men of what we now call the Renaissance—were neo-pagans who had rejected God. On the contrary, they gave their religion a new set of symbols with which to express itself. The humanization of Christ, already begun in the sculptures at Reims and elsewhere, was taken to its final stage by the artists of the Renaissance. The Madonna and Child took on the comfortable reality of a bourgeois household. But there was much more to this new middle-class culture. Affluence often leads to conservatism and intellectual caution. This was not the case in Italy. There, the old order of church and feudal nobility formed the conservative element. The merchant classes, looking for new ways to display their wealth and power, became patrons and supporters of a new secular art and learning. The adventure of the Crusades had revealed to many the poverty of Europe's material culture. The great cities of the Levant exhibited secular luxuries unknown in Europe. Such travellers as Marco Polo brought back reports of distant states full of wealth and trade, of learned men and beautiful things. The merchant classes were quick to reach out for anything that, by its luxury or beauty, signified their own escape from the stifling twilight world that had been Europe before the Crusades.

The city itself, in the architecture of its churches, in its public and private buildings, looked for a new language with which to mark the break with the past. Many architects found it in antiquity, in the ruins of Imperial Rome. So, too, did sculptors and painters. This search in the debris of the ancient world was part of the quest for an essentially *European* past, for a native greatness to set against the contributions of Arab and Mongol, but it did not mean that the riches of the East were rejected. Even in architecture, the elegant form of the minaret was translated into the bell-tower, the campanile of many Italian towns.

The influence of the East on the new middle-class culture came by many routes, by the trade in actual objects which were later copied by Italian craftsmen, by the observations of travellers and merchants, and so on. But there is one possible source to which scholars have so far devoted scant attention—the presence of Asians in many Italian towns. There is testimony of this in, for example, a painting done by Giotto in Florence about 1317, which shows Arab figures in such realistic detail that they could only have been drawn from life. Many other examples are to be found in other Italian towns. Ambrogio Lorenzetti's 'Martyrdom of the Franciscans', now in the church of San Francesco, Siena, was completed in 1331 and depicts Mongols and Chinese with some accuracy. It is known that there was a fairly substantial trade in Tartar (that is, Mongol and Chinese) slaves to act as servants in Italian homes in the fourteenth and fifteenth centuries. Many, but by no means all, of these slaves were young women. That there were men of consequence and learning amongst them is not at all improbable; one of the figures in the Lorenzetti painting appears by his dress to be a kind of mandarin. It seems reasonable to assume that, apart from adding a colourful and exotic element to the urban scene and some interesting racial strains to the population, some of the slaves may well have helped to transmit ideas and techniques.

By whatever means, a great many technical discoveries, major and minor, entered Europe during this period. Most of them were Chinese in origin. They included such devices as blowing-engines for furnaces, and lock-gates on canals. Lock-gates were first known in Europe in the middle of the fifteenth century, but they had been developed in China—where hydraulic engineering was a sophisticated science—many centuries before. The Chinese also possessed, from very early times, a highly developed metal industry whose products were applied to bridge-building. The suspension bridge made of bamboo cables is of considerable antiquity in many parts of Asia, where it is still common today, and the first iron-chain suspension bridge seems to have been constructed at some time between 589 and 618. The first successful bridge of this kind to be constructed in Europe did not come into being until 1741— though the idea was first proposed about 1595. The first segmental arch bridge, on the other hand, reached Europe much earlier. Its predecessor still stands at Chao-hsien, in the Chinese province of Hopei; modern though it looks, it was built in 610. Those responsible for the first segmental arch bridges in Europe— such as the Ponte Vecchio, spanning the Arno at Florence (1345)— must have been influenced by pioneer Chinese expertise. Indeed, the fame of China's technicians persisted until the seventeenth century, and Peter the Great of Russia, in process of modernizing his country, called in Chinese engineers in 1675 for his bridge-building projects.

Such technological contributions as these—even such apparently banal objects as the wheelbarrow—helped to shape the industrial base on which European science was to build its dominating position. But Chinese *scientific* ideas did not penetrate the European mind. There are several reasons for this. Practical inventions or discoveries are comparatively easy to transmit, because they do not have to pass through the filter of cultural attitudes. If a technological invention fulfils a need, no one queries the theory behind it on religious or ideological grounds. Scientific ideas, on the other hand, are concerned with the nature of phenomena, with analysis and exegesis. In late medieval Europe, the demands of theology still inhibited scientific inquiry; European science had to break through the hard shell of Christian dogmatism before it could move forward. In most respects, Chinese scientific thought had nothing in common with that of Europe, and even if Chinese ideas had, in fact, been transmitted to Europe they would have been found unacceptable. But they were *not* transmitted until after the Jesuits reached China—and by then European science had already escaped from most ecclesiastical restrictions.

In the visible symbols of culture, in the *luxe privée* of the rich, nothing was likely to be rejected for theological reasons. Pope and bishop had as little objection as the merchant to accepting exotic fashions. Some of these had appeared quite early, and had a comparatively short life. The hennin, that tall conical hat with a muslin veil hanging from its peak—which to most people today is the only recognizable female 'fashion' of the Middle Ages—was very popular in China between the eleventh and the fourteenth centuries. Since it appears in Europe in the fifteenth century, it is not unreasonable to argue that it was brought by some of the female slaves of Mongol and Chinese origin. One scholar has suggested that beauty-patches and the crinoline were also Asian in origin, but the evidence, though persuasive, is vague.

There is, however, no real question about the origin of fine textiles. Though silks and brocades were imported from China and from the Muslim world, quality and cost restricted their use. Popes and saints might still be buried in imported cloths covered with pagan symbols, but the demand for fine textiles had produced a new industry in Italy. Chinese-type silk-weaving machinery was apparently being used by Italian craftsmen in such cities as Lucca towards the end of the thirteenth century—the period, in fact, of easiest communication between East and West. Many of their designs came from oriental models—Chinese dragons and Persian peacocks abound, and there are stylized flowers, fruits and palm-leaves as well as abstract shapes. Many of the motifs were a legacy from the studios of Palermo, which had been encouraged by the Norman kings and the Hohenstaufen emperor Frederick II. But the Italian weavers drew on a whole new repertoire of exotic forms, even, as in the case of one late fifteenth-century example, on a design originating in India—though this probably came through Persia rather than by the new sea routes currently being opened by the Portuguese. At about the same time, Florence began to export figured silk fabrics to the Near East, manufactured especially for that market in oriental styles. This could be one of the earliest examples of adapting industrial production to the requirements of the overseas customer.

The seventeenth century—which witnessed the entrenchment of the bourgeoisie—also saw a wider distribution of those objects of luxury which had once been reserved for the aristocracy. Carpets, for example—unknown in England until about 1500 and even after that seen only among the appurtenances of royal portraits—appeared in the next century adorning the tables of Dutch merchants. Soon, they were common enough to be walked

upon. Many of these carpets came from Turkey; the establishment of the Ottoman Turks in the former possessions of the
Byzantine empire resulted in a considerable increase in the carpet
trade with Europe. An imperial carpet factory was set up at
Constantinople in the sixteenth century and, from there, a vast new
design vocabulary found its way into Europe. Many of the carpets
imported had the characteristic colour which later came to be
known as 'Turkey red'.

Turkey's domination in the Levant gave her a monopoly of the
transit trade with farther Asia. And a very profitable monopoly
it proved to be, as Europe's demand for luxury goods continued
to increase steadily throughout the sixteenth century. Portugal
did break the Turkish monopoly in the spice trade, although not in
many other exotic products. Venice, that curiously Eurasian city,
still controlled much of Europe's commerce with the Turks;
the word *argosy*—often used to describe a vessel laden with riches
—is derived from the name of Ragusa in Dalmatia, which was an
important Venetian trading-post. England, stimulated by the
bright sun of the Elizabethan age, stretched out a hand to Asia
with the Levant Company, which was granted its charter in 1581
after the conclusion of a commercial treaty with the Sultan of
Turkey.

From Turkey, a new drink was introduced into Europe. This
was coffee, whose name in most European languages is a version
of the Turkish pronunciation—'kehveh'—of the original Arabic
name. The Turks adopted the idea of coffee-houses, which soon
spread to Europe and became the meeting-places of politicians
and men of letters. One English traveller noted in about 1610
that the Turks were fond of a drink which was 'black as soot and
tasting not much unlike it!' But in spite of such strictures, the first
European coffee-house was opened in Oxford in 1650. London's
first coffee-house seems to have been the enterprise of a man from
Ragusa who had been brought to London by a Turkish merchant
to prepare coffee for him personally, and the first coffee-house in
continental Europe was publicly opened in Marseilles in 1671.

The men of letters who frequented these new meeting-places
were influenced by the East, as their predecessors had been.
Many fables in popular literature had had their origin in India.
Best known of all were the various versions of the *Tales of Pilpay*

(or *Bidpai*) which came to Europe through the Arabs. In Arabic they were called *Kalilah wa Dimnah*, from the names of the two jackals who play a leading role. A German version, made in 1481, was one of the earliest of printed books. In the sixteenth century, the tales appeared in Italian, and from that language they were translated into English. Other stories of Indian origin were annexed by European writers, the plot of the three caskets in Shakespeare's *Merchant of Venice* being one of the more familiar examples.

In an earlier chapter, it was described how Eastern forms entered Europe by way of Spain and were spread in the poetry of the troubadours. The picaresque novel is an example of a similar dissemination of Arabic styles. Such influences as these helped to release European literature from the corset of didactic forms and to produce new types of secular writing. The effect of Eastern forms is sometimes obvious—as in the animal tales which were based upon the fables of Bidpai. In other instances, it is much more subtle. But the area in which Europe's poets and writers could express themselves was gradually being widened.

From the East, and essentially the Arab East, came new ways of presenting works of literature so that they could be elegantly housed in the libraries of the rich. During the fifteenth century, when Venice was the main channel of Islamic influences, book-binders in Italy adopted Eastern styles, including the flap that folds over to protect the fore-edge. European craftsmen had been producing blind-tooled book covers for many years, but it was Muslim bookbinders settled in Venice who enriched the stamped decorations by filling the sunken parts with gold. They introduced, too, oriental designs which are still used on fine leather bindings today. 'Marbled' patterns, for endpapers and book edges, were another innovation. These came from Turkey and were not produced in Europe until the end of the seventeenth century, though the technique was known a century before. Francis Bacon wrote that the Turks 'take diverse oyled colours, and put them severally [in drops] upon water; and stir the water lightly, and then wet their paper with it, and the paper will be waved and veined, like . . . Marble'.

The inclusion of oriental figures, and the wide use by Italian artists of motifs originating in the Near or Far East, demonstrate the painters' delight in the increased range of decorative expression suggested by textiles, metal-ware and other *objets de luxe*. These motifs were widely disseminated and widely copied, especially after the introduction of printing. Pattern books containing original Eastern designs and adaptations of them were immensely influential from the sixteenth century onwards. But what of the direct influence of Eastern pictorial art on European painters? Such influence implies more than just the superficial use of exotic animals or foliage. These can be found scattered throughout Italian painting from the thirteenth century onwards. To be directly influenced the painter must have seen examples of Eastern art and recognized something of their aesthetic purpose. There is no satisfactory evidence of actual paintings having been brought to Europe before the seventeenth century—when Rembrandt, for example, was interested enough to make copies of Indian Mughal miniatures. But it is possible to discern, in a number of earlier works, a use of Chinese forms which betrays knowledge of Chinese pictorial art. There is certainly no reason why Chinese paintings should not have been known in Italy. Although Marco Polo did not mention Chinese art at all, other travellers and merchants may have taken more interest. The Mongols certainly disseminated Chinese paintings, which were copied in Persia and, later, Turkey. The characteristic treatment of landscape by painters of the Sung dynasty—which preceded that of the Mongols —supplied inspiration to the unknown painter of a triptych in the Academy at Siena. This dates from the late thirteenth century, and in the central subject trees and rocks are used as they are in Chinese art, to create a timeless landscape where the narrative may take place. That same landscape, at once harsh and mysterious, appears in Leonardo's 'Virgin of the Rocks'. The whole painting is an exercise in shadow. The cave is haunted by it. Shadow menaces the landscape. The Chinese were masters of chiaroscuro long before it was used by European artists, and it is not unreasonable to believe that they passed on something of their art to Europe.

Paper and printing are the scaffolding of the modern world. The passage of the first from China to Europe is easily traceable, but in the case of printing the line of transmission is uncertain. There is, however, a body of inferential evidence from which the general pattern can reasonably be established.

The beginnings of printing in China are comparatively well documented. The first type of printed book, produced by inked impressions from wooden blocks, had its origin in the Chinese practice of taking inked rubbings from stone inscriptions. An example of this kind of thing can be seen in the illustration of a horse of the Han period following page 87. By the seventh century, single sheets and roll-books were being produced from specially carved stone blocks. In fact, even after woodblock printing was well established in China, rubbing from stone was still the orthodox way of transmitting Confucian texts. The expansion of printing was a result of the spread of Buddhism. After the fall of the Han dynasty in the third century, China, like Europe, entered an age of darkness. When she emerged from it, after some four centuries of anarchy and civil war, Buddhism—which offered a way out of the agony of everyday living—was already established. The 'barbarians' who ravaged China had carried with them the iconography of Buddhism; they were the great transmitters of the Indo–Greek image. Soon Buddhism penetrated painting, and with the establishment of the dynasty of the T'ang in the seventh century, art and religion came together. From this synthesis emerged the need to duplicate sacred texts and sacred pictures in order to achieve the widest diffusion, and the need was satisfied by the printed image.

The beginning of actual printing from wooden blocks is not satisfactorily established. It can, however, be dated approximately to the reign of the emperor Ming Huang (722–56). There are no surviving examples, perhaps because this period was followed by revolution and a subsequent persecution of Buddhists, when a great number of shrines and libraries were destroyed. The earliest *dated* example of a Chinese block-printed book is from the year 868. It was discovered in 1907 by Sir Aurel Stein, in Tun-huang in Kansu province. There, in one of a series of caves decorated with frescoes, a secret chamber was found piled with manuscript rolls in an almost perfect state of preservation after being sealed up for many centuries. Among the manuscripts was a printed copy of the Buddhist classic the *Diamond Sutra*, consisting of six sheets of text and another, shorter one with a woodcut, pasted together to form a roll sixteen feet long. At the end was printed the statement that the book was 'reverently made for universal distribution by Wang Chieh on behalf of his two parents on the 15th of the 4th moon of the 9th year of Hsien-Tung (11 May 868)'. It is now in the British Museum. The spread of printing in Europe after Gutenberg has very close parallels with that in China. China had its revival in the era of the Sung. In Europe, printing ushered in the Renaissance. Both were a direct consequence of the large-scale production of the printed image.

Printing in China was not confined only to religious texts. For about four centuries before printing even began in Europe, the Chinese had been printing paper money in vast quantities; the existence of paper currency was noted by a number of European travellers, including Marco Polo. This period—when the Mongol power was spreading to form a great bridge between Europe and China—was of crucial importance to the diffusion of printing, for it was soon after the end of the Mongol era that the first primitive block-prints appeared in Europe.

While traders and travellers from Europe were aware of the existence of paper currency they did not comment on the fact that it was printed; they were interested only in the fact that it was *money*. Neither were they particularly concerned with books. But playing-cards were quite another matter. Significantly, playing-cards are one of the first forms of block-printing in Europe. Games involving the use of cards can be traced back to about 969 in China. Many games entered Europe during the period of the Crusades, but the first verifiable allusions to games played with cards are concentrated in the years between 1377 and 1382. By 1397, such games had become so popular in Paris that workmen were prohibited from playing cards on working days, and soon the ecclesiastical authorities were preaching against them as tools of the Devil. The dates relating to cards are of considerable importance when they are compared with those for *religious* block-prints, which are first known in the last years of the fourteenth century. By 1418 they had reached an advanced stage of technical sophistication. The first printed playing-cards also date from the end of the fourteenth century. By the middle of the next century, a number of German towns were exporting cards to places as far away as Sicily. It seems likely that the craftsmen engaged in printing playing-cards also produced the religious block-prints.

In Europe, as in China, the diffusion of religious images formed the main incentive for block-printing; the first prints, too, were of pictures, not text. But in the early part of the fifteenth century, printed pictures and printed texts appeared, and finally there came the first of the block-*books*. Though scholars are still arguing about dates, it seems likely that such books were being produced before movable type came into use. In Europe, in fact, the stages in the development of printing which led to Gutenberg's 'invention' compare reasonably accurately with those in China, just as the incentives in Europe—a new intellectual curiosity and a general desire for change and innovation—have their parallel in the Sung renaissance of the tenth century.

The routes by which Chinese block-prints entered Europe cannot be established beyond doubt. A good case can, however, be made for the theory that at least one of the routes went through Russia. During the Mongol period, the market of Novgorod on the River Volkhov was an important entrepôt for goods from the Far East. There, the merchants of the Hanseatic League—a loose federation of North German towns which dominated the northern trade routes—had one of their *Kontore* or counting-houses. Playing-cards were probably included in their merchandise. Persia also has a claim. Although Islam offered a barrier to the extension of printing—for Muslims maintained that, as the Koran had been given to them in a *written* form, copies must also be written by hand (and printing was not in fact accepted in the Islamic world until 1825)—records of block-printing at Tabriz in Persia do exist, and include the printing of paper money. In the fourteenth century, there was a substantial European population in Tabriz, and while there is no documentary support for the contention that block-printing entered Europe either by this route or through Novgorod, there is good circumstantial evidence. It is, in any case, easier to accept either possibility than to believe that block-printing in Europe was an independent invention, made at the time when intercourse between Europe and China was at its peak.

This is the background to the invention of movable type in Europe, usually credited to Johann Gutenberg of Mainz, somewhere about 1440. Movable type had been used in China for about four hundred years before this. Type production and type-setting were described during the second half of the eleventh century, and in 1313 a more detailed description was published. Several hundred units of type, cut in hardwood, have been discovered in the caves at Tun-huang—well along the way to the West. But there was a hundred years' delay between the closing of the trade routes, when the Mongol dynasty in China collapsed, and the use of movable type by Gutenberg. For this reason, some scholars have rejected the idea of a westward transmission of movable type from China. There is certainly no concrete evidence for or against, but the trade routes were never completely closed. Information still passed between China and Europe, even if only as hearsay. Europe had already followed the Chinese pattern as far as the block-print; even without material examples the next stage was inevitably towards movable type. The distinctively European contribution to the technology of printing was to lie in alphabetic type and the printing-press.

In one sense at least, the development of firearms and the invention of printing turned Europe in upon itself. They became the principal weapons of change, above all of violent change. The history of Europe turns from wars of conquest overseas to civil wars, wars with guns, and wars with books and broadsheets. The Renaissance and the Reformation are sagas of escape from the unease of the times. Their significance lies in the fact that neither was an escape into obscurantism. They differ from each other in the sense that one rejected contemporary reality while the other sought to change it. But the vitality with which the men of the Renaissance made their rejection helped the process of change. Without the art of printing neither the Renaissance nor the Reformation could have taken place, for both were consequences of the democratization of education that the printed word brought about. In the last decades of the fifteenth century, a large number of printed books and pamphlets was produced, but even more significant, perhaps, was the recognition of the value of printing for propaganda.

Luther, that dynamo of the Reformation, first began his attack upon the church in Latin, but he soon realized what a weapon the printed word could put into his hand. It was a weapon whose power could only be realized through use of the common tongue.

Luther's propaganda was directed not at churchmen but at ordinary people—and it had therefore to be written in the language of ordinary people. The fourteenth century had already seen the rise of vernacular literatures—Chaucer and Dante, for example, for the first time wrote in the everyday tongue—but the printed word was the great fertilizer of vernacular literature. The mind of Europe was to be irrigated with ideas and information, and the printer was to become the unacknowledged legislator, the moulder of events, the craftsman of revolution.

On the whole, this great period of gestation cared little or nothing for the East. The Renaissance, in effect, turned its back on the Orient, annexing instead a particular vision of the antique world. This did not, however, mean that the men of the Renaissance were not acutely aware of the existence of the East. Italy, the epicentre of the Renaissance, always faced the East—the East of the Greeks, of the Byzantines, and, after the fall of Constantinople in 1453, of the Turks. But although it looked essentially for exotic detail, for decoration rather than substance, no filter is fine enough to prevent the seepage of ideas. The Renaissance, for all its Classical face, was alive with influences from the East, often disguised, their source almost always unrecognized.

At the Reformation, the legacies of the East were almost exhausted, at least as far as the inventions which were to form the foundation of Europe's scientific and technical progress were concerned. The opening of the East by Portuguese navigators brought luxuries, both material and spiritual, but little else. When the West was once again beginning to reach out for renewed contact with the East, when the transmission of ideas was to become comparatively easy and certainly direct, the East had already given the most seminal of its gifts. In the genius of Leonardo da Vinci, for example, can be seen a mind stretching forward into the new world of *European* technology, a prophet charting the coasts of the future.

Not only technical inventions were absorbed into the new world that was in process of parturition in Europe. Such inventions were, of course, more readily transmitted than scientific ideas, because their immediate utility was not only obvious but desirable; merchants and others could see their purpose without concerning themselves with the theory behind them. But scientific ideas need prepared ground in which to germinate. The Arabs, the great transmitters of Chinese technology, had been interested in Chinese scientific thought, but Europe was too excited by its discovery of the Greek classics to pay attention to Muslim works on Chinese and Indian science. Throughout the formative period of European science, this barrier remained to block off contributions from the Far East. Nevertheless, in at least one case, technical inventions must have carried with them certain scientific implications. These are reflected in European astronomy.

The great Danish astronomer Tycho Brahe (1546–1601), who possessed several Arabic astronomical works, took from the Chinese not only the equatorial mounting for his telescope but also their method of measuring the position of stars in the heavens. The Chinese method, using equatorial co-ordinates, differed radically from that used by the Greeks, and is still the method favoured by modern astronomers. Nor did the Chinese ever envisage the universe in the way of Europe's Ptolemaic system, as a series of concentric spheres; they held that stars and planets were lights suspended in infinite empty space. The Europeans who propounded the same idea towards the end of the sixteenth century were not necessarily aware of this, but when Chinese ideas later became widespread, they seemed to endorse the validity of the new system. Two thousand years of Chinese observations are still proving useful to Western astronomers in the 1970s, notably in the case of pulsars.

Of Bacon's three great discoveries—than which 'no empire, no sect, no star, seem to have exerted greater power and influence in human affairs'—there remains the magnetic compass. Of the uniquely Chinese origin of this there is no question.

The first recorded use of the magnet is in the ancient art of geomancy, of divination by observing points or lines on the earth or on a plate. In Han times, the diviner used a metal plate and a lodestone spoon. In the work by Wang Ch'ung published in A.D. 83 the spoon is described as a 'south-controlling spoon', and it is said that, when thrown on to the plate, it will always point to the south. The spoon was made from lodestone, the magnetic oxide of iron, and shaped like the constellation of the Northern Dipper or Great Bear. Its form can be seen even today in the

Chinese porcelain spoons which Westerners find so awkward for eating soup in Chinese restaurants.

The essential step from the use of magnetism in divination to its use in the compass is not easy to trace, but the earliest description of a lodestone used as a floating pointer occurs in a compendium of military techniques dating from 1044. One of the earliest forms shows a piece of lodestone embedded in a wooden fish floating in water. There are also examples of dry suspension, where a little wooden turtle with a lodestone inside is balanced on a sharpened stick.

The route by which the magnetic compass came to Europe is, again, undocumented. Whether it came by way of the Arabs or along the northern land routes is a matter for speculation. The earliest known European mention of magnetic polarity dates from about 1180, the earliest Arab one from a work of 1282. But the first description of a *pivotal* compass is that of Peter Peregrinus of Picardy in 1269, a significant date in relation to the progress of Mongol expansion. It is possible, therefore, that the *idea* of the magnetic compass may well have been transmitted along both routes. In any case, the thirteenth century inaugurated a new era in navigational science, an era which prepared the way for the great Portuguese voyages of discovery in the fifteenth.

The use of the compass spread rapidly. Sea-charts of the Mediterranean prepared at the end of the thirteenth century gave a much more accurate image of the position of the coasts and islands than earlier maps had done. These portolans, as they were called, could not have been made without the compass. Many of them were produced by the Genoese, and it was such men as these who were called to Portugal by Henry the Navigator so that the Portuguese might sail out into the Atlantic with the most up-to-date navigational aids. They sailed first to Madeira in 1419, then on to the south, edging always farther, their charts covering more and more of the coasts and seaways.

As the European nations followed one another along the route to the Indies, knowledge of the countries of the East increased. The old view of Asia, its rulers and its peoples, slowly began to change. The travellers who had moved along the land routes to China and India had gone in fear and wonder. Their eyes could accept and even record reality, but their imagination was quick to see dragons. Friar Odoric de Pordenone, whose narrative is full of facts, still cannot resist spawning legends of hills snow-white on one side and coal-black on the other; of the Old Man of the Mountains, in whose garden he found four thousand two hundred human souls imprisoned in the bodies of apes and cats! It was from Odoric, from William of Rubruck and from John of Plano Carpini that Sir John Mandeville quarried the fables and wonders of his own *Travels*. His work, like that of Marco Polo, belongs in essence to the literature of wonder, a style of writing about the East which still persists today. But the eastward expansion of the Portuguese produced a new kind of literature: that of appraisal. Portuguese and Spanish travellers now wrote narratives which were almost completely objective in their approach. The early Jesuits in China —Ricci, Trigault and Martinius—produced what were on the whole sober and factual accounts.

Generally speaking, however, it was the traveller with a commercial mind, an eye for profit rather than the picturesque, a desire to trade rather than to convert, who was responsible for the new literature. Many travellers of this type were Dutch or English. One of them was Peter Mundy, who left England in 1636 and sailed eastwards to Goa, Singapore and finally to the Portuguese enclave of Macao on the South China coast. His narrative is simple and straightforward. An indefatigable observer, he noted both the unusual and the everyday in his sketch-book. Mundy was impressed by the Chinese hatred of foreigners, by their cowardice and their greed. But he also saw that China was rich and peaceful, a land ripe for commercial exploitation.

The Dutch were in contact with the East before the English were, and it was through Holland that portraits of China came to Europe towards the end of the sixteenth century. The first illustrated reports of European embassies to China were published in Holland. In the second half of the seventeenth century, an immense number of illustrations, covering most aspects of life in the countries of Asia, began to make their appearance and, with the narratives that accompanied them, were quickly published in other European countries.

By the middle of the seventeenth century, a new trend in books about China was becoming apparent. The Jesuit propagandists were to create a new image of the country, one which the hard-headed merchants and sailors must have found it very difficult to reconcile with their own observations. The Jesuits in China were to have a profound influence on the European mind in the eighteenth century. Their industry was tremendous, and letters packed with information on all subjects flowed from their pens to be avidly read in Europe. These works—designed primarily as weapons against the Dominicans, who were disputing Jesuit methods of conversion in China—were produced to justify the attempt to assimilate Chinese ethics into Catholic doctrine. Jesuit writers praised the civilization of those whom they hoped to convert. Theirs was the literature of adulation, frequently uncritical, but always calculated. Some of its effect will be described in the next chapters. It also produced, in scholars such as the Frenchman François Fénelon (1651–1715), a revulsion against China. But Fénelon was an early exception and could not stem the growing passion for things Chinese.

Fénelon, however, is of more than passing interest in the present context. At the beginning of this chapter, Francis Bacon's words on the subject of printing, gunpowder and the magnet were quoted. Bacon, writing early in the seventeenth century, was not aware that these great discoveries came from a source outside Europe. Fénelon, writing at the beginning of the eighteenth century, reveals in one of his *Dialogues des morts* (published posthumously) that he knew very well the source of printing and gunpowder.

The conversation, sub-titled 'Sur la Prééminence tant vantée des chinois', is between Socrates and Confucius. Fénelon's dialogue is heavy with scepticism. In support of his argument, Confucius parades the inventions of the Chinese. But surely, Socrates points out, these are nothing to be proud of. Gunpowder served only to destroy mankind, printing had not brought happiness. Even porcelain 'must be set down to the credit of your soil rather than of your people'. The list continues through architecture, painting and lacquer. Confucius is the one who is humbled.

But Fénelon, the unorthodox cleric and one-time tutor of an heir to the throne of France, was not in sympathy with his age. He sought remedies for the diseases of his time in the world of Ancient Greece. He saw a dangerous model for Europe in the ever-growing infatuation with the dream of Cathay as a country of happy and contented people. His faith in the legacies of Hellas was to be shared by others who, even at the height of China's triumph over the European mind, were to act as a *maquis* against the tyranny of the sinophiles.

IV

The Dream of
Cathay

Occupé sans relâche de tous les soins divers
D'un gouvernement qu'on admire,
Le plus grand potentat qui soit dans l'univers
Est le meilleur lettré qui soit dans son empire.

> Inscription to the frontispiece portrait of the 'emperor
> Kien-Long', in *Mémoires concernant l'histoire . . . des
> chinois* (1776)

Of late, 'tis true, quite sick of Rome and Greece,
We fetch our models from the wise Chinese,
European artists are too cool and chaste,
For Mand'rin only is the man of taste.

> JAMES CAWTHORNE, *Essay on Taste* (1756)

All between float milky-ways of coral islands, and low-lying,
endless, unknown Archipelagoes and impenetrable Japans.

> HERMAN MELVILLE, *Moby Dick* (1851)

The most interesting link of the Japanese theatre is, of course,
its link with the sound film, which can and must learn its
fundamentals from the Japanese.

> S. M. EISENSTEIN, *The Cinematograph Principle
> and the Ideogram* (1928)

Confucius Conquers Europe

In the late seventeenth and eighteenth centuries, Europe became infatuated with a vision of Cathay as legendary in its way as Mandeville's had been. In study and salon, the Chinese vogue swept all before it. The seventeenth century was an age of expanding curiosity in a rapidly expanding world. Men wanted answers and they were confident that answers were somewhere to be found. They turned first to what was, for Christians, a great reservoir of revealed truth—the Bible. Scholars and theologians, inspired by new scientific experiments, by the researches of antiquaries, by discoveries overseas, began to examine their Bibles for new interpretations. They sought for the universal language they were convinced had existed before Babel. Some believed it might be Chinese; by elaborate and totally unfounded argument they came to the conclusion that China had been peopled by the children of Noah before the confusion of tongues. It was even suggested that Confucius was a Christian prophet. Controversies sparked off by such conclusions survived well into the eighteenth century. Fundamentally, they represent an attempt to fit China into that universal history whose outlines were drawn from the Bible. It was perhaps China's antiquity which most influenced Europeans, the continuity (as they believed) of its institutions, and the peaceful and stable government that seemed always to have existed. This image was already established by 1660 and in the following years China also became renowned for superior morality. In the person of Confucius all these qualities were combined. The Jesuits were responsible for this—in their missionary endeavours in China they had tried to create an autonomous Christian church with its own rites, and Confucius was fundamental to this ideal. Jesuit propaganda in Europe stressed his role as a teacher whose code of ethics was implicit in the nature of Chinese government. They made Confucius into a prince of philosophers, and the Confucian *literati* into scholar-governors. The European philosophical climate proved receptive, and the Jesuits flooded Europe with translations of the Chinese classics and Confucian writings. In 1687 a compendium of these, *Confucius Sinarum Philosophus*, was dedicated to no less a person than Louis XIV of France.

Confucius did not help the Jesuits much in what came to be known as the 'rites controversy', but the sage was avidly taken up by the philosophers of the European Enlightenment. The first was the German thinker Leibniz (1646–1716). As early as 1697, he was referring to Confucius as 'the king of Chinese philosophers'. During a visit to Rome, he had made the acquaintance of the Jesuit father Grimaldi, who had worked in China. From the information he received then and later in correspondence, Leibniz proposed the universal system of natural philosophy first expounded in his *Novissima Sinica* of 1697. He also called for close cultural relations with China. 'I almost think it necessary that Chinese missionaries be sent to us to teach us the aim and practice of natural theology as we send missionaries to them to instruct them in revealed theology.' Leibniz pointed out the beneficent effect the rules of Confucius had had on private and public life in China and went so far as to suggest that 'if a wise man were to be appointed judge—not of the beauty of goddesses but of the goodness of peoples—he would award the golden apple to the Chinese'. He founded the Berlin Society of Science for the 'opening-up of China and the interchange of civilizations between China and Europe', and even suggested that France should construct a canal at Suez in order to open up a shorter sea route.

The enthusiasm of Leibniz communicated itself to others. One, Christian Wolff, made out such a passionate case for Chinese morality that he was expelled from the Prussian dominions for atheism. Wolff, following Leibniz, taught the doctrine of 'pre-established harmony', a view of the universe in which the greatest possible variety was held together by the greatest possible unity, a concept very close to that of the Chinese. This doctrine was explained to Frederick William I of Prussia, who was obsessed with his army, as meaning that, if the king's tallest grenadier ran away, he could not fairly be punished, because in running away he was merely conforming with the laws of pre-established harmony. The king ordered Wolff on pain of death to leave the country within forty-eight hours!

The essence of the gospel of the Enlightenment, as expressed by

Leibniz and Wolff and many others who followed them, was the need for socially purposeful action—that is, action in harmony with the human spirit and natural morality. This was indeed the Confucian concept of the virtuous act. Furthermore, there was nothing incompatible with Christianity in this concept; on the contrary, the philosophers and the Jesuits believed that the god of Confucius was the same god as theirs. But from the theological faculty of the University of Paris, the centre of Jesuit enthusiasm for China, came a constant flow of praise for Confucian ideas, much of which was expressed in what can only be described as heretical terms.

It was in France that Chinese ideas were to have their greatest effect. There was every reason why this should have been so. The reign of Louis XIV had imposed a rich but pompous rigidity on thought and art. The *roi soleil* might relax enough to allow an occasional chinoiserie to enliven his court, but the climate of his age was staid and stifling. Before he died, old, pious and lonely, in the second decade of the eighteenth century, a new world had begun to break through. Faith was giving way to scepticism, symmetry to exuberance, dullness to gaiety, the formality of the throneroom to the licence of the *fête champêtre*.

The philosophers, too, moved into a gayer world—though they did so with great seriousness. They looked at God not with unquestioning acceptance but with rational inquiry. They contemplated society, and sought to change it by the exercise of virtue. They gazed at China, and saw Reason's kingdom of heaven. They discovered, in Confucius, someone who had thought the same thoughts as they, two thousand years earlier, and who had come to conclusions which, they believed, ordered the happy state of affairs in China. The philosophers of Europe knew nothing of other Chinese thinkers such as Lao-tse, or of Taoism with its magic, mysticism and irrationality. Looking through the refracting lens of Jesuit propaganda, they saw only Confucius, and not China. Theirs was the chinoiserie of the study, the counterpart to that of the salon.

It was Voltaire, that impresario of the exotic, who made Confucius into the archetype of the eighteenth-century rationalist. Confucius, he wrote, 'appeals only to virtue, he preaches no miracles, there is nothing in [his books] of religious allegory'. The

Jesuits had indeed made a convert in Voltaire, but one who, with enthusiasm, turned against them the knowledge they had taught him. The Jesuits had, in fact, by stressing the importance of natural law in practical politics, put into the hands of eighteenth-century thinkers ammunition for the defence of both enlightened despotism and the old concept of absolutism. Voltaire and those who drew inspiration from him were, above all, enamoured with the view of the philosopher as king. 'Go to Peking,' exclaimed one. 'Gaze upon the mightiest of monarchs; he is the true and perfect image of Heaven.'

Voltaire thought he saw in Frederick the Great of Prussia the enlightened despot of his hopes. But Frederick was not concerned with a country he confessed to knowing nothing about. 'I leave the Chinese to you,' he wrote to Voltaire in 1776, '. . . along with the Indians and Tartars. The European nations keep my mind sufficiently occupied.' No eighteenth-century monarch would, in fact, have dreamed of employing philosophers in important offices of state—which, in effect, was what Voltaire was advocating, on the mistaken assumption that such a system of government existed in China. Their lack of success in practical politics did not discourage Voltaire or the rest of the sinophiles, however, and their advocacy of Confucius continued unabated. It was to be left to another, more practical, thinker to give China some real influence upon affairs.

This was François Quesnay (1694–1774), physician to Madame de Pompadour who was herself an enthusiast for things Chinese. Fittingly, her doctor soon came to be known, at least by his admirers, as the 'Confucius of Europe'. Quesnay erected a system of political economy with which he hoped to save the absolutist French monarchy from the dangers that were already facing it, and published his plans in *Le Despotisme de la Chine*. He and his followers—the Physiocrats, as they were called, from the Greek word for nature—believed implicitly that society should be governed according to 'natural' laws. Agriculture, he maintained, was the sole source of wealth and therefore the only subject for taxation. In his *Tableau économique* (1762), Quesnay ingeniously translated Chinese doctrine into mathematics. But it was ingenuity wasted. The King of France was no more interested in the example of China than was the King of Prussia. Other forces, too, were active and were eventually to triumph, changing society not by reform, but by revolution.

Like France, England had by no means been immune to the glamour of Confucius. In the second half of the seventeenth century, Sir William Temple had claimed that 'the kingdom of China seems to be framed and policed with the utmost force and reach of human wisdom, reason and contrivance'. It was a Utopia, he claimed, far surpassing the imagined ideals of such men as Plato. But, though Confucius did have his admirers—who for a time included Dr Johnson—such panegyrics did not inflame the English. Dissenting opinion was soon heard. One writer, as early as 1694, dismissed the maxims of Confucius as mere pastiche, with which 'good Sense and tolerable experience might have furnished any Man'. When Voltaire and Quesnay were creating their ideals, the Chinese vogue amongst English scholars and men of letters was already dying. China had become little more than the land of tea. This was because a new literature of hardheaded appraisal had begun to appear. In 1743, Captain George Anson touched briefly on the coast of China during a voyage around the world, and was treated with the usual Chinese contempt for foreigners. His sharp eye was quick to observe the shortcomings of the administration. The magistrates, he wrote, 'are corrupt, their people thievish, and their tribunals crafty and venal'. Although Anson's strictures were denied by Voltaire, they provided splendid ammunition for the anti-sinophiles and his book was widely distributed. These and similar revelations did not, of course, undermine the reputation of Confucius overnight, but they did cast doubt on the Jesuit view of China and the interpretations which had been based upon it. Towards the end of the eighteenth century, a distinguished French man of letters was able to assert that the moral doctrines of the Chinese were exactly suitable for a 'herd of frightened slaves'.

Their uncritical acceptance of the Jesuit view of China laid European sinophiles open to attack the moment the authenticity of that view was in doubt. The church of Rome had already condemned the Jesuits; the English were engaged in proving that, even if such a China had existed in the past, it certainly did not exist today. European thinkers who looked upon Confucius mainly as an ally of reaction soon had facts with which to attack the enemy. Rousseau, the grit in the oyster of mid-eighteenth-century thinking, condemned China as a terrible example of good manners corrupted by science and art. Of the Chinese he wrote: 'There is no sin to which they are not prone, no crime which is not common amongst them. If neither the ability of its ministers, nor the alleged wisdom of its laws, nor even the numberless multitude of its inhabitants, has been able to protect the realm against subjection by ignorant and rude barbarians, of what service have been all its wise men?' It was to counter this view that Voltaire wrote his play *L'Orphelin de la Chine*, 'Confucian Morals in Five Acts' (1755). He prefaced it with a letter to Rousseau which began: 'Sir, I have received your new book against the human race . . .'

But the tide was already running against Confucius. Montesquieu, in his *De l'Esprit des Lois* (1748), questioned the benevolence of the Emperor of China's despotism and suggested that China's 'public tranquillity' was no more than the product of a climate 'which naturally disposes the inhabitants to slavish obedience'.

When it became clear that a sizeable proportion of China's population was not Confucian at all, but followed the Buddha or Lao-tse—whose philosophies had been described by the Jesuits as idolatrous—China's reputation sank even lower. In England in 1778, the *Monthly Review* described the beliefs of Lao-tse as 'such effusions of nonsense as surpass the most extravant ravings that ever were heard in the cells of Bedlam.' The experiences of Lord Macartney, sent on an embassy to the Emperor of China in 1792, struck the final crippling blow at the legend of China. England, already embarked on the first stage of her imperial journey, was to drown the Chinese myth for ever in a wave of contempt and abuse.

A large part of the legend had already crumbled long before the Macartney mission. Those philosophers who had hoped to convince Europe's monarchs that their only hope of survival lay in a benevolent despotism on the Chinese model had been ignored by the men they wished to save. The monarchs merely treated such suggestions as they did the chinoiseries of their palaces, as a pleasant gloss on the business of living. The sinophiles never really considered the people as worthy of their proselytizing endeavour—why should they, when they sought to model Utopia on their own view of China, on an administration of philosophers by whose virtue the happiness of the people was inevitably assured? The sinophiles were not egalitarians; if they thought of equality at all, it was in terms of the equality of talent. They believed implicitly in the Confucian principle that a virtuous administration, operating within the harmony of natural law, was the only way to stability. They were not revolutionaries, but reformers.

The Chinese model of an absolute monarchy, however benevolent, could have no appeal for men who looked to the concept of popular sovereignty as a counter to, for example, the abuses of the *ancien régime* in France. The advocates of democratic liberalism were not prepared for any enhancement of absolutism. They looked to an elected parliament as a means of universal happiness, and the Declaration of the Rights of Man was their reply to the ideology of enlightened despotism. As the blade of the guillotine fell on the neck of Louis XVI in January 1793, it severed the head of Confucius as well as that of the King of France.

In the fall of Cathay, however, what might be called the Classical underground also played its part. The discovery in the second half of the eighteenth century of the ruins of Herculaneum, Pompeii and Palmyra revived interest in the Classical world—the world of Greece and Rome. Plutarch began to displace Confucius. Just as the men of the Renaissance had sought out their European past in defence against the East, so did the men of the late eighteenth century. Some even suggested that the Chinese themselves had derived their civilization from Ancient Greece. 'The Greeks,' wrote Christoph Meiners, professor of philosophy at Göttingen in 1778, were 'the people who really shed light upon the dark places of the earth . . . illuminated eastern Asia even earlier than western and northern Europe.' This suggestion was of the same order as those designed to prove that China had been an Egyptian colony, or that the inhabitants of Tierra del Fuego were none other than the descendants of wandering Koreans. There were ingenious claims, too, that Chinese writing was of Phoenician origin. But, so low had the opinion of Chinese culture fallen in the minds of European scholars that even these theories were scornfully dismissed as valuing China too high. It was a natural reaction against the uncritical worship of China, but a reaction also based fundamentally on ignorance. In such circumstances, there was no middle way between fulsome praise and total contempt.

The exotic, however, never loses its appeal. The lost worlds of Greece and Rome, the Noble Savage in his primitive paradise, the sensual secrets of the harem, the mysterious gods and fabulous Golcondas of Hindustan—all continued to capture the imagination of philosophers and men of letters. Confucius, after conquering Europe, was defeated and virtually forgotten until modern times.

Yet though China ceased to be a model for European society, a legendary, exotic China still held its own in literature—even if it was the literature of entertainment rather than instruction. One of the first roles of China in European literature had been to supply observant travellers whose innocent eye could penetrate the recesses of European society. The Oriental observer was a well-established device in political satire. There had been a Turkish spy as early as 1687. Montesquieu had used two Persians to anatomize French life in his *Lettres persanes* (1721). The use of a Chinese traveller by such men as the Marquis d'Argens in his *Lettres chinoises* (1739) and Oliver Goldsmith in *The Citizen of the World* (1762)—one of the last of this genre—was not just a concession to current fashion. It did reflect that belief in the particular virtue of China which the philosophers found so attractive. As the cult of Confucius declined, the Chinese observer returned home and stayed there until in 1901 he paid a short return visit to European literature in *The Letters of John Chinaman* by the English philosopher G. Lowes Dickinson.

Fashions, however, have remarkable qualities of persistence. Charles Lamb paid his delicate tribute to China in a *Dissertation upon Roast Pig* (1823), and Coleridge created in *Kubla Khan* (1797) an imaginary China more enduring than that of the medieval travellers. Goethe—who was not only the presiding genius of his age but an encyclopedia of its intellectual excitements—wrote occasional chinoiseries even as late as 1826. But the general development in the nineteenth century was one of scorn for China, sometimes amused—as in the case of the American writer Bret Harte's wily *Heathen Chinee*—sometimes vicious. The harsh contempt for the Chinese which was felt by so many Westerners in the nineteenth century was almost entirely a product of missionary Protestantism and the disgust it could barely conceal for civilizations other than that of the West. The Victorian mind took a gloomy view of the heathen it proposed to drag into the kingdom of Christ. The image of the Chinese as a sinister and inscrutable people with marked criminal tendencies is a product of that view.

The mysterious Doctor Fu Manchu, who helped to create the Chinaman of comic papers and the cinema, was first immortalized by the novelist Sax Rohmer in 1916. He still leers at us from the covers of paperbacks. And why not, when many men in the West believe that equally mysterious and sinister Chinamen, plotting to conquer the real world, sit inscrutably today in the heart of the Forbidden City of Peking?

The Chinese Madness

Just as the Jesuits in China, by exporting their rose-coloured view of a Confucian Utopia, created a chinoiserie style of thinking in the minds of European philosophers, so Dutch and English merchants provided the basis of a chinoiserie style for artists and decorators by importing oriental textiles, porcelain and lacquer. Both the thinking and the decoration were essentially European, a projection of European desires rather than an imitation of Chinese reality.

Though the 'Chinese madness', as the satirists called it, was to reach its height in the middle of the eighteenth century, the taste for oriental *objets de luxe* had begun nearly two hundred years before. Delicate Ming porcelain had been brought to Europe by the Portuguese in the sixteenth century, and attempts had been made to reproduce it. It was, however, regarded as no more than an interesting and exotic curiosity until the flow of oriental merchandise increased, and brought with it some of that discrimination which marks the connoisseur and the collector. At the beginning, only the very rich could afford Eastern wares but, as the fashion grew, so did the demand. The European craftsmen who tried, by imitation, to satisfy it, laid the foundation for the vogue of chinoiserie. Of great importance were the designs themselves. Early in the seventeenth century, two engravers—Mathius Beitler, a Dutchman, and Valentin Sezenius, a Dane—produced sets of oriental-style designs which were, perhaps, the first indication that fantasy was soon to take over from imitation.

But before imitation gave way to fantasy, there were technical as well as design problems to be overcome. About the middle of the seventeenth century, a group of factories at Delft in Holland began producing vessels decorated in blue and white in imitation of Ming ceramics. European potters, however, did not at first have the secret of oriental porcelain. Attempts to discover it were made, and wares produced at a factory in Saint-Cloud in France were said to be indistinguishable from the real thing; unfortunately no specimens from before 1700 survive.

It was at Dresden in Saxony that the secret was finally discovered. The elector, Augustus the Strong (1694–1733), was so enamoured of oriental porcelain that China was said to be 'the bleeding-bowl of Saxony'; Augustus was rumoured to have spent one hundred thousand thalers on porcelain in the first year of his reign and to have exchanged a regiment of dragoons for forty-eight porcelain vases belonging to the King of Prussia. In such circumstances, the discovery of porcelain must have been the salvation of the state. Two alchemists in Augustus's employ had been instructed to make gold; they produced hard-paste porcelain instead—which turned out to be almost as profitable. In 1712, Augustus established the Royal Porcelain Manufactury at Meissen, a few miles outside Dresden, and its wares soon began to flow into the china-cabinets of Europe. As any cult must have an image, so Meissen produced the *pagod* or *pagoda* figure of the Chinese god of happiness—a squat, round-bellied fellow with open mouth, whose light-hearted laughter echoed the essential gaiety of chinoiserie.

The carefully kept secrets of Meissen soon leaked out, as did the influence of its designers and decorators. Before the middle of the century, there were factories in many European countries, all with their own chinoiserie styles. These styles had, in fact, begun to develop even before Europe discovered how to manufacture porcelain. Large quantities of the genuine Chinese article had been imported, unpainted, for decoration by European craftsmen in the prevailing taste.

Delight in the hard, smooth and shining surface of porcelain was not satisfied by such small items as statuary, vases and teapots. Porcelain panels soon came into use as a decoration for interior walls. Augustus the Strong, whose craving for chinoiserie appears to have been as total as that of a drug-addict, planned a pleasure-house where every room was to be panelled with porcelain on walls and ceilings. This plan was never realized, but others were. In Naples, at the royal residence at Portici, a complete porcelain room was constructed between 1757 and 1759. Later moved to Capodimonte (in 1886), it was made up of over three thousand interlocking pieces of porcelain.

If the porcelain room is considered as the shrine of the cult of chinoiserie (and practically everything is possible in the *rêve chinois*), the teapot is its sacred vessel and tea its sacramental wine. In the second half of the seventeenth century, with the lacquer and the porcelain, the oriental textiles, and the travel-books whose illustrations had such a profound influence on the European image of China, there came a mysterious herb. Travellers in China had recorded its qualities in glowing terms. With their advertising already done for them the Dutch East India Company imported first samples and then, in about 1650, commercial quantities. Within a few years, tea had become a major item on the bills of lading of ships trading with the Indies. The English, soon to be known as a nation of tea-drinkers, quickly took to the new herb. The English East India Company's imports expanded from a cautious twenty-three pounds in 1666 to twenty thousand pounds a year by the end of the century. And with tea-drinking came the ritual objects—kettles, pots, cups, caddies, and tables to put them on. A petition of the Joiners' Company of London shows that large numbers of these last were imported from the East— 6,852 in the five years between 1696 and 1700.

Lacquer-ware, sometimes plain but usually decorated, had been among the first imports from China. Indeed, imitations were already being made as early as the first decade of the seventeenth century and possibly even before then. By the end of the century, the taste for lacquer was widespread. Louis XIV, that arbiter of princely taste, had given it the imprimatur of Versailles; the dark glow of lacquer panels, with their chinoiserie designs in gold and brilliant colours, was at once sumptuous and exotic. Much of Europe's lacquer furniture came through Holland, which imported it from Japan, where the lacquer was of a finer quality than in China. Once again, demand exceeded supply; imitations appeared and found a ready market. 'Japanning' became so fashionable that it was even thought a suitable occupation for young ladies, and the designs produced by Stalker and Parker in their *Treatise* of 1688 were probably intended for a growing number of amateurs. But the art of japanning reached its height in the hands of French craftsmen, particularly of the family of Martin.

The men of the late seventeenth and early eighteenth centuries —the era of baroque—enjoyed their 'China-ware' in baroque terms. It was the *richness* of lacquer, the *texture* of porcelain that attracted them. Porcelain vases were mounted in European ormolu; lacquer cabinets were placed on massive stands of gilded wood, heavy with putti and swags of foliage. This was an attempt to fit the products of the East into the current conception of the East—a place of fabulous riches and magnificence. The China of fairy-tale, of gaiety, was still to come. When it did come, in the 1730s, it soon displaced richness with frivolity, heaviness with fragility. Furniture became as light and as airy as the imaginary landscapes with which it was often decorated. The designs were not so much exotic as irrepressible. The wooden bells on the corners of the curving roofs gave off a tinkling sound; the strange forms of rustic furniture refused to conform. This was the essence of rococo, that vast sigh of relief at escape from a sombre and constricting world. Artists and designers broke away from the mathematical rigidity of Classicism into free and twisting forms, and from dark colours to delicate tints. The dresses of fashionable ladies reflected this change. They adopted light-coloured silks, which soon became the fashion all over Europe as the elegantly dressed dolls used by French merchants to display their wares reached even the smallest courts of Germany. French silks and fabrics had early reached a high standard of quality; Chinese dyeing techniques seem to have been known as early as 1699, and Chinese dyes offered the weaver a new range of colours. The most delicate of these were a luminous yellow-gold and the so-called 'Chinese green'. People with limited money to spend on chinoiserie decoration were even supplied by the fabric manufacturers with an economical means of doing out their rooms à la mode de Chine. Toiles, particularly those from the factory at Jouy near Versailles, could be used to cover walls.

These toiles were often printed (originally from copper plates and in one colour only) with scenes of fragile pagodas and other motifs copied from engravings by Watteau, Boucher, Huet and Pillement. The latter's designs were widely copied for textiles, wallpapers, and even marquetry. Pillement's work has survived and today is again being used for wallpaper. Watteau produced the first rococo chinoiserie designs as early as 1719. In them he set the tone for Europe—priests and pagodas, parasols, and temples open to the sky. They contain the spirit of rococo, they are fantastic without being grotesque, mysterious but without any feeling of menace. The chinoiserie of the age of baroque provided inspiration for the artists of the age of rococo. From it they created an entirely new vocabulary, one which articulated the spirit of the times. Their work was primarily decorative, for the houses of the new aristocracy still displayed a classical front—although even there, there was a lightening of feeling. Chinoiserie was an intimate style, the style of a society concerned not with creating a grand impression but only with enjoying itself.

The architecture of chinoiserie was an architecture of pleasure, its buildings intended for relaxation and gaiety. China, or at least the China the eighteenth century was aware of, offered no acceptable style of architecture for *public* building. To the rococo mind, Chinese architecture was exotic and therefore frivolous. Augustus the Strong erected an 'Indian' pleasure-house at Pilnitz and a 'Japanese' palace at Dresden with spreading Chinese roofs like those of the Imperial Palace at Peking. (The eighteenth century was quite impartial in its attributions. India, China and Japan were all the 'gorgeous East', and therefore interchangeable.) Frederick the Great built himself a chinoiserie tea-house at Potsdam. In Germany, the Landgrave of Kassel constructed an entire Chinese village. In 1799, Ferdinand IV, king of the Two Sicilies, built the Villa Favorita in Palermo, an unexpectedly successful marriage of chinoiserie and Palladio. The Prince of Wales, later George IV, considered in 1803 erecting a Chinese pavilion at Brighton, but chinoiserie was really no longer fashionable and the prince finally decided on what Humphry Repton called the 'architecture of Hindustan'. The Chinese taste, however, ran agreeably riot inside.

The Chinese mode was eminently suitable for small pavilions, for summer-houses and follies. And what better setting than that peculiar hybrid, the Anglo–Chinese garden. The relation of the Anglo–Chinese garden, not the least extravagant manifestation of the Chinese vogue, to the gardens of China has long been argued. But one thing is reasonably sure—reaction to that highly formal disciplining of nature which had been made fashionable by le Nôtre in France, and copied elsewhere by princes anxious to emulate the Sun King, provoked what Horace Walpole was to call a 'whimsical irregularity' in garden design. Sir William Temple had suggested a 'wild garden' as early as 1685, 'where the beauty shall be great, and strike the eye, but without any order or disposition of parts that shall be commonly or easily observed'. Strict regularity in the layout of trees and shrubs began to be abandoned early in the eighteenth century, although this was more a result of the romantic landscapes of Claude Lorrain, Poussin and Salvator Rosa than of the Chinese example. Some protagonists of the 'natural' garden, however, believed that it did have the approval of the Chinese. William Chambers, who had sketched a few buildings at Canton when he travelled as supercargo on an English East Indiaman, described the true Chinese garden (which he had never seen) and laid out those at the Botanical Gardens at Kew, near London. He was, however, the first to attempt some scholarly imitation, rather than parody, of Chinese buildings. His work was tremendously influential, and when the French took up the English garden they used Chambers's descriptions to prove that its origin was really Chinese. Nature tamed but not subdued, ornamented— as if to confirm the provenance of the garden's design—with chinoiserie kiosks and bridges, became the ambition of the princes and nobles of Europe. The 'natural' garden of meandering paths and serpentine streams was, for the sophisticated urban aristocracy, an evocation of the simplicity of that pastoral life whose apotheosis was the *ferme ornée* in which Marie-Antoinette, symbol of a dying world, played at being a shepherdess.

The essential fantasy of the Anglo–Chinese garden was underlined by the absence of Chinese plants and flowers, which were mostly unknown in Europe before the end of the eighteenth century. There was, perhaps, a pool of goldfish—Madame de Pompadour is said to have possessed one of the first goldfish in Europe—but the majority of the flowering shrubs, winter jasmine, *Camellia reticulata*, and many others, only appeared in time to embower the gloomy neo-gothic of the Victorian middle classes.

Occasionally, chinoiserie moved out of the salon and the private garden into the streets. In Italy the elaborate spectacle of the annual carnival—for which such cities as Rome, Venice and Florence were famous—would hardly have been complete without its chinoiserie floats and the rich, oriental dresses of the revellers. When Augustus the Strong visited Venice in 1716, a junk bristling with parasols sailed down the Grand Canal. In Rome, decorated floats rumbled past the crumbling monuments of classical antiquity and fireworks outlining chinoiserie designs burst in the air

THE DREAM OF CATHAY

like magic fountains. Shadow-plays, known in France as *ombres chinoises*, became a popular entertainment. 'Chinese' cafés opened their doors. On the brink of the revolution, a *redoute chinoise* was established in Paris in 1781, where Chinese pageants and Chinese illuminations could be seen. It is, perhaps, significant that the chinoiserie idea came late to popular entertainment, at a time when the rich were turning towards the simpler but no less fantastic life of the model dairy and the workshop.

The theatre, on the other hand, had been quick to reflect the vogue for China. At the court of Louis XIV, Chinese masques (of a sort) were acted in the late seventeenth century. The Chinaman, or what was taken to be a Chinaman, joined Harlequin and Pierrot in the players' repertoire. The Sun King himself appeared in a masque wearing a costume described as half Persian and half Chinese. The first appearance of chinoiserie on the *public* stage seems to have been a performance in 1692 by the Comédie-Italienne of Regnard and Dufresny's *Les Chinois*—though the character who claims to be a 'Chinese doctor' does not appear until the second act, when he informs the audience that he has just come hot-foot from the Congo! In England, after David Garrick's *Chinese Festival* failed in 1755—not through public dislike of China but because of objections to the French dancers who had been imported for it—Chinese entertainment virtually disappeared from the stage. One serious play was performed: Arthur Murphy's *The Orphan of China* (1759), which was an adaptation of the Chinese original from which Voltaire had taken his *Orphelin de la Chine*. In 1753, there had been an operatic version of this, entitled *L'Eròe cinese*, with music composed by Metastasio. But Carlo Gozzi's *Turandot* (1761), with its then uncharacteristically harsh view of the East, was to have the longest dramatic life; it was probably the combination of barbarity of plot and delicacy of language which inspired Schiller's adaptation in 1801 and the two modern versions in operatic form by Busoni (1918) and Puccini (1924).

Chinoiserie drama, opera and literature, though light and insubstantial, did reflect the widespread feeling which expressed itself in decoration, in gardens and in architecture. It would be strange if this had not been so, for the essence of rococo chinoiserie was that it was an *entertainment*. China even penetrated into the world of prophecy—the *tarot* system of foretelling the future had come from the East with the gypsies, and chinoiserie decoration on *tarot* cards was to add yet another element of the bizarre to the fantasy of the Chinese madness.

By about 1770, the future of chinoiserie itself was not too difficult to prophesy. In England by the middle of the century it had already come under heavy attack; the assault was two-pronged, from Classical purists, and from the supporters of the Gothic Revival. In Europe, the Classical style was popularized by discoveries at Herculaneum, Pompeii and Palmyra, while the English Gothic Revivalists—although they had enjoyed a flirtation with chinoiserie in buildings and furniture decorated with both Chinese fretwork and pointed arches—turned away from further misalliance into interpretation of the grim world of northern Gothic, an apparently *nationalist* architecture suitable to a small island in process of turning itself into a great empire.

In France, chinoiserie died with the *ancien régime*. Napoleon, intent on creating a new empire, saw that its majesty could be expressed in neo-Classicism and its universality in the exotica of Egypt and India, both of which he intended to conquer. Chinoiserie could not survive a combined assault from Hellas and the quest for empire, although it did make the experiment of becoming more restrained.

The dream of Cathay, however, was not yet over. In Germany, little Chinese follies continued to be built into the first decade of the nineteenth century. England had a revival under the Prince Regent. In the United States a pagoda from a design by Chambers was erected in a park in Philadelphia in 1827; and the New Haven railway station, built in 1848, included Chinese in its curious mixture of styles. In the 1830s another vogue for rococo chinoiserie appeared in England and France to satisfy the Romantic craving for the exotic, and later the new bourgeoisie, snug in the comforts of the age of industry, began to yearn for the forgotten graces and lost fantasies of earlier times. The new vogue for Cathay was to be short-lived—though more and more real Chinese objects were finding their way into the home—but in the middle of the nineteenth century, as the armies of England and France at Peking sent the Summer Palace of the emperors of China up in flames, a new vision of an exotic Eastern kingdom was being revealed to the European mind—the empire of Japan.

A Floating World

To eighteenth-century Europe, Japan was not a separate place. It was part of that empire of Cathay that meant porcelain and lacquer and Confucius. This lack of geographical exactitude was partly a result of the legendary nature of Europe's view of Cathay; an imaginative landscape hardly needs topographical definition. But it was also a fact that, since the expulsion of the Portuguese in 1638, Japan had been closed to all foreigners except the Dutch, who were allowed to live in and trade from an island ghetto off Nagasaki. The Dutch kept Europe supplied with lacquer and porcelain—but did not clutter the European image of Japan with facts. The Jesuits, before their expulsion, had shown Japan to be an intelligent and civilized nation—but this was before the massacre of the Christians in the seventeenth century. Swift had sent Gulliver on one of his travels to Japan—but it appeared to be a country whose frontiers marched with those of Laputa. Only in the early years of the nineteenth century did a few works of observation begin to appear.

Japan itself, however, still remained impenetrable, avoided even by the foreign whaling-ships which operated in its waters, until in the 1850s the Western imperialists took a hand. The steamship was their instrument, and the coaling-station its driving force. The United States, anxious to protect her trade in Eastern seas, needed a coaling-station in Asia; that need, coinciding with a period of revolutionary change inside Japan, made it possible for Commodore Perry and his gunboats to enter Tokyo Bay on 8 July 1853. Japan soon opened itself up to Western ideas and techniques, and the West itself settled down to a period of japonaiserie which was to have an important effect on the course of European art.

In the early summer of 1860, a Japanese mission arrived in the United States to ratify treaties between the two countries. The mission visited a number of American cities and in New York was given, according to one newspaper, 'decidedly the most magnificent display our city has ever seen'. In the crowd that watched these envoys from the empire of the Rising Sun was the American poet Walt Whitman, who saw the 'swart-cheek'd two-sworded envoys/Leaning back in their open barouches, bareheaded, impassive', as the Orient came to pay its respects to an America which was about to step out on its imperial mission. But Whitman was premature in his dream of manifest destiny; others preferred to take the exotic as it came. The old device of the oriental observer was revived to satirize American life; the American impresario Phineas T. Barnum added Japanese coins and lanterns to his wonderful exhibitions of the bizarre. But soon the Civil War came, and when the next flood of japonaiserie flowed into the United States it was to derive from Europe.

Shortly after trade relations were established with Japan, fans, lacquer boxes, embroideries, and vases of bronze were imported into Europe in ever-increasing quantities. In England, the exhibits in the Japanese Court at the International Exhibition of 1862 aroused considerable attention. 'Truly,' wrote one Gothic enthusiast, 'the Japanese Court is the *real* medieval Court of the Exhibition.' Soon rooms full of Japanese objects were to be found in almost every middle-class home. In France, too, the rage for japonaiserie was soon established. In 1862, Japanese ambassadors were received by the Emperor Napoleon III, but Japan's most significant envoy—the colour print—had already arrived in France in the form of wrappings round vases and fans.

The first man in France to discover *ukiyo-e*—the painting of the floating, fleeting world—is hidden by myth, but the most acceptable story is that the engraver Félix Bracquemond, one day in 1856, discovered in the possession of the printer Delattre a volume of prints by Hokusai which had been found in a crate of porcelain. Bracquemond is said to have carried the volume around in his pocket for the rest of his life. A year or so later, the painter Claude Monet acquired his first Japanese prints in le Havre, and the brothers Edmond and Jules de Goncourt were also to become early collectors as well as zealous propagandists. But these discoveries might have meant nothing; they might have had as little effect as Chinese art had had on the chinoiseries of Watteau and other painters in the eighteenth century. The rage for real Japanese objects, and for japonaiserie, amongst the fashionable of the Second

Empire was as superficial as the Chinese madness which had affected the court of Louis XV.

Artists in the eighteenth century had been largely circumscribed by their patrons' wishes. The French Revolution did not free them from that patronage but it did liberate their minds. The Romantics were to see the greatness and anguish of the human predicament in heroic terms; Realist painters such as Gustave Courbet and Honoré Daumier were to wed the heroic tone to a plebeian naturalism. But in the middle of the nineteenth century new experiments were in progress, characterized by an increasing interest in sensibility, in the emotions, and in the psychological processes of artistic composition and appreciation. To those who sought a new theory of art—and of literature—the revelation of Japanese colour woodcuts acted as a catalyst. Artists who called themselves 'Impressionists' took the Japanese print as a justification of their new view of reality. They borrowed subject-matter and technique from this source; one even exclaimed that the Japanese were 'the first and finest Impressionists'. But what in fact *did* they find? In odd perspectives and unbalanced composition, a release from academic formalism. In unusual and brilliant colours, an excuse for their own palettes. In stylization, a case against the representational art of the academies. They found, as the critic Ernest Chesneau put it in 1878, 'confirmation of their own personal way of seeing, feeling, understanding and interpreting nature'. The earliest effects can be seen in Manet's 'La Chanteuse des rues' (1862), with its flat colours and stark, unsentimental portrayal of the figure. Other painters—Monet, who was addicted to Japanese fans; Degas, who adopted strange angles of view in many of his ballet scenes; all the Impressionists in fact—took something different from the Japanese print to use as an instrument of their own genius. It is perhaps ironical that what so attracted the Impressionists to the Japanese block-print was the photographic immediacy with which it appeared to capture the reality of the moment; it was precisely this element to which Japanese connoisseurs took exception, because it lacked universality and truth!

It was not only painters who grasped at what Jules de Goncourt called '*japonisme*'. Literature—and literary thinking—were as much affected. Zola, for example, was an enthusiastic collector. In Manet's portrait of him, there is a Japanese screen, a Japanese print, and a print of Manet's own 'Olympia'. Zola's staircase was decorated with other Japanese prints whose erotic subject-matter he described as 'furious fornications'. The naturalism of the Japanese prints fitted well with Zola's concept of 'scientific' realism; it was their instant reality which he found so appealing. But Zola believed that real life lacked order and shape and that it was necessary to give it form, not by *composing* a scene but by viewing it from an unusual perspective, as the Japanese artists did. This belief was shared by the Goncourts, who were also influenced by the subject-matter of Japanese prints. The prints enshrined actors and geisha—the pop idols of the ordinary Japanese. The Goncourts took, as their characters, the courtesan and the acrobat.

So fertile was Impressionism that it profoundly influenced literary movements as opposed to each other as Naturalism and Symbolism. Many Symbolist poets adopted Impressionist techniques, calling their poems 'impressions' and frequently using Japanese allusions. There was also a real attempt actually to *imitate* Japanese poetic style. This development was significant, because it began to move literary *japonisme* out of the exotic towards a genuine appreciation of Japanese forms. The publication in 1910 of an important anthology of Japanese literature, in translation, inspired French poets like Paul Fort and Paul Eluard to imitate even the syllabic arrangements of the Japanese nature lyrics known as *haiku*. One authority has suggested that the discovery of *haiku* by French poets was as important to them as was the discovery of the sonnet to the poets of Renaissance England.

From even this brief survey it can be seen how *japonisme* entered the veins of French art. The excitement Japan caused in Paris, the capital of the world of art, soon spread out to other parts of Europe and to America. In England and the United States, the great missionary of ideas was an American painter who had studied in France and lived most of his adult life in England— James McNeill Whistler.

Whistler had gone to Paris to study painting and, probably through his acquaintance with the artist-engravers of the time— Delacroix, Bracquemond and Meryon among them—soon developed an enthusiasm for Japanese prints, and began avidly to collect porcelain and curios. In 1859 he moved to England. There, five years later, he painted his 'Arrangement in Rose and Silver: La Princesse du Pays de la Porcelaine', in which the flowing lines of the princess's clothes clearly reflect the influence of the block-print. Essentially the painting was a work of exoticism, an exercise in japonaiserie. But Whistler's interest went further. He also advocated plain walls and light colours for interior decoration; in his own house in Chelsea he had rich yellow and white walls, plain curtains, Japanese matting and a few select paintings and pieces of porcelain. In his contrast of exoticism and simplicity, Whistler saw Japanese art not only with the eye of an Impressionist but with that of a prophet of *art nouveau*. From imitation, he gradually absorbed the best aspects of the Japanese prints and transformed them into a distinctive personal style.

This transformation can be seen at its best in his studies of London's Battersea Bridge. One of these, modelled on a print by Hiroshige, he called 'Nocturne in Blue and Gold'. The art histor-ian John Ruskin, taking offence at what he felt to be insincerity and superficiality, accused Whistler of 'flinging a pot of paint in the public's face'. In the subsequent libel action Whistler won a farthing damages, but was ruined by the costs of the action. William Morris described Whistler's painting as 'the impression on a very short-sighted person of divers ugly incidents seen through the medium of a London fog'; but then Morris thought Burne-Jones was the greatest painter of his time.

Whistler's use of such titles as 'Nocturne', 'Harmony' and 'Symphony' demonstrate how Impressionism united the work of artists, writers, and even composers such as Debussy. For probably the first time in European cultural history, the arts intermingled in a profound and mutually refreshing way. Whistler's views, like his paintings, aroused controversy. He fancied himself as a writer of style, and directly influenced some of the writers he gathered around him. But the poet Swinburne was so affected by Whistler's statement that 'the story of the beautiful is already complete— hewn in the marbles of the Parthenon—and embroidered, with the birds, upon the fans of Hokusai—at the foot of Fusayama', that he felt forced to remind Whistler's hearers that they were 'not in a serious world; that they were in the fairyland of fans, in the paradise of pipkins . . . [surrounded by] all the fortuitous frippery of Fusayama'. Swinburne, however, belonged at the end of an old tradition, not at the beginning of a new—and he resented the coming change.

The Victorian middle classes in England and France, undeterred by the arguing of intellectuals, continued to enjoy their Japanese madness. In 1862, the same year as the great Japanese display at the London International Exhibition, there opened in Paris a shop selling oriental goods. By the time of the *Exposition* of 1878, France was flooded with monstrous lacquer cabinets, vases, lamps and *jardinières*, glistening furiously in the gaslight. Real Japanese fans mingled indiscriminately with home-produced cloisonné enamel. The largest market was for furniture decorated with bamboo fretwork and paintings of geisha, butterflies, and the rest of the repertoire of japonaiserie, but Japanese inspiration was, in spite of this, stimulating a new attitude towards design, an impulse away from the over-stuffed, over-ornamented furniture so characteristic of the times to a simplicity of line which was to be almost stark in its elegance.

The depth of the Japanese craze is perhaps best seen in two of the operettas of Gilbert and Sullivan, *Patience* (1881) and *The Mikado* (1885). The first parodied such writers of the aesthetic movement as Oscar Wilde, as well as the mania for 'All one sees/ That's Japanese'. *The Mikado*, however, besides being a satire on the England of the day, recognized the strength of popular enthusiasm for japonaiserie. The libretto even contains Japanese phrases —translatable, in one case, as: 'You devil! With fright, with hiccups! Hey! Hey!' *The Mikado* had an enormous success, though it drew a formal protest from the Japanese ambassador, and it spawned a large progeny of pseudo-Japanese plays.

The effects of Japanese art were being absorbed into the changing climate of taste. Japan was only one of the stimuli, but it did play an important role. The Great Exhibition at the Crystal Palace in London in 1851 had released a wave of criticism of design in the industrial arts. This criticism came from two diametrically opposed directions. Some critics hated the machine and wanted to return to handicrafts; William Morris was the leading exponent of this school. On the other hand, there were designers who looked forward to the art of the machine itself. The former gazed backward to a romanticized Middle Ages, the latter ahead to the modern world of technology. But it was Morris who liberated the designer and taught him to look for sources in other cultures as well as in the past. Though Morris *was* a liberator, his own inclination was to replace the ugliness of Victorian decoration with a fake medievalism which was almost as stifling. Towards the end of the reign of Queen Victoria—a reign which had muffled the arts in bombazine—there grew up a desire for freedom, light and gaiety which was not very different from that which had inspired the artists of the age of rococo. Delicately coloured Eastern silks, imported by the London drapery store of Liberty, had wide sale in the 1890s. Artists and designers who had at first rejected the Impressionists' interpretation of the Japanese print now looked at it and other Japanese objects again, and discovered a stylization of line and decoration which was to have considerable influence both on the movement known as *art nouveau* and on post-Impressionist painting.

The essentials of *art nouveau* can be seen in the work of such painters as Beardsley, Toorop and Klimt; in the posters of Alphonse Mucha; in the buildings of Victor Horta, Louis Sullivan and Gaudí; in the embroidery of Hermann Obrist; and in the stations of the Paris Métro designed by Hector Guimard. Fundamentally, the style is complicated and sinuous. Flower-like forms writhe extravagantly, but with great delicacy and interior discipline. The fantasy is highly formalized, an assertion of that asymmetrical essence of nature which is a concept implicit in the Japanese view of reality.

In France in the early 1880s, while the rage for japonaiserie was dying, painters were on the threshold of discovering new aspects of the Japanese colour print from which to draw inspiration. It is significant that the influence of Japanese art in Europe should have been so varied, as varied in fact as the artists who responded to it. The reaction of the post-Impressionists was of a uniquely different order from that of the Impressionists, though, in essence, it was very similar to that of the decorators of *art nouveau*. They reacted to style and, in particular, to the Japanese artists' disregard of what in the West were the basic academic rules of design. On this new level of influence, the effect of Japan is both less obvious and yet more profound than in the case of the Impressionists or even the practitioners of *art nouveau*. Because of this, much of it passes unnoticed. Yet in the work of Toulouse-Lautrec, for example, the Japanese influence is immediately apparent when his work is juxtaposed with that of the Japanese masters of the colour print.

Lautrec is known to have collected *ukiyo-e*, perhaps under the influence of his eccentric father, but certainly with the encouragement of painters such as Degas with whom he associated. He made sketches from Japanese prints, but in only one of his paintings is his debt to the East fully acknowledged. In his 'Les Ballets des *Lotus*', there is a group of Japanese heads in the foreground. The real stylistic effect, however, can be seen in Lautrec's method of composition, with its falsified perspective, flat areas of colour, and strongly flowing lines. His posters have the immediacy—and economy—of Japanese prints at their finest. They have the uncompromising lack of entanglement in a fleeting moment, captured without contrivance, and certainly without the involvement of criticism or flattery. Other painters were indebted to Japanese art in minor but none the less real ways. Some broke free from artificiality—like Renoir, whose 'Les Parapluies' has obvious affinities with Utamaro's 'Girls on a Bridge'.

Van Gogh and Gauguin, on the other hand, clearly and obviously acknowledged their debt to Japan. The Japanese print in Van Gogh's self-portrait in the Courtauld Institute, London, has more than symbolic significance. He even went so far as to copy, a little freely, Japanese prints such as Hiroshige's 'Ohashi Bridge in the Rain'. Van Gogh first discovered Japanese prints in Antwerp and in 1887 organized an exhibition of them in Paris. It was, however, in Provence that he really felt the touch of Japan. The countryside seemed as beautiful as Japan, 'for clarity of atmosphere and gay colour-effects'. In a letter to his brother Theo, in 1888, he talked of the Japanese artist as a man studying a single blade of grass, but: 'This blade of grass leads him to draw every plant, and then the seasons, the wider aspects of the countryside, then animals, then the human figure.' In many of Van Gogh's paintings—such as 'Boats at Saintes-Maries' (1888)—the pattern and the large areas of resonant colour immediately betray Japanese influence, and he even used oriental reed pens in order to imitate the technique of the Japanese masters.

Gauguin, in 1888, began to work in a style known as *cloisonnisme* or *synthétisme*. This had literary beginnings, and was closely affiliated with the work of poets such as Rimbaud. The aim was to express ideas, moods and feelings, in bright colours, decoratively and abstractly. One of the movement's principal members, Émile Bernard—who claimed to have founded it—said categorically that the study of Japanese prints had encouraged the impulse towards a new simplicity. The sources of Gauguin's inspiration included Romanesque carvings and Gothic sculpture, but some of his works were directly influenced by Japanese art. In 'The Vision after the Sermon', the figures of Jacob and the Angel are based on a pair of wrestlers by Hokusai. The painting has no touch of japonaiserie, but Camille Pissarro criticized Gauguin for copying elements from the Japanese—though his own work was also undoubtedly affected by the same influences.

The effect of the Japanese print lasted well into the present century. Painters such as Bonnard, who, a year before Toulouse-Lautrec, had produced, for a Champagne firm, a poster with a distinctly Japanese feel; Vuillard; and the Belgian painter of terror, James Ensor; all these responded in their different ways to the most fruitful of all Europe's cultural imports from the East.

Europe's image of Japan was, of course, largely formed by the Japanese print, and by objects specially produced in Japan to satisfy European taste. It was not just a nineteenth-century version of the *rêve chinois*—for one thing, Japan was accessible to travellers in a way China had never been—but the discovery of the country produced no revolutionary political philosophies, no new vision of man and his world, as the ideas of Confucius had done in the eighteenth century. Sir Edwin Arnold—who produced a prolix, and now fortunately little read, poem on the life of the Buddha—also wrote enthusiastically in praise of the Japanese woman of pleasure, the 'Musmee' (*musume*).

> The Musmee's heart is slow to grief
> And quick to pleasure, love and song.

Rudyard Kipling, whose work is a mirror of the apparent contra-dictions of English Victorian attitudes, looked at Japan with the eye of cultural humility. 'Japan is a great people,' he wrote. 'Her masons play with stone, her carpenters with wood, her smiths with iron, and her artists with life, death, and all the eye can take in. Mercifully she has been denied the least touch of firmness in her character which would enable her to play with the whole round world. We possess that—We, the nation of the glass flower-shade, the pink worsted mat, the red and green china puppy-dog, and the poisonous Brussels carpet. It is our compensation.' Such attitudes frequently surprise people who are unaware of the flexibility of the Victorian temper. But on the whole, the travellers of the late nineteenth century brought back one or other of two stereotypes of Japan. It was either a fairy-tale country, inhabited by a toy-like and polite people, or a land of cruel, militaristic and treacherous men. Both images still survive today.

Some writers, of course, created their own popular images of Japan. The most important among them was Julien Viaud (1850–1923), who wrote under the pseudonym of 'Pierre Loti'. He took an ugly view of Japan, and his most popular book *Madame Chrysanthème* (1888), combined, as one critic has put it, 'the most trivial exoticism with a conscienceless imperialism'. Loti regarded 'marriages' between French naval officers and Japanese women as a kind of dirty joke and although in Puccini's opera *Madame Butterfly*—which was based on the book—the ugliness is obliterated by honeyed music, Lieutenant Pinkerton's desertion of his bride is basically just as offensive as anything in Loti's original.

The Anglo-Irishman Oscar Wilde viewed Japan with quite a different eye. He delighted in oriental detail, in creating verse pictures alive with colour. He was, in fact, an isolated precursor of modern poetry. Wilde's Japan—Impressionist in style and thought—was kept alive in the works of the American journalist Lafcadio Hearn (1850–1904), who became a naturalized Japanese, but it was another American, Ernest Fenollosa, who was to attempt a unification of Eastern and Western experience and who was to have an important effect upon the poetry of modern times. Fenollosa 'cannot be looked upon as a mere searcher after exotics', said Ezra Pound. 'His mind was constantly filled with parallels between Eastern and Western art. To him the exotic was a means of fructification.' When Fenollosa died, the Japanese sent a warship to convey his ashes to Japan. Pound himself was deeply influenced by Impressionism—Whistler's Impressionism—and by the *haiku* lyric form which he used in many shorter poems as well as, more freely, in the first thirty of the *Pisan Cantos*. When, under the influence of some manuscript notebooks given to him by Fenollosa's widow in 1912, he produced an *Essay on the Chinese Written Character* (1920), he reached back to join hands with those who, in the seventeenth and eighteenth centuries, had believed that Chinese was the language spoken by man before Babel. Fenollosa viewed Chinese characters (which are also used for the Japanese language) as stylized pictures—objects pictorially expressed. Unfortunately, though this was very probably the case far back in the mists of time, they are now so obscure as to be unrecognizable. Pound used Chinese characters in his poems as a sort of magic picture, totally unrelated to their proper meaning and significance. Their use as a poetic image he defined as 'Listening to Incense'.

Pound misunderstood the nature of the Sino–Japanese written character, but he produced from it a fruitful and meaningful technique. So, in another medium, did the Russian motion-picture director Eisenstein. In his theoretical essay *The Cinematograph Principle and the Ideogram*, Eisenstein saw the written character as a vehicle for the direct presentation of meaning. It was the key, he wrote, 'to a cinema seeking a maximum laconism [conciseness of style] for the visual representation of abstract concepts'. In practice, Eisenstein took many of his techniques from the Japanese *kabuki* theatre—the 'cut', 'disintegration', 'slow motion', and the 'super close-up'. He used Japanese prints as a justification for the latter. Had they not, he asked, 'used super close-up foregrounds and effectively disproportionate features in super close-up faces'? Eisenstein's techniques are common-place today but his pioneer work fulfilled very much the same function in the cinema as that of the Impressionists when they brought Japan into literature.

Eisenstein's use of the Japanese *kabuki* was unique until after the Second World War, but that other example of Japanese drama, the *No*, was translated and had a comparatively early effect, particularly on the plays of the Irish writer W. B. Yeats, the French man Paul Claudel, the German expressionist Bertolt Brecht, and the American Thornton Wilder. Again, such writers used Japanese models to satisfy the urge to borrow form and technique, and widen the frontiers of Western drama. They shared with the painters and writers of the end of the nineteenth century a growing feeling of pessimism about the creative forces of Western culture. This was, in part, a reaction against the growing dominance of science and technology which had already begun to press upon the Western writer and artist in the middle of the nineteenth century. The *philosophes* of the eighteenth century had looked to China for ready-made Utopia; the modern world—and the Impressionists are just as much as part of it as today's artists and writers—looked to 'unspoiled' cultures for refreshment and regeneration.

Both China and India have affected Western man's view of his world, but it is Japan, partly by the historical accident of the timing of its discovery, which has been most influential in literature and art. Once more today—save in the continuing exotic image of Japan which remains in *The Teahouse of the August Moon* and the novels of James Michener—Japan appears as a meeting-place of East and West. Because her rulers in the Meiji era (1868–1912) realized that, to save themselves from Western imperialism, they must retain a distinct national identity and yet take much of the West's material culture, some Westerners now believe they see in Japan that mingling of cultures which they regard as ideal. It is a belief that may well prove as exotic as its predecessors—for it is a characteristic of the mutual discovery of East and West that each has taken from the other only what it hoped to find.

V

The Crescent and the Lotus

Wer den Dichter will verstehen
Muss in Dichters Lande gehen;
Er im Orient sich freue
Dass das Alte sei das Neue.

GOETHE, *West-Östlicher Diwan* (1819)

The bard whom pilfer'd Pastorals renown,
Who turns a Persian Tale for half-a-crown.

ALEXANDER POPE on Ambrose Philips

The real source of all tongues, of all thoughts and utterances of
the human mind . . . everything—yes, everything without
exception—has its origin in India.

FRIEDRICH SCHLEGEL, letter to Ludwig Tieck

If the wild bowler thinks he bowls,
Or if the batsman thinks he's bowled,
They know not, poor misguided souls,
They too shall perish unconsoled.
I am the batsman and the bat,
I am the bowler and the ball,
The umpire, the pavilion cat,
The roller, pitch, and stumps, and all.

ANDREW LANG, parody of EMERSON, *Brahma*

Out of the Arabian Nights

Of all the Asias that have attracted Europe by their mystery and splendour, the Near East—the Muslim East, that is—was the first to take on a genuine sense of geographical reality. In part, this was a legacy of the Crusades. Though that extensive period of contact did not produce any large quantity of descriptive literature, it did give to Europe some experience of a different civilization. From this experience, the Latin West took on a new dynamism. Islam, which was for some time in retreat under the pressures of both East and West, of Crusader and Mongol, revived under the Turks and began to menace Europe in the fifteenth century as the Mongols had appeared to do in the thirteenth.

When Constantinople fell in 1453 to the Turkish conqueror Mehmed II, and Athens—the Holy City of the Renaissance thinkers—was captured three years later, a great chorus of lamentation went up from European humanists. The sacred soil of Hellas had been profaned. This feeling coloured the whole Western view of the Turks until modern times, although it did not cut Europe off completely from the Islamic world. Humanists might recoil in horror from the conquerors of Greece, but kings and merchants were not above doing business with them. Indeed, the Turks acted as transmitters of a number of ideas and techniques from farther Asia. But their very presence, whether as an ally or as a possible enemy, inspired curiosity about their dominions and those of other rulers who might perhaps be a threat to them.

The Crusades had produced some of the materials of romance; factual history had been turned into fabulous legend. The theme of border warfare between Christians and Muslims in Spain inspired the *Song of Roland* as early as *c.* 1100; there were works glorifying the Crusaders, Peter the Hermit, and Godefroy de Bouillon. But, on the whole, they had little *direct* influence on European literature. There are, however, close affinities with Arabian tales in the story of the Holy Grail—perhaps the most impressive version of which was composed by the Franconian knight Wolfram von

Eschenbach at some time between 1200 and 1217—and a number of genuine oriental tales, probably transmitted orally by merchants and others, penetrated the European mind. 'The Squire's Tale', for example, in *The Canterbury Tales* by Geoffrey Chaucer (? 1344–1400), is undoubtedly an 'Arabian Nights' story. Later, as the Turks advanced in Europe, there was a new outburst of heroic propaganda, and the Elizabethan dramatists in turn mirrored a revived interest in the Levant. The East—mainly the Muslim East —became an almost conventional setting for seventeenth-century tragedy. It was a region of mystery, of cruel monarchs and strange, doomed loves. The vogue was exploited by such writers as Madeleine de Scudéry, in her famous novel *Artamène ou le Grand Cyrus* (1653), and by the Genoese Gian-Paolo Marana, whose *L'Esploratore Turco* (or 'Turkish Spy') was presented in manuscript to Louis XIV in 1683, and widely translated. Marana's book was the first to use the device of the 'oriental observer', through whose eyes European institutions could be examined and criticized.

The 'oriental romance' reached its height in the eighteenth century, when France was to play a particularly creative role. Under Louis XIV, France had set the fashion for Europe in literature as well as in practically everything else; classical forms, systematized by the French critic Boileau in his *Art poétique* (1674), had constrained writers and poets. At the turn of the new century, however, a desire for new forms of expression began to come to the surface. Though it was China that was to play the dominant role in the eighteenth century, the Muslim East—and Turkey and Persia, in particular—exercised an important influence in the early years of the century.

The catalyst was Antoine Galland's rendering of *The Thousand and One Nights* (1704–17). This expurgated and Frenchified version had an immediate success. The reading public was entranced by the rich colouring and exotic settings of the tales. Galland's work was translated into English, and had as much success in England as in France. Soon, in order to satisfy the demand, pseudo-translations of other 'works' appeared and the Orient became more and more a legendary place, fashioned by the imagination of industrious writers who turned out tales of caliphs, kadis and jinns to order.

The Muslim East was to supply a rich vein of language, metaphor and inspiration for eighteenth-century writers. Not all were romancers or weavers of exotic tales, but all produced in one form or another an idealization to suit their purpose. *The Thousand and One Nights* was only one of many sources. Travellers' descriptions were another. These enjoyed a great vogue, in some cases justly so. Those of Bruin and Chardin were the most popular, and helped— with their descriptions of institutions, thought and religion—to influence both satirists and scholars. Chardin was a French protestant who had fled to England to escape persecution in 1681. He was knighted and became a fellow of the Royal Society. His narrative was first published in 1686 and reprinted in 1711, 1723 and 1775. On the whole, however, actual *knowledge* of the Muslim East barely increased between Chardin's time and the end of the eighteenth century. The men of the Enlightenment did not find in the Muslim world any revelation which might help to reform European society; they discovered it instead in the Jesuit interpretation of China. But the early narratives of travellers in the Levant helped to create interest in the East for its own sake.

A combination of reliable information about the East with the literary technique first seen in Marana's *Turkish Spy* was used by the French political writer Montesquieu (1689–1755) in his *Lettres persanes*. In this book, two Persians visiting Paris exchanged letters with each other and with their friends at home on the manners, customs and institutions of contemporary French society. The device of the foreign visitor allowed Montesquieu, who published the book anonymously, to conceal his own opinions, as well as to make use of factual information about Persia by way of comparison. It was this book, with its only faintly concealed deism and materialism, which perhaps more than any other opened up the Age of Reason. Montesquieu, with his descriptions of the harem, was able to add sexual titillation to social criticism— thus, no doubt, extending the range of his potential audience. The eighteenth century displayed a lascivious and continuing interest in the sexual customs of Muslims, and it is possible that such descriptions as those of Montesquieu, and certain parts of *The Thousand and One Nights*, may well have helped to establish the *contes licencieux* of such writers as Crébillon *fils*.

It was not only polygamy and espionage which attracted writers, and the public, to the Muslim East; the life of the prophet

Muhammad also had its fascination. Legends of his life were current in Europe from the time of the early Crusades, and possibly earlier, and traces of them can be found in Dante's *Divine Comedy*. William of Tyre, the chronicler of the deeds of the Crusading knights, also produced a *History of the Muhammadan Princes from the appearance of the Prophet*. The first translation into a Western language of the Koran—the Holy Book of Islam—was made by an Englishman, Robertus Retenensis. Completed in 1143, it enjoyed a wide circulation in manuscript copies. Four centuries later, this medieval Latin version was set up in print at Basle. Other translations undoubtedly existed, but, at least until that of André du Ryer (1647), most were inspired by hostility—Christian hostility—and were full of inaccuracies. In the eighteenth century, however, as the threat of the Turks receded, a more favourable attitude developed. Certainly, the idea of a heaven populated with beautiful girls whose virginity was miraculously restored every day—an idea which had the authority of the Koran—must have had considerable appeal, though no one seems to have turned Muslim in order to savour it. But when Voltaire wished to attack religious fanaticism in general (without offending the pope) he used, as a basis, the life of Muhammad. And when he wanted to portray a virtuous pagan and an unfortunate Christian girl—a restatement of the theme of *Othello*—he called his heroine *Zaïre* and set the scene in the Turkish dominions. These and other plays, as well as his novel *Zadig* (almost every Near-Eastern character in eighteenth-century literature had a name beginning with Z), influenced English writers. But what in France produced penetrating satire, perhaps because of the fundamental unease of French society, in England resulted in the moral tale.

Earlier eighteenth-century English writers like Defoe, Addison and Steele, looking for new literary forms in which to disguise their didactic intent, had welcomed the oriental tale and quietly anglicized it. Until the first victories of Robert Clive in India and his conquest of Bengal (after 1757), the English were not, however, greatly interested in the East as a *place*. Despite English writers such as Lady Mary Wortley Montagu, they remained fundamentally insular. In 1718, Lady Mary returned from two years in Constantinople where her husband was British Ambassador with Turkish costumes, knick-knacks and paintings, and started a craze which in literature produced a vast number of highly imaginative oriental tales. This vogue ultimately reached such a pitch that Goldsmith, in his *Citizen of the World* (1762), used his Chinese observer to ridicule both the authors of Arabian tales and such readers of them as the English lady who exclaimed: 'Oh, for a history of Aboulfaouris, the grand voyager; of genii, magicians, rocs, bags of bullets, giants and enchanters; where all is great, obscure, magnificent, and unintelligible!' The fashion, like all fashions, went into decline—although not before it had produced Samuel Johnson's *Rasselas* (1759)—and the oriental tale, as a form, is usually discounted by literary critics, perhaps because the quality of the writing is so often poor. There is, however, one exception in William Beckford's *Vathek* (1786), a fusion of oriental subject and imagery with the Gothic 'tale of terror'. It was written in French by an Englishman whose imagination was warmed by the exoticisms of both East and West, and whose desire to move away from reality—in space to the mysterious East, and in time to the Middle Ages—anticipated two of the most important elements in the Romantic movements of the next half-century.

At the end of the eighteenth century, a new discovery of the Muslim East—and of a civilization much older than that of Islam —was taking place. In 1799, the French army under Napoleon Bonaparte landed in Egypt. With him on the campaign Bonaparte took a large number of scholars and so founded the science of Egyptology. One of those scholars was D.-V. Denon, who, with the aid of Egyptian motifs, was to try to create a decorative style which would commemorate both Bonaparte's Egyptian campaign and the glory of the new French empire. He did not succeed— Napoleon's taste leant more towards the Classical—but a number of articles in the Egyptian taste did have considerable vogue. The principal motifs include the lotus-leaf, sphinx heads, lion supports, and even crocodiles and serpents.

Denon's book, *Voyage dans la basse et la haute Égypte*, was published in France and England in 1803. English furniture designers such as Thomas Hope and Thomas Chippendale the younger were attracted by the style. But by 1807 the fashion had caught on in England to such an extent that, in his *Household Furniture*, Hope warned designers 'never to adopt, except for motives more weighty than a mere aim at novelty, the Egyptian style of ornament'. The Egyptian influence lasted in England until 1826, but in France it hardly survived the fall of Napoleon. The French acquaintance with Egypt and Syria had, however, set in motion an interest in the Muslim East, which was to be intensified by the French campaign to conquer Algeria which began in 1830.

At the end of the eighteenth century, Europe was still profoundly ignorant of the real nature of Islamic literature and thought. In 1771, Sir William Jones translated into English a poem or *ghazel* of the fourteenth-century Persian poet, Hafiz. This and his Latin *Commentaries on Asiatic Poetry* had, with *Vathek*, considerable effect on such English poets as Byron, and in turn influenced poets in France and Germany. But the oriental elements in English Romanticism, acquired from scholarly reading, rarely formed more than a picturesque background. Sir Walter Scott made of the Crusades once more the stuff of romance. *The Talisman* (1825) and *Count Robert of Paris* (1831) were widely read and admired in both France and Germany. The reliance of English writers on the new oriental scholarship reached its peak in Thomas Moore's *Lalla Rookh* (1817) which had wide and lasting popularity. Moore is said to have secluded himself for two years in order to absorb Eastern ideas and images, and he claimed total verisimilitude for his characters. His claim is quite unjustified, and his long poem merely a sentimental arabesque.

It was in Germany that the influence of genuine Muslim literature was to have its greatest effect. In the late eighteenth century, poet-scholars such as Herder, the Schlegels and Hamman let loose into German literature a great flood of Eastern poetry. Goethe, wearying in his old age of the complexities of a Europe turbulent with social change, turned to the Orient for relief. He found in Persian poetry what he saw as a delightful sensuality combined with a deep, mystical philosophy. The product of his excitement— as well as of his acquaintance with a fascinating young woman, Mariane von Willemer—was a collection of gay, spiritualized love-songs with the title *West-Östlicher Diwan* (1819). The decorations were 'in the Persian style', but the poems themselves were not imitations. Goethe created a new idiom to express his ideas and to affirm, at the same time, his belief in the ideal of a cosmopolitan literature.

Goethe's contemporaries, however—men such as von Platen

(1796–1835)—imitated the forms of Persian poetry slavishly. 'These poor poets,' said Heine, 'eat too freely of the fruit they steal from the garden groves of Shiraz, and then they vomit *ghazels.*'

In France, the influence of the East renewed itself in a less scholarly form than in Germany. Scott and Byron were its models, and its Orient had all the glittering barbarity of the *Arabian Nights.* Victor Hugo, whose energy pulsated through French literature for so much of the nineteenth century, claimed: 'In the age of Louis XIV, all the world was Hellenist; now [1829] it is orientalist.' But Hugo's Orient was the same as that of Byron, an imaginary landscape, and his principal 'Eastern' work, *Les Orientales*—from whose preface the above quotation is taken— bears little relation to reality. One contemporary French critic had actually travelled in the Near East and remarked of Hugo's series of poems: 'To write *Les Orientales* without knowing the East is like making a rabbit stew without the rabbit.'

Other French writers, notably Théophile Gautier (1811–72) and Gérard de Nerval (1808–55), were rather more under the influence of Germany than some of their contemporaries. Their orientalism was secondhand, but they felt a sympathy with the East which did have some reflection in their work. Gautier's attitude to literature, however, was such as later came to be described as 'art for art's sake'. It was summed up in his answer to the question: 'What is the *use* of that?' Gautier replied: 'Its use is that it is beautiful. Is that not enough?' His Orient was an Orient of externals, almost as exotic as the monster-haunted world of Mandeville. Nerval, how-ever, was deeply concerned with philosophy and mysticism and read widely in the works of scholars. But even in his case—and the East was familiar to him, not only through books but through actual travel—the Orient remained superficial.

It was, however, painted by both artists and writers in glowing colours. The East of the Romantics was essentially a *visible* world, a sensate experience filling the eye and the emotions with rich and intoxicating images. These images found their most vibrant expression in the works of Eugène Delacroix (1798–1863) in such paintings as 'The Death of Sardanapalus'—which was based upon a tragedy by Byron. Delacroix visited North Africa in 1832 to feel the Orient at first hand, but his exoticism still remained uninformed by reality. The sensuality of the Muslim East had already, in 1814, inspired the painter Ingres (1780–1867) to produce his 'Odalisque'. With it, he began a cult still being expressed by Manet nearly fifty years later in his 'Olympia'. Critics said that, with his 'Odalisque', Ingres had 'put painting back three hundred years'. The eighteenth-century dream of women, nubile and adept, waiting on the whim of some Turkish nobleman, lived on in the imagination of the monogamous West, and still does today. Other painters—Decamps (1803–60), for example, who was called the 'discoverer of the Orient'—produced scenes with considerable attention to the truth. But the appeal was still to the exotic; this was the strange and cruel world of the romancers.

Around the middle of the century, however, a change was taking place, and it was a change which owed its origin to a combination of archaeology and arrogance. The nineteenth century—the century, that is to say, of the middle class, the 'Christian' manufacturers, the missionaries and the 'saintly' soldiers and empire-builders—was obsessed with the Bible. Commentaries were legion, and interest in the 'lands of the Bible' profound. Discoveries in Palestine and in Mesopotamia were to influence the attitude of Western peoples towards Islam and Islamic culture. It was not discoveries about the world of Muhammad that exerted the fascination, but discoveries about the world of Christ. Everyone seemed anxious for confirmation of the reality and physical truth of the Bible stories, in witness that the waters of Babylon still flowed and that the foundations of the tower of Babel might still exist, concealed beneath the shifting sands.

The excavation of the great monuments of the pre-Islamic past —of Nineveh, for example, so excitingly uncovered by the Englishman Layard in the middle of the century—offered proof of the Bible and caught the world's imagination with its wonders. This was the place of which the Lord had spoken to Jonah. 'Go to Nineveh, that great city, and cry against it; for their wickedness is come up before me.' The discovery of Nineveh helped, in effect, to restate the old medieval contrast between Christian and Muslim, but this time the *European* situation was very different. Now the Europeans, with their factories and their gunboats, their industrial optimism and their overseas empires, were arrogant with a new sense of power and superiority. To the Victorians, the legacy of Islam was nothing compared to the legacy of Biblical times, and the modern Muslim was merely a dirty peasant in dire need of Christ's teaching. Even such a romantic and intrepid traveller as Sir Richard Burton could not reduce the contempt of the Victorians, however much he might appeal to their sentimentality. It was, perhaps, to this same sentimentality that Edward Fitzgerald's *Rubá'iyát of Omar Khayyám* (1859) owed its popularity. Fitzgerald's masterpiece is not a translation but an evocation in English of the tone and feel of a Persian poet dead eight hundred years. It is perhaps the first example of an Eastern poet's being absorbed into the heart of Western literature.

Works and reports on travel and archaeology influenced at least one major novelist, Gustave Flaubert (1821–80). In 1862, after a visit to Tunisia four years earlier and a wide reading of scholarly works, he published his novel *Salammbô*. Though it is a tale set in ancient Carthage, its source was the East of the Romantic painters, with its rich palette of barbaric colour. But Flaubert's novel was much more than a romance. *Salammbô* had what one French critic has called '*une modernité archéologique*', a mingling of the imaginative and the documentary.

On less romantic levels, the Muslim East had a continuing, though relatively unimportant, influence. The Turkish bath, no longer exotic, heated the skin rather than the blood; Islamic shapes decorated the Victorian mantelshelf, but shared it with Benares brass-ware and Japanese fans—tributes from a conquered Asia. The source of coffee, even of 'Turkey' carpets, moved to the West Indies and the European factory. A Turkish restaurant offered no more than an exotic style of decoration which might also be found in the expensive *bordellos* of Montmartre, simulating the sensuality of the harem for jaded appetites.

Yet, all around, echoes of the Islamic style remained, assimilated into Victorian Gothic architecture. There had been a revival of the Gothic style in Europe in the second half of the nineteenth century, although Britain had gone into its neo-medieval period somewhat earlier. There, indeed, it was in decline after 1865, though Gothic buildings continued to be constructed. In France, the revival was given impetus by the architect Viollet-le-Duc (1814–79), who believed that the Gothic thirteenth century had been 'the century

143

of the people'. He was a ruthless restorer of churches as well as a persistent propagandist for the use of iron—that magic metal of the industrial revolution—in building construction. In his work arches, tracery patterns, pierced battlements, and all the other examples of borrowing from Muslim sources which had been absorbed into early Gothic are united with the constructional techniques of the modern world.

But what might perhaps be called—in all its possible meanings—'a flowering of the Arabian Nights', can be seen in the work of the Spanish architect Antonio Gaudí (1852–1926). He, too, started off as a Gothic revivalist, but he ended as the architect of nightmare. His work has been described as 'amazing', 'fascinating' and 'horrible', and his buildings are like those one might expect to find in an enchanter's garden—always in process of turning into something else, even into something alive. Gaudí's work is almost exclusively found in and around Barcelona. The Parque Güell, a kind of garden suburb, is entered past a minaret, and the parapets of the walks curve wildly, orientally, menacing the pedestrian with their unexpectedness. His masterpiece, the Church of the Sagrada Familia, begun in 1882 and still in progress, began in an almost conventional Gothic. But as each storey rose, the forms distorted until they disappeared altogether. Crowning the east façade are four tall sugar-loaf spires, like the minarets of a Tunisian mosque eroded by some magical wind.

North Africa also had its effect on that painter of the magical Paul Klee, who visited Tunisia in 1913 and maintained that the experience had a profound influence on all his work. As well as providing the subject of such paintings as 'The Great Dome' (1927), the Orient was absorbed into Klee's own enchanted world, that world where the simple nightingale becomes a 'twittering machine'.

All these are examples of genius. Except for the work of Gaudí—which can hardly pass unnoticed by the inhabitants of Barcelona—they do not necessarily impinge upon everyday life. But the Muslim Orient has made more than one contribution to popular entertainment. The sport of horse-racing—a pleasure which unites rich and poor—owes much to the Arab horse, which was particularly noted for its staying power. Its use by Turkish cavalry was greatly admired by their European opponents, but the Turks strictly controlled the export of this strategic war material. Captured horses were highly prized in Europe, and usually found their way into the stables of kings. The English were particularly quick to recognize the value of the Arab, and the English thoroughbred horse is a mixture of Barb (from North Africa), Arabian and Turkish breeds.

In many ways, the Arabia of the *Arabian Nights* lived on. Often it provided local colour for those classic works of imperialism, stories of the French Foreign Legion. But it was in the cinema that the exoticism of the Near East had its apotheosis. The dream-factories of Hollywood and other countries took on Scheherazade as their script-writer. The cunning sheikhs of Araby—symbols of sexual potency—soon leered from cinema screens, enticing white women into their tents with the lure of *frissons* apparently unavailable in cold Western bedrooms. Genii were released—in Technicolor—from their bottles, and magic carpets still have an appeal even in the age of supersonic jets. The cinema itself was sometimes decorated to resemble a Moorish palace—the final meeting, perhaps, of the dream with the dream.

But though the sheikhs of the Persian Gulf now pump up the oil for their Aladdin's lamps, and though their harems are transported in Cadillacs, this merely increases that tension between the mundane and the marvellous which forms the essence of the fairy-tale.

The Fatal Ring

After the fall of the Roman empire India virtually disappeared from the European consciousness. Exotic products of Indian origin still made their way to the West, Indian tales and Indian numerals filtered through Arabic culture, but direct intellectual commerce was not possible. The hearsay of merchants and the scanty information contained in some of the surviving works of Greek historians were not improved upon until Marco Polo visited southern India at the end of the thirteenth century on his way home from China. His narrative contained very little hard fact, though he did record the burning of Hindu widows with their husbands and called the Hindu priestly caste of the Brahmins the most truthful men in the world. The next reports also came from a Venetian, Nicolò Conti (*fl.* 1419–44), who described religious festivals and customs, but no more information became available until some years after the Portuguese had arrived in India at the end of the fifteenth century.

Most of the new information was to be contained in narratives of travel and the reports of missionaries. But it was commerce not culture that opened up the Indies. The cargoes brought back by the adventurers of Holland and England were touched with high romance—vezino, quicksilver, lignum aloes, cubeb, amomum, galague, musk, silks, and pearls as large as doves' eggs. The words have an almost incantatory quality and they certainly cast a spell on the European imagination.

From the latter part of the sixteenth century onwards, a great deal of reasonably well-informed travel literature—much of it from Dutch and, later, English sources—was let loose upon Europe, but tales of the 'wealth of the Indies' remained so seductive that when the English sent Sir Thomas Roe as ambassador to the Mughal emperor Jahangir, in 1615, they expected him to receive a generous handout from the emperor. Jahangir gave Roe only a female slave ('a grave woman of forty years'), a male criminal, and a wild boar; Roe recorded in his diary that the emperor's munificence had amounted to 'hoggs flesh, deare, a theefe and a whore'.

Roe's experience, however, scarcely ruffled the imaginative view of India. Merchants, hard-headed men whose only philosophy was that of the counting-house and whose imagination was bounded by visions of profit, might concern themselves with reality, but poets were already laying the foundations of a literature of empire. The Portuguese had early been influenced by Asia, and the playwright Gil Vicente (c. 1470–1537), had already begun to express a feeling for imperial glory. But the laureate of Portuguese expansion was Luiz Vaz de Camoëns (?1524–80), whose poem *Os Lusiadas* (1572) celebrated the conquest of the sea and the meeting of two worlds. Camoëns's epic of a new Crusade reflected the same mixture of knightly chivalry and desire for riches as had animated the old. Though he had been a soldier in the East, his India was only the background in a tapestry of Portuguese exploits —reality converted into high romance.

> *Que gloriosas palmas tacer vejo.*
> *Con que victoria a fronte lhe coroa,*
> *Quando sem sombra vãa de medo, ou pejo,*
> *Toma a ilha illustrissima de Goa!*
> *Despois, obedecendo au duro ensejo*
> *A deixa, e occasião espera boa,*
> *Com que a torne a tomar; que esforço, e arte,*
> *Vencerao a fortuna, e o proprio Marte.*

(To bind the brow of the victor, the palms of Goa offer their leaves. Like a bull or a lion he charges the Muslims and puts them to flight.)

Elsewhere, it was travel literature which inspired poets and dramatists. John Milton (1608–74), even in his blindness, could feel the glowing colours of Asia so deeply that there appeared no better parallel for the 'royal state' of Satan than the splendour of the 'gorgeous East'. *Paradise Lost* (1667) is alive with Indian images and names acquired from the works of travellers.

> Of Cambalu, seat of Cathaian Can,
> And Samarkand by Oxus, Temir's throne,
> To Paquin of Sinaean kings, and thence,
> To Agra and Lahor of Great Mogul.

Later in the century, two famous French travellers, Tavernier and Bernier, published vivid pictures of the Mughal empire. Their reports confirmed the visions of poets.

It should be stated [wrote Tavernier in his *Six Voyages en Perse et aux Indes* (1676)] that the Great Mogul has seven magnificent thrones, one wholly covered with diamonds, the others with rubies, emeralds or pearls. The principal throne . . . resembles in form and size our camp beds. Upon the four feet, which are very massive and from twenty to twenty-five inches high, are fixed the four bars which support the base of the throne, and upon these bars are ranged twelve columns, which sustain the canopy on three sides. . . . Both the feet and the bars, which are more than eighteen inches long, are covered with gold, inlaid and enriched with numerous diamonds, rubies and emeralds.

The Mughals, a foreign dynasty established by conquest in 1526, were followers of Islam, and Europeans visiting India usually accepted the Muslims' view of the native Hindus as degraded and superstitious. This did not divert imaginative writers, who were interested primarily in an exotic vocabulary and continued to draw on the fables of Bidpai. La Fontaine (1621–95) admitted borrowing from the 'Indian sage Pilpay', though the works of the sage came to him through a Persian source. Although the ground was being prepared, it was not until the end of the eighteenth century, and the revelation of Sanskrit literature, that India began to have a direct and profound effect upon European literature.

The most important early work on Hinduism and its rites was that of Rogerius, *De Open-Deure tot het Veborgen Heydendom*, published at Leyden in 1651. This included the first adaptation into a Western language of a Sanskrit work—a collection of lyrics by the poet Bhartrihari (died *c.* 651). It was not a translation but a paraphrase in Dutch prose of a paraphrase in Portuguese, made by a Brahmin in the Dutch settlement of Pulicat near Madras. It was only in the second half of the eighteenth century, however—when works of travel, journals, memoirs, histories and communications increased enormously—that Europe began to assemble an exotic and fascinating image of India. Very soon, India displaced China as the fount of all civilization. Voltaire was convinced (in 1775) that Western astronomy and astrology had come from the Ganges. The astronomer Jean-Sylvain Bailly (1736–93) maintained that the Brahmins had been the tutors of the Greeks and therefore of Europe. Commentators became convinced of the great antiquity of Indian culture, but they did not have access to its equally ancient literature. The existence of the literary language, Sanskrit, was known quite early, as were Indian scripts, but it was difficult to find a Brahmin willing to teach the 'holy language' to a European. Nevertheless, Europe was being prepared for an important revelation when the wonders of Sanskrit literature were finally exposed to view.

When it came, it was as a by-product of the extension of British rule in India. Warren Hastings, the first Governor-General in Bengal (1734–85), was engaged on drawing up a code of laws for the East India Company's Hindu subjects and decided that an accurate knowledge of ancient Sanskrit law-books was essential. Nathaniel Halhed (1751–1830) translated a *Code of Gentoo* [that is, Hindu] *Laws* from a Persian rendering, but it was left to Sir William Jones (1746–94), the real pioneer of Sanskrit studies, to make a direct translation of the *Codes of Manu*. Jones had been appointed a supreme-court judge in Calcutta in 1783, where in the following year, with the active encouragement of Warren Hastings, he founded the Asiatic Society of Bengal. The first direct translation from Sanskrit to be published in Europe (1785) was, however, made by Charles Wilkins (1749–1836). It was of the *Bhagvat-Geeta* [*Bhagavad-gita*], a series of dialogues between the god Krishna and the hero, Arjuna, which are expressed in extremely esoteric terms. Wilkins in his preface remarked that 'the text is imperfectly understood by the most learned Brahmins of the present times', and it could scarcely have been expected that Westerners unacquainted with Hindu religion, philosophy and history would gain much from it. Wilkins's version did not therefore have any immediate effect. The real revelation came from William Jones's translation in 1789 of the play *Sacontala* [*Sakuntala*] or *The Fatal Ring* by the dramatist Kalidasa (*c*. 400). The translation was originally made into Latin, as Jones maintained that 'Latin . . . bears so great a resemblance to Sanskrit, that it is more convenient than any modern language for a scrupulous interlineary version.' He then translated it out of Latin into English. It was from the latter version that translations into other European languages were made. Jones added no notes and only a very short preface, perhaps assuming that his English readers had already learned a good deal about Hindu mythology and Indian life from the publications of the Asiatic Society.

Such works were, without doubt, known to English writers and poets. For them Jones was a fountain of ideas bursting out at a time when the desire for change was growing. The revolution in France which began in 1789 had its effect even in England. Although the social order there had displayed remarkable stability since the English revolution of 1688—the Augustan values had not been shaken even by chinoiserie, and Confucius had been properly kept to the salon—a reaction against the rule of Reason was in progress. It took many forms. The *idea* of revolution, of liberal democracy, was one; the retreat into the Picturesque another. Byron's East, for example, was partly an expression of political opposition and moral non-conformism, a metaphor of revolt. For Shelley, the East was more than a collection of colourful stage-props or an extension of the poet's vocabulary; in *Adonais* (1821), his mystical pantheism is rich with Hindu overtones:

> The One remains, the many change and pass;
> Heaven's light for ever shines, Earth's shadows fly;
> Life, like a dome of many-coloured glass,
> Stains the white radiance of Eternity,
> Until Death tramples it to fragments—Die,
> If thou wouldst be with that which thou dost seek!

Wordsworth too spoke with a Hindu voice when he wrote:

> A motion and a spirit, that impels
> All thinking things, all objects of all thought
> And rolls through all things.

It is, however, significant that, except in a number of minor cases, Indian philosophy hardly penetrated English literature. It was as if England's direct involvement in India inhibited anything more than the most superficial acceptance of Indian culture. Certainly, in the first three decades of the nineteenth century, there grew up with great rapidity contempt for Indian society and Indian morals, and, as a consequence, for Indian philosophy.

The English experience of India did have an effect upon architecture, though that effect was very limited and hardly influential. The expansion of Britain's rule had attracted artists to visit the new dominion, and many of their drawings of scenery and buildings were published in aquatint, a particularly 'romantic' method of reproduction giving results similar to an original water-colour. Very soon, the English imagination was being enthralled by the 'splendour of minarets and pagodas that shone out from the depths of [India's] woods'. Thomas and William Daniell, whose *Oriental Scenery* was published between 1795 and 1807, illustrated many Indian buildings, and Thomas himself collaborated on an Indian villa at Sezincote in Gloucestershire (1806). He designed a temple, a bridge and a fountain, while Samuel Pepys Cockerill, Surveyor to the East India Company, produced the plans for the house itself. At the height of the Chinese madness, exteriors had remained Classical while the rooms inside were adorned with chinoiserie. At Sezincote, the outside became a version of an Indian palace, while the interior remained classically restrained.

In 1807, George, Prince of Wales, went to see Sezincote and was much taken with it. He had already employed William Porden to design stables for his pavilion at Brighton, and these bore a distinct resemblance to Sezincote. Porden may well have received advice from Thomas Daniell. After seeing Sezincote, the prince commissioned the landscape gardener Humphry Repton, who had laid out the gardens there, to advise on rebuilding the Brighton pavilion in the Indian style. Repton's designs were not carried out, as the prince was short of money, but, in 1815, with John Nash as architect, he resurrected his project for rebuilding. The result was a harmonious blend of aquatint India—the India of delicate domes and minarets—and concave spires. It was a fairy-tale in stucco which fortunately survives in almost its original glory today.

Brighton Pavilion was not universally admired, but the American impresario, Phineas Barnum, had it adapted—rather loosely—for his own home, 'Iranistan', in Bridgeport, Connecticut. The prince's pavilion was to have an even more curious successor at Alupka in the Crimea. This was designed for Count Worontzow-Dashkov by the English architect Edward Blore and was an amalgam of the oriental and the Gothic, of Brighton Pavilion and Windsor Castle. It was constructed between 1837 and 1840 and still survives. Apart from a mid-nineteenth-century effusion at Cintra in Portugal, these are the only examples of the India of dreams, fairy-tale palaces from an Indian Nights' Entertainment transported to the daylight of the West.

In Germany, the enthusiasm with which the Romantics were to grasp at India and Indian philosophy owed much to Johann Gottfried von Herder (1744–1803). Herder's reverence and adulation ('O Holy Land, I salute thee, thou Source of all Music/Thou voice of the Heart') helped create the Romantic image of India. Although his view was originally derived from travel books, his attention was later drawn to Wilkins's translations and then to Jones's *Sacontala*. Herder is a bridge between the rationalism of the Enlightenment and the mystical world of Romanticism. His attitude remained Western; like Voltaire he looked to the East for a system of ethical values which he could adopt for his own didactic purposes. In his preface to the second German edition of *Sacontala*, Herder warned his readers not to be disturbed by the marvellous elements, by gods walking the earth, or the personification of nature. These were, he maintained, delineations of authentic experiences. Here on the Ganges, said Herder, on that river of Paradise, the Golden Age exists. Nothing could have been more appealing to the young Romantics, to the brothers Schlegel, to Novalis, Tieck, Schleiermacher and others, who yearned for a new vision of life and happiness. 'It is to the East,' wrote Friedrich Schlegel in 1800, 'that we must look for the supreme Romanticism.'

In 1802, Schlegel journeyed to Paris, then the European centre of oriental studies where the French scholar Anquetil-Duperron had published (1801–2) in a queer jargon of Latin, Greek and Persian—a version of the *Upanishads* which had caught the attention of the German philosopher Schopenhauer. In Paris, Schlegel learned Sanskrit from an Englishman, Alexander Hamilton, who had been caught in France on his way home from India by the outbreak of the Napoleonic War and detained in Paris as an enemy alien. By November 1803, Schlegel was able to claim that he had become such an expert copyist of Sanskrit characters that he could earn his living in India as a scribe!

In the reaction of German writers to India there were two distinct strains. Schlegel represented a longing for harmony between the arts and sciences, for that unity of religion, philosophy and art which had been broken by the 'progress' of Western civilization. Those who followed him thought they saw, in the inextricable mingling of the human and the divine, of all wisdom in the everyday which is the essence of Hinduism, the presence of the Golden Age. Through a synthesis of the cultures of East and West, it seemed that the profoundest revelation of the human spirit might be attained. To a politically divided Europe and a nationally divided Germany, the legendary Hindu world offered a concrete ideal—the integration of personal, social and political life. It was an image just as mythical as that of the romancers. Both embroidered truth and, in doing so, exoticized it almost out of recognition. The artist, dissatisfied with actual appearance, added an extra dome or two. The Romantics, enamoured with legend, gave it the status of the real.

Ironically, the Romantics' desire to give their view—which was based on the most limited appreciation of Sanskrit literature—a scholarly basis only brought about its destruction. The urge to know more of Sanskrit literature unfiltered by translation led instead to a study of comparative linguistics which, though it left an important legacy to oriental studies, was unconnected with thought and devoid of passion. Cold scientific inquiry into words withered the Romantic ideal. The early Romantics, indeed, were interested not really in India but rather in the intellectualized emotion they felt for its culture. In 1808, disillusioned by the time he finished his most important work, *Über die Sprache und Weisheit der Indier*, Friedrich Schlegel deserted India for Roman Catholicism, one universal creed for another, an Eastern mythology for a European. Others, however—among them Friedrich Majer (1772–1818) and the philosopher Schelling (1775–1854)—kept the image alive.

Not all German writers were engulfed by the myth of India. Goethe—always saved from drowning in the exotic by his attachment to the serenity of Greek myth—rejected the Indian gods as repulsive, dark and menacing, half human and half beast. But he received *Sacontala* with enthusiasm, and the Prologue to *Faust* Part I is modelled upon that of Kalidasa. The only other traces of Indian themes in Goethe's work are found in *Der Paria* ('The Pariah', or 'Untouchable') and *Gott und die Bajadere* ('God and the

Dancing-Girl'). In the latter work, Goethe, who found Indian mythology unhealthy, was not above idealizing *suttee* or widow-burning. Friedrich Schlegel, though condemning *suttee* as a law, praised it as a voluntary demonstration of ultimate love, and the poetess Karoline von Gunderode (1780–1806) transformed the custom into an almost erotic rite. The dramatist Schiller (1759–1805), in whose journal *Thalia*, the German translation of *Sacontala* first appeared, found his ideal of beautiful femininity in Kalidasa's epic. Schiller borrowed from another work of Kalidasa (*The Cloud Messenger*) in his play *Maria Stuart* (1800), when the exiled queen calls on the clouds to carry greetings to the land of her youth.

The Romantic image of India had a comparatively short life in German literature. Schlegel's disillusionment helped to discredit it, but it by no means died. India was to supply to E.T.A. Hoffmann (1776–1822) a fantastic imagery for stories which convincingly unite the wondrous with the common-place, magic with reality. For Hoffmann, Sanskrit was a magical language, whose script resembled the forms of nature (*Der goldene Topf*, 1813).

Hoffmann transfigured the image, absorbed it into his own mythology. But Heinrich Heine (1799–1856), who called himself the last Romantic, was torn between idealism and irony, between longing and the awareness that it could never be satisfied. The Ganges, that mystic river which flowed through the hearts of Romantic writers, still kept its attraction. The poet ached to fly there with his love. The gentlest people in the world lived on its banks, and the most beautiful women (*Über Polen*, 1822). Essentially, however, Heine merely gave the status of symbolism to the commonplaces of Sanskrit literature—the sacred river Ganges, the lotus-blossom, and love of animals. The spell that India had cast over the minds of the early Romantics was, in fact, broken.

Their vision of India had satisfied a particular longing in the minds of the German Romantics. At a time when the world of Europe appeared to be crumbling, they searched for a means by which to shake themselves free from its cultural disintegration. Basically, they were looking for that unity of art and religion which they believed had existed in the European Middle Ages, for an identity of man with nature. But their aim was even bolder—it was to discover the unity of all mankind. 'Asia and Europe,' claimed

Friedrich Schlegel, 'together make up a single indivisible whole.'
Thus the myth of India was part of a primal myth, saturated with
lost innocence, enriched by the unselfconscious dialogue of God
and man. In effect, the German Romantics were groping in the
recesses of their own souls. As Novalis put it:

In the temple of Sais, a man once lifted the veil of the goddess
And found—O wonder of wonders!—and found concealed
   there—himself.

At the beginning of the nineteenth century, travellers' tales and
the revelations of scholars introduced new themes into French
literature just as they had done into German. The legend of the
pariah produced two plays, one by Casimir Delavigne in 1823,
which was an immense popular success, and the other by Michel
Beer in 1825, which was given a performance at Weimar and
praised by Goethe. In 1810, an opera by Etienne Jouy was
produced. Jouy had one advantage: he wrote from actual experience of India. He had spent his youth there as a soldier, and some
of his work has a sense both of place and of history. The costumes
for the opera were based upon a dress—presumably a sari—
supplied by 'a young lady from Chandernagore' then living in
Paris. In 1813, Jouy's tragedy *Tippu Sahib* was performed. It concerned the Sultan of Mysore (ruled 1782-99), who had tried to
enlist French help against the expanding British, but had been
granted no more than a small number of volunteers and the dubious honorific of 'Citizen Tipu'. His defeat by the British helped to
end Napoleon's dream of an oriental empire. But in spite of Jouy's
attention to detail, the play had no sense of involvement in distinctively Indian circumstance.

In fact, the impact of India upon French literature and literary
thought was almost entirely superficial—a touch of colour, an
exotic phrase, an occult thought, but very little more. This was so
even though a growing number of French oriental scholars were in
close and personal contact with the poets and writers of their day.
One could hardly have expected from French writers of the early
nineteenth century an involvement as deep or as positive as that
of the German Romantics, in spite of the important role they
played in the formation of French Romantic thought. There is a

vital difference, not only of time but of intellectual climate, between the German Romantics and their French successors. The French Romantics were not, in fact, successors at all; it is only that inexact word 'Romantic' which makes them appear so.

The first French Romantics were preoccupied not so much with ideas as with form. They were enemies of the neo-classicism that had stifled creativity during Napoleon's reign. The battle that took place between members of the audience at the first night of Hugo's play *Hernani*, in 1830, was a battle between protagonists of the Classical and of the Romantic. The Romantics won. Their victory brought a new freedom of speech, of subject, and of treatment. It also released extravagance and gaiety and, above all, that capacity for enjoyment which was so lacking in German Romanticism.

Because of all this, India remained only one of several sources of exoticism—fascinating, certainly, but no more so than the Near East or North Africa. Théophile Gautier, the epitome of French Romanticism, made a ballet of *Sacontala* (1858), and in his novel *La Partie Carrée* (1848) had in mind the Indian sect of the Thugs, who murdered travellers for their possessions and the glory of their goddess, Kali. Nerval went deeper; in 1835 he adapted for the stage an Indian drama by Sudraka, a contemporary of Kalidasa, *The Little Clay Cart*. There were others, too, who made an occasional Indian foray—Parnassians such as Leconte de Lisle (1818–94), and Symbolists like Paul Verlaine (1844–96). Joseph Méry, whose novels *Les Damnés de l'Inde* and *La Guerre du Nizam* went into many editions, was referred to by contemporaries as the most Hindu poet who ever existed, although few critics would agree with this judgement today. The explanation lies with Gautier, who described his own attitude—and that of his contemporaries—when he wrote that he was a man for whom the visible world existed. It was *with the eye* that French writers looked at the Orient, and few of them looked beyond the outward appearance.

India also had some influence upon American writers and poets. This came about almost entirely through the Scottish historian and essayist Thomas Carlyle (1795–1881), and his translations and criticism of the German Romantics. In one of his essays, published in 1830, Carlyle gave enthusiastic acclaim to the work of Friedrich Schlegel, and in another to Novalis. England was, in fact, in the throes of a new period of oriental scholarship, though—as it roughly coincided with a growing contempt for India amongst British administrators there—it did not have the same impact as the earlier revelations of Sir William Jones and others. It did, however, inspire one English writer, Thomas de Quincey, to the most superb mixture of fascination and disgust for the East known in Western literature, *Confessions of an English Opium-Eater* (1821–2). This, in turn, attracted Charles Baudelaire, who translated the book into French. The effect of these two responses to the East, those of Carlyle and De Quincey, reached American literature through Ralph Waldo Emerson (1803–82).

The 'Transcendentalist' school of American literature, which included Margaret Fuller and Theodore Parker and influenced such other writers as Hawthorne and Thoreau, was a reaction against puritan prejudices, materialistic philistinism, and utilitarianism. Its sources were an odd mixture of Plato and Swedenborg, German idealism, Carlyle, English poets such as Coleridge and Wordsworth, and translations of oriental literature. Emerson, the movement's principal figure, was well acquainted with Sanskrit texts and his idea of an omnipresent deity and of the human personality as a passing phase of universal Being is contained in what is almost a paraphrase of part of the *Bhagavad-gita*—his poem *Brahma*. Emerson's lines:

> If the red slayer think he slays,
> Or if the slain think he is slain,
> They know not well the subtle ways
> I keep, and pass, and turn again

are certainly reminiscent of Krishna's words to Arjuna: 'He who deems This to be a slayer and he who thinks This to be slain, are alike without discernment; This slays not neither is it slain.'

The American transcendentalists were, in effect, the true heirs of the early German Romantics. Unlike their French contemporaries, they were immensely serious—and essentially humourless—in their search for universal truth. They were, too, often pedantic, prolix and extravagant. There is nothing in their work of the gaiety and enjoyment, of the colour effects which saturate French literature. For the missing gaiety, it is necessary to go to the mansion of that merchant of the exotic, the circus-proprietor and dealer in marvels, Phineas T. Barnum. His house, 'Iranistan', was finished in 1848 and was followed by a number of rather less ambitious imitations.

In more general terms, India and its philosophies scarcely ruffled the surface of American culture. This was possibly because, in creating a *national* literature in the nineteenth century, American writers were able to draw on the recent excitements of nation-building, on the greatness and tragedy of American life, instead of on the European tradition. American writers, when they finally came into direct contact with an Asian culture, did so in Japan, with significant and lasting effects.

In Germany, the image of India continued to appear in literature, but it was never to recapture the glitter and excitement of the early years of the nineteenth century. In France, India could hardly compete with the glamour of the Muslim East. In England, missionaries and reformers plastered the image with mud.

It was unfortunate for India that the expansion of British rule there should have coincided with great social changes in Britain. Though the servants of the East India Company in its early days had settled comfortably into India, patronizing both the Hindu and Muslim religions impartially and generally leaving Indian society untouched, a new generation of officials began to arrive in the country in the early years of the nineteenth century. They took with them a very different attitude. Their Christianity was an activist faith. They knew they were right, and they proposed to save India from the dark sea of paganism in which it was un-doubtedly drowning. These new men saw in the excrescences of Hinduism—in the burning of widows, in female infanticide, in the ritual robbery and murder of the Thugs—the face of Anti-christ in all its horror. Inspired by their own ideology, they pushed aside any suggestion that Hinduism might have relieving virtues. To them, awareness of the Christian God was all important; above all, awareness of His revealed Word. The extension of literacy was therefore one of the first tasks. Education would spread know-ledge, of the Bible and of the works of God. The reformers began what can only be described as a smear campaign against Hindu institutions and philosophy. Lord Macaulay (1800–59) symbolizes the contemptuous ignorance of those who sought to anglicize India. Attacking Hindu ideas with glorious disdain and all the fatal majesty of his booming prose, he maintained that they consisted of

'medical doctrines which would disgrace an English farrier—
Astronomy, which would move laughter in girls at an English
boarding-school—History, abounding with kings thirty feet high,
and reigns of thirty thousand years long—and Geography, made up
of seas of treacle and seas of butter'. It was Macaulay's view 'that a
single shelf of a good European Library was worth the whole
native literature of India'. Many Indians accepted his foolish
criticism. Such an attitude on the part of India's British rulers
undoubtedly lowered Hindu literature in the estimation of
Europe, and it was an attitude that was never really discarded by
the British themselves until the end of their empire. In 1877, the
apotheosis of British rule took place at Delhi, when Queen
Victoria was proclaimed empress of India. The popular literature
produced by this new age was to be the literature of expatriate life,
of *British* life in India. The *Jungle Books* and *Kim*, by Rudyard
Kipling (1865–1936), have a genuine feeling for India that is often
overlooked, but most examples of Anglo–Indian literature are
narrow and parochial in their outlook.

Fortunately, scholarship survived. In 1870, there began in
France the publication of the *Bibliothèque Orientale*, and four years
later, in London, that of the *Sacred Books of the East*, which, under
the editorship of Friedrich Max-Muller (1823–1900) were to make
Hindu scriptures available to ordinary readers for the first time. In
1875 was published James Fergusson's *History of Indian and
Eastern Architecture*, the first important work on the subject and
one which still has merit today. But interest in Indian art in the
second half of the nineteenth century was primarily confined to
the so-called 'industrial arts', and it was left to the twentieth
century to begin a genuine discovery of the art of India, a discovery which is still far from being complete.

At the same time as the renewed interest in Hindu literature,
there emerged an interest in Pali, the language of the Buddhist
scriptures. Although Buddhist ideas had penetrated into early
Christianity, the very existence of the greatest of all Indian ethical
teachers was almost completely unknown in the West until the
nineteenth century. But the Buddha had penetrated Christian
hagiography—in disguise.

One of the most popular religious romances of the Middle
Ages had been that of *Barlaam and Josaphat*, which relates the

conversion of an Indian prince, Josaphat, by the Christian hermit Barlaam. The story is in fact a Christianized version of the life of the Buddha, and the name Josaphat is a corruption of the word *Bodisat*. The early Greek text of the story was thought at one time to have been compiled in the eighth century by a certain John of Damascus. From Greek, it was translated into Arabic, and it was from this language that translations were made into a number of European tongues. The original Greek was probably a version of the *Lalita-Vistara*, a Sanskrit work of uncertain date. Somewhere around the fourteenth century, Barlaam and Josaphat were canonized, and in the *Martyrologium* authorized by Pope Sixtus V at the end of the sixteenth century there appeared, for 27 November, 'the holy saints Barlaam and Josaphat of India, on the borders of Persia, whose wonderful acts St John of Damascus has described'.

By the middle of the nineteenth century, oriental scholars were uncovering some of the Buddha story. Brian Hodgson, the British Resident in Nepal who spent over twenty years there prior to 1843, had collected a vast number of Buddhist manuscripts. James Prinsep, another Company servant, had deciphered inscriptions of the Buddhist emperor Asoka. In 1844, Eugène Burnouf published his immensely influential *Introduction à l'histoire du Bouddhisme Indien*. R. Spence Hardy's *Manual of Buddhism* appeared in 1853, and a popular life of the Buddha, by Barthélemy Sainte-Hilaire, in 1858. These were followed by many others, but they had laid the foundations for a new interest in India on the part of a number of authors, artists, and composers. The Reverend James Gardiner, writing about 1860, acknowledged that Buddhism contained some excellent moral principles. But he still felt the distaste of the age for anything heathen, and expressed it with the authentic ring of exoticism. Buddhism, he wrote, had 'spread like an upas-tree over immense regions of Eastern Asia, shedding a withering and destructive blight over all that dwell in its shadow'. Buddhist ideas were not as creative in their effect on Europe as those of Hinduism had been, but they can be traced in the works of Richard Wagner and of Tolstoy, in the dream-world of the French painter Odilon Redon (1840–1916), and—perhaps at their most mysterious—in Hermann Hesse's novel *Siddartha* (1922).

27   *An eighteenth-century view of Confucius (pp. 103–11). The sage stands incongruously but symbolically in a European library.*

Le Heros de Ferney.
au Theatre de Chatelaine

28   *Voltaire playing the part of Genghiz Khan*
     in his play L'Orphelin de la Chine
     (pp. 105–7).

29   *A Chinese sail-assisted wheelbarrow.*

30   *The landscape of an imagined China; an*
     eighteenth-century chinoiserie fabric (p. 115).

*31   The Chinese, sinister and cunning; Sax Rohmer's
Dr Fu Manchu* (p. 111).

*33   European fantasy. The Pleasure House of Augustus
the Strong, Pilnitz* (pp. 113 and 116). ▶

32   *A lacquer design by Stalker and Parker, 1688* (p. 114).

34   Inspiration: 'Moon at Ryogoku at Dusk', by
     Hiroshige.

35   Adaptation: 'Old Battersea Bridge', by Whistler
     (pp. 123-4).

36 *Close-up from* Ivan the
Terrible, *by Sergei Eisenstein.*

37 '*Close-up' of the actor,*
Ichikawa Danjuro, by
Kunimasa (p. 130).

38 *The church of the Sagrada Familia, Barcelona*
    (p. 144).

39/40 *The decorative page (right) was designed by Goethe himself* (p. 140).

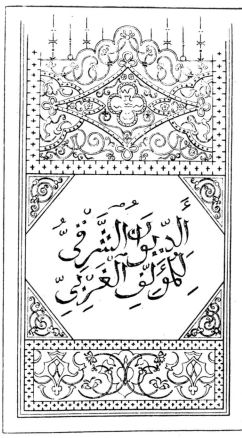

41 *The popularity of Omar Khayyám was such that, in this advertisement published in 1904, the poet is seen enjoying something more than his usual loaf of bread, flask of wine and book of verse! The caption reads: 'No one can ever be lonely where there is a gramophone' (p. 143).*

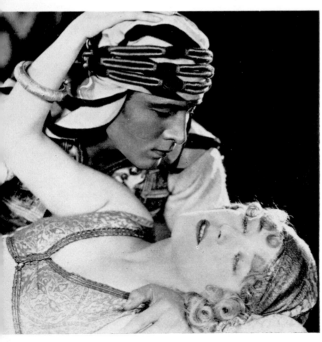

42 *The call of the desert; Rudolf Valentino in* Son of the Sheik *(p. 145).*

43 The marriage of East and West. South façade of the Alupka Palace, Crimea (pp. 151–2).

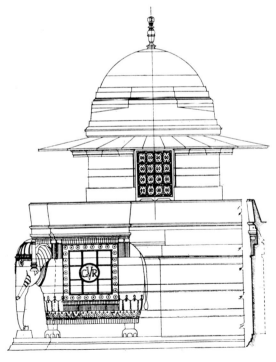

44 Pastiche. Sir Edwin Lutyens's indoiserie design for a guardroom. Viceroy's House, New Delhi (pp. 168 and 195).

45 Above: *View of Tonk in the Rajputana. Original watercolour.*

46 Below: *Aquatint from No. 45, with romantic embellishments added by the engraver* (p. 151).

47 *A European version of the Buddha story; Barlaam and Josaphat* (pp. 159–60).

48 *A discovery of the West. Three modes of transport as seen by the innocent eye.*

49   *The Opium War through French eyes*
     (pp. 181–2).

50   *Napoleon through Japanese eyes* (p. 193).

A seventeenth-century Mughal painting, using a landscape from a European original (p. 191).

A Japanese view of Westernization. Left: *complete;* centre; *partial;* right: *none* (pp. 202–3).

53 *'Primitive' spaciousness. A street in Tokyo before Westernization.*

54 *'Progressive' clutter. The Ginza, Tokyo, early twentieth century (pp. 195–6).*

Unlike China, India did not produce in the European mind an image easily translated into the visible. While the country was still comparatively unknown, exports to the West consisted mainly of textiles. Much of their desirability lay in their texture, in, for example, the incredible fineness of muslin. Most of the repertory of 'Indian' designs which were acceptable in Europe turn out, on investigation, to have been supplied *from* Europe. As early as the seventeenth century, the English East India Company was sending out what can only be called 'indoiserie' designs—'indiennerie', though more correct, sits less comfortably on the tongue—to be reproduced by Indian craftsmen. Very soon, European factories were producing their own imitations which were about as authentic as their chinoiserie equivalent.

Europe retained some affection for these 'Indian' designs, but other *objets de luxe* had little effect. This was partly due to the dominance of chinoiserie and the Classical, but a more immediate cause was the character of the English 'nabob', the East India merchant who, having made his fortune, returned to spend it in Britain. The earlier English merchants in India had returned home and settled down to a life in the country very little different from that of any successful merchant who had never travelled farther than London. But the later 'nabob', living at high luxury in India, began to consider himself a gentleman. In England, commerce and trade were considered incompatible with gentility, so the returned 'nabob' did not vaunt his trade, the source of his wealth; he sought to ape the English nobility, to live in a Palladian house and indulge in the current English fashions. He might bring back a few Eastern wares—though these were usually Chinese—and a black servant or two, but on the whole his desire for acceptance made him conform. He neither created nor influenced fashion.

Such 'Indian' influences as there were came from the objects themselves. The most persistent theme is the 'Kashmir' pattern. European taste affected the design of the Kashmir shawl, once a very expensive luxury. France, in particular, offered a considerable market in the nineteenth century, and patterns devised in Paris were sent out to Kashmir for reproduction by native craftsmen. The popularity of the Kashmir shawl, which was artificially endowed with all the superficial mythology of the exotic—an elaborate and non-existent symbolism being attributed to its patterns—soon inspired imitations. These were first produced at Norwich in England in 1784, not as real shawls but as embroidered neckcloths intended for export to America. Edinburgh followed and, later, about 1808, Paisley. At the beginning, attempts were made to bring to Britain the 'shawl-goat' which produced the extremely soft wool that was one of the principal attractions of the Kashmir product. All the attempts were unsuccessful, however, and British weavers had to be content with substitutes.

In France, as in Britain, the fashion for Kashmir shawls was widespread. The Empress Josephine, a leader of fashion, possessed between three and four hundred of them. Demand created imitation, and the first French-made shawls appeared in 1804. By the middle of the nineteenth century a conflict of authenticities was taking place. In Kashmir itself, the trade was dominated by French merchants working from their own European pattern-books. In France, shawls were being produced with designs supposedly imitating genuine Kashmir. These, in turn, were being copied by Scottish weavers at Paisley! By 1860, the true Kashmir product had become inferior to European imitations and when the French market disappeared after the Franco–Prussian war of 1870–1 and there was a sudden change in taste, the industry in Kashmir collapsed—though the 'Paisley pattern' survives triumphantly to this day.

In 1851, the Great Exhibition of the Works of Industry of All Nations was held inside the Crystal Palace, then in Hyde Park, London. From that time onwards, similar vast demonstrations of industrial and economic optimism were held regularly in the principal capitals of Europe. They were, in effect, religious ceremonies in honour of the machine and its accomplishments. Though these accomplishments were many and wonderful, they failed to offer any aesthetic quality. Their products, covered with coarse and overcrowded designs, demonstrated a conspicuous lack of artistic sensitivity. But the exhibitions were extremely important in that they included examples of what the Victorians called the 'industrial arts' of Eastern countries. The contrast between the vulgarity of Western design and the delicacy of some of the Eastern exhibits helped to arouse a renewed interest in the East.

There was certainly an enchantment about some of the more exotic exhibits. Théophile Gautier, in London to report on the 1851 Exhibition for the newspaper *La Presse*, wrote: 'I have seen Lahore, Calcutta, Kashmir, Benares, Hyderabad under the crystal bell at Hyde Park,' and went on, 'I recognized my native country.' Indian designs began to appear again in brassware, textiles and even in jewellery, but they had no deep influence upon European art, for they did not express any particular concept of 'reality' as the Japanese colour print did. The Manchester textile industry, indeed, fathered a magnificent series of volumes on *The Textile Fabrics of India*—at the same time as Manchester's own products were destroying indigenous Indian crafts. In the final analysis, India's artistic legacy to the West was almost entirely confined to the Paisley pattern, to Benares brassware, and fretted woodwork, the bric-à-brac of the middle-class home.

On other levels, the British connection with India did have some effect. The returning 'nabobs' and their Civil Service successors introduced into British cookery a number of typically Indian dishes. The first European mention of 'curry' seems to date from around 447, but Indian curry—as experienced by Europeans in India—contains an essential ingredient which was, in fact, introduced into India by the Europeans themselves. Chilli, or red pepper, had been taken there by the Portuguese. In 1773, curry was a speciality in at least one London coffee-house. By the middle of the next century, it had received the accolade of that theologian of English cookery, Mrs Beeton. Mulligatawny soup, whose name is a corruption of the Tamil word for pepper-water, is still put up in cans, while Indian pickles of fearsome fieriness disguise the tastelessness of modern commercial cold meats.

It has been suggested that the English cult of cleanliness—which is quite modern—may well have originated with Englishmen returned from India. The Hindu love of washing was one of the things most remarked upon by observers in the eighteenth century.

To sport, that other allegedly English cult, India contributed polo which had been introduced there by the Muslim conquerors; the Mughal emperor Akbar drew up the first known code of rules. The English, however, discovered it in a primitive form in the hill state of Manipur in Eastern India in the middle of the nineteenth century, and the first public game in England seems to have been played in either 1870 or 1871. To this day, the technical terms used betray their origin.

The common-place pyjama of today also had its origin in India. Europeans there were quick to adopt Indian fashions, especially if they were comfortably adapted to a hot climate. The loose trousers tied round the waist were of Indian Muslim origin, and the British used them as a garment for relaxing and sleeping in. They were known as long-drawers, Shulwaurs, or Mogul-breeches. A Vandyke portrait of the first Earl of Denbigh shows him out shooting in pyjamas. The English word comes from the Hindi—*pai-jama*—which means, literally, 'leg-clothing'. The wearing of pyjamas only became common after about 1900.

Generally speaking, the influence of Asia upon Europe in recent centuries has had few destructive consequences, at least for the West. But, in one sense at least, Asia exacted a terrible revenge for her exploitation by colonialist Europe. A line *can* be traced from early Hindu ideas of racial purity to the crematoria of Dachau and Buchenwald. European racial theories—many of them originating in the mind of the diplomat and orientalist Arthur de Gobineau (1816–82)—were to prove a terrible and bloody sequel to nineteenth-century exoticism.

In his book, *Essai sur l'inegalité des races humaines* (1853–5), Gobineau expanded, with a wealth of data, a racial theory of history. He argued that races were inherently unequal, that by intermingling with other races they changed character, and that the white races, especially the Aryans, were superior to all others. From the 'history' of the Indo–Aryans, a tribe of light-skinned and blue-eyed nomads who invaded northern India some time about 1500 B.C., Gobineau drew many of his ideas about racial purity and degeneration. The Indo–Aryans were extremely conscious of their colour and evolved savage laws to preserve themselves from the defiling blood of the dark-skinned people they had conquered. Ultimately, the Aryan invaders of India had been forced to take women from among the dark inhabitants in order to increase the numbers of the ruling élite, but though they developed the most sophisticated mechanism of social control ever devised by man—the system of 'caste'—they did not save the race and were ultimately conquered by more virile white men from the West. Gobineau pointed at contemporary India, which he described as decadent, to demonstrate what happens to a race which fails to protect the purity of its blood. Nevertheless, said Gobineau, of all the white races, the 'Aryan' family was 'the most noble, the most intelligent and the most dynamic'.

During the nineteenth century, the discovery that a number of European languages had something in common with Sanskrit led to the view that all these languages had a common 'Aryan' root. Though this was explicitly denied by Gobineau, he transformed a rejected philological truth into an anthropological falsity. The 'Aryan' race existed, but apparently 'Aryan' languages did not. Of all Aryans, the Germanic tribes were the purest. They had spread themselves over Europe and given it the dynamism of the 'pure Aryan essence'. Gobineau's theories were published at the time of an evil flowering of anti-Semitism in Germany, and Gobineau exercised considerable influence on philosophers such as Nietzsche. But his principal legacy was to a violently pro-German Englishman, Houston Stewart Chamberlain (1855–1926), the son-in-law of Richard Wagner. Chamberlain, in his book *Grundlagen des neunzehnten Jahrhunderts* (1899), amalgamated the conclusions of Gobineau with those of the philologists and declared that the German race was composed of those who spoke the German language—as nonsensical an idea as suggesting that an English-speaking Chinese from Hongkong is English by race. Hitler and the theorists of National Socialism took Chamberlain's and Gobineau's ideas and made one the basis of Germany's irredentist claims and the other that of their oppression of the Jews. From both, they assembled support for the idea of a German–Aryan master race.

Richard Wagner (1813–83) was one of the first Germans to recognize the force of Gobineau's ideas and, in 1881, published an introduction to his work. But Wagner was also drawn to India, however 'decadent' it might appear to Gobineau. In his attempt to find new operatic forms, to get away from what he called 'the tyranny of convention personified by Louis XIV', Wagner had turned to pagan myth, to 'Germania, that true flower of the Aryan race'. At the same time, he believed implicitly in the idea of predestination, and for this he turned with enthusiasm to Indian philosophy, as presented by European scholars. He was particularly attracted by the Buddhist ideas he acquired from a reading of Burnouf. Wagner's correspondence with Mathilde

Wesendonk (his love for her inspired *Tristan und Isolde*) is saturated with Buddhist ideas. Indeed, Indian ideas, both Buddhist and Hindu, became part not only of Wagner's work and thought but also of his life. Although transformed to suit his aesthetic and patriotic purpose, some of his Indian sources can be discerned in the libretti which he wrote himself for his operas.

In *Parsifal* (1882), Wagner used an episode from the *Ramayana* of the Hindu poet Valmiki (*c.* 400 B.C.). In the *Ramayana*, a huntsman fires an arrow at a pair of curlews and kills the male. The poet, who appears in his own tale, is inspired by the complaint of the female curlew to lay a curse on the huntsman. In Wagner's opera, Parsifal kills a male swan and is in turn accursed. There is more here than the mere borrowing of a scene, for there is a direct similarity between the story of the opera and that of the *Ramayana* in the idea of the sin that can never be expiated. There are many other examples of the influence of Indian ideas upon Wagner, but they are usually less obvious. He seemed, however, to absorb them into everything he wrote, creating perhaps the only real synthesis of India and Europe. Wagner's world view embraced East and West, and transformed them into the materials of a universal drama. In this way, he perpetuated the ideal of the first German Romantics.

Others too, were looking to the East for a revelation which might transform the world. In the early part of the century, the real nature of Indian metaphysic was only imperfectly understood, and it was not thought to be of much value. The English wit Sydney Smith summed up the current attitude in 1835. 'The departure of the wise men from the East,' he said, 'seems to have been on a more extensive scale than is generally supposed, for no one of that description seems to have been left behind.' But as the century grew older, and more information became available, India appeared to offer a fruitful field to Europeans who found orthodox religion unappealing and were exploring the occult to satisfy their appetite for miracles. Some, like Madame Blavatsky (1831–91), found the source of wisdom in great (and mythical) teachers residing at some imprecise location in the Himalayas. The Theosophical Society, which she founded in 1875, propagated an elaborate esoteric philosophy owing much to Hinduism, though it was a Hinduism dressed up in Christian terms. The second president of the Society, Annie Besant (1847–1933), was to play an important role in Indian nationalism. So, indirectly, was the Russian novelist Tolstoy (1828–1910) who, finding no answers in Western thought to the problems that exercised his mind, turned to a study of Christian theology and Eastern religions. Tolstoy always proclaimed his debt to Indian philosophy and, from Buddhism, took the concept of non-violence which he adapted to the needs of modern political man. Through his influence on Mahatma Gandhi, he helped to send it back to India, where it is still considered as the instrument which gave India independence from British rule—a belief as romantic as any in the long dialogue between India and the West.

Behind European Romanticism lay dissatisfaction with the situation of man. The longing for new and exotic worlds, for worlds of magic, was a response to the pessimistic view of things-as-they-are. The industrial progress of nineteenth-century Europe seemed to many to be a diminution rather than a fulfilment of man. Certainly, it destroyed the 'harmony' of man with nature, for technology and science were the instruments of man's growing domination over his environment, weapons in a war *against* nature. Westerners dissatisfied with the Christian god—the god who was invoked at the launching of battleships, and by armies on the march—looked more and more to the East for a religion divorced from politics. At the end of the nineteenth century, a new breed of wise men from the East set out to conquer new worlds. They did not succeed, but they did more to create a popular image of India than all the oriental scholars. Of these men the most important was Swami Vivekananda (1862–1902).

Vivekananda, a disciple of the inspirational visionary Ramakrishna (1836–86), wrote in English and virtually created the vocabulary in which Indian ideas are expressed in the West. His followers were many and they presented a view of India— spiritual, non-violent, brimming over with the secrets of life— which today still inhibits any proper appreciation of India by the West. Indian art, Indian politics, sometimes even Indian politicians, are judged by the metaphysical criteria of mystical philosophers and their Western devotees. It is, perhaps, the ultimate irony of Romanticism that Westerners expect from India a spirituality and a high-minded ethical purpose which they would be the first to deny had practical application in the modern world, and that Indians themselves do everything to encourage the expectation.

The irony has its monument in the city of New Delhi. Before the British moved their capital there in 1912, seven cities had crumbled to make it a necropolis of earlier conquerors. With characteristic contempt for Indian architecture and tradition, Britain created a monument not only to her rule, but to the Romantic image. The indoiserie buildings of Sir Edwin Lutyens and Sir Herbert Barker, highly unsuitable for the climate of northern India, are an incongruous and mediocre mixture of styles, but independent India has continued to erect massive hybrids in the same idiom.

In the West, Indian philosophy is fashionable. The affluent still yearn for revelations from the East even if they are reluctant to practise its austerities. Books pour from the presses, statesmen practise yogic exercises, meditation takes its place with marijuana as an agent of release. Yet the basic longing remains unchanged, however much it may be vulgarized by the glossy magazines. With Novalis, the searcher still hopes that, hidden behind the veil of the goddess, there lies his own, real self.

VI

The Discovery of
the West

What we have to learn from the barbarians is only one thing: solid ships and effective guns.

> FENG KUEI-FEN, *Chiao-pin-lu k'ang-i* (1860)

The very thing India lacked, the modern West possessed and possessed to excess. It had the dynamic outlook. It was engrossed in the changing world, caring little for ultimate principles. . . . It paid little attention to duties and obligations and emphasized rights.

> JAWAHARLAL NEHRU, *The Discovery of India* (1946)

In these capitals, London, Paris and Amsterdam, live people virtually without peer in the world. . . . Their prosperity is probably due to the excellence of their political system.

> HONDA TOSHIAKI, *Seiiki Monogatari* (Tales of the West) (1798)

Resistance to the flood-tide of Western civilization is vain: she is quite merciless to those who ignore or disobey her. Western civilization pierces the mountains, soars in the skies, sees and illuminates all things, from the invisible atoms to the stars.

> KAMAL ATATURK, *Speech at Inebolu* (1925)

The Kingdom of Christ

When Vasco da Gama landed in Calicut on the west coast of India in 1498 and was asked what he had come for, he is said to have replied, 'Christians and spices.' The Portuguese saw themselves as soldiers of Christ as well as traders, businessmen as well as agents of God's will. And they could prove it. On 7 June 1494, Spain and Portugal had signed the Treaty of Tordesillas, splitting the world between them. They had fixed a dividing line north to south through the Atlantic Ocean, 370 miles west of the Cape Verde islands, and the treaty had been confirmed by the issue of a Papal Bull. Pope Alexander VI Borgia appointed the Kings of Portugal and Spain as his emissaries in the lands of the heathen, and thus expressed the theory that the Papacy was the centre of a spiritual empire destined to unite the world, with the Pope as priest-emperor and vicegerent of God on earth. It is important to understand this, because it gave the Portuguese impact on Asia the aura of a grand crusade. The heathen lay under the certainty of eternal damnation, on the very edge of the pit; it was the *duty* of the Portuguese to snatch them—however much they might resist—into the arms of Christ and His salvation.

The Portuguese expected to find Christians already in India. When da Gama was escorted through Calicut, he thought he had found them, for he was invited into a building which he took to be a church. Seeing a statue of a woman, he asked who it was and thought he heard the name of Mary. Kneeling down, he gave thanks for his safe arrival. But the statue was probably that of the Hindu goddess Kali, known in Western India as Mari Ama, 'the Mother of Epidemics'.

The tradition that there was a church in India founded by the Apostle Thomas was well known in the West. According to legend, the 'doubting disciple' had landed at the port of Musiris on the coast of Kerala in A.D. 52 and had been murdered by the priests of a temple of Kali at Mylapore, near present-day Madras, twenty years later. In the sixteenth century, the Portuguese found what was said to be the saint's tombstone, and his remains are allegedly enshrined in the cathedral of São Thomé today. According to another theory, the apostle's body was transferred to Edessa in Syria. All these stories are apocryphal, though they were widely accepted in Europe, and the Christians of Malabar still maintain the apostolic origin of their religion.

Da Gama accepted the presence of Christianity, though the Portuguese later became much more sophisticated and realized that the 'Christianity' they had found in India was heretical, at the very least. There is no evidence that they knew the source of the heresy to be not a falling away from the original orthodoxy of St Thomas but a sequel to the Nestorian dispersion of the fifth century.

Something of the extraordinary story of the Nestorians has already been given in earlier chapters. They produced not only philosophers and theologians but physicians and statesmen. At one time during the hegemony of the Mongols, it even appeared that Nestorian Christianity might conquer Asia. The Nestorians did more than propagate their religion. They were transmitters of civilization. Very little of that aspect of their work can be discerned in India, but relics of their influence crop up in the most unexpected places. When the intrepid French missionaries Huc and Gabet visited Lhasa in 1842, they were shocked to observe a resemblance between Catholic and Lamaistic rituals. In secret Tibet, they found the mitre, the crozier, the chasuble, and the censer with the five chains. All of these have since been traced to Nestorian influences.

Within the areas they came to rule the Portuguese made many conversions. A number of these resulted from the desire of those discriminated against by the rigid Hindu social order to find a place in the world of their conquerors. Out-caste and low-caste Hindus thought that, by adopting the religion of their rulers, they could win new social status (and preferential treatment). It was to these castes that St Francis Xavier, the Apostle of the Indies, addressed himself. Xavier arrived in Goa, the capital of Portugal's Asian possessions, in 1542. He made many converts by equating the suffering of the poor with their ignorance of the love of the true God. His ten-year mission was carried out, quite unwittingly, in a manner which the Asian peasant readily understood. Barefoot and in ragged habit, black of beard and eye, Xavier radiated that passionate certainty of communion with the gods which is the hallmark of the holy man throughout the East. Many Portuguese felt that Xavier thus diminished the splendour of the European in Asia. 'The white people will be despised by the natives, because of him, for only if they see us splendid and magnificent conquerors will we be able to impress upon them that we are a superior race.'

The Portuguese were pleased to convert the heathen. Even at their most ruthless, they were always conscious of their crusade as long as it did not interfere with profit. They thought, however, that threats were better than example, and in 1560 the Inquisition was established in Goa. Hindus, Muslims and Christians were subject to its calculated oppression. Between 1595 and 1610, the archbishop, Menezes, moved also against the Nestorian Christians.

This was the dark side of Portuguese Christianity, symbolized by the baroque, black stone façade of the palace of the Inquisition at Goa. But there was a lighter one. The Society of Jesus, of which Xavier had been one of the founders, decided that it would be simpler to convert the *rulers* of India rather than the people. If they and the intelligentsia could be brought into the Christian fold, the rest would surely follow. For this task scholars, not mystics, were needed, diplomats rather than saints. At the court of the Mughal emperor Akbar, Portugal was usually represented by Jesuit diplomatists. The Fathers Acquaviva and Monserrate, who reached Akbar's court in 1580, tried in the time they could spare from their ordinary business to convert the emperor to Christianity. Akbar's tolerance, and the apparent consideration he gave to their sermons and discourses, tempted them to announce to Rome that his conversion was imminent but unfortunately they had failed to understand the nature of Akbar's mind. He believed that there were many ways to the same God, and that a tolerant attitude towards them all would help to stabilize the state. He was, in fact, not interested in conversion to Christianity, only in knowing more about it. Nor was he particularly impressed by what he heard.

Having failed with India's ruler, the Jesuits turned to the Hindu priestly and scholar caste, the Brahmins. Though the Portuguese had learned a good deal about *popular* Hinduism, they knew nothing about the inner core of Hindu metaphysics.

By the end of the sixteenth century, the knowledge that there existed Indian philosophical ideas of considerable depth and complexity was reasonably widespread, but these ideas were thought to be either an offshoot of Greek transcendentalism or, as one late seventeenth-century scholar decided, 'it might be . . . that in former times the Indians heard of Christianity, and that their religion is an imperfect imitation or corruption of ours'.

Acceptance of the possibility of a common root of ideas led the Jesuits, convinced that conversion from the top was the surest method of spreading Christianity, to begin an investigation into Brahminical beliefs. Their aim was, firstly, to demonstrate the inferiority of these to Christian beliefs, and then to devise a syncretism, some reconciliation between Christianity and Brahminism—just as Aquinas, in the *Summa Theologica*, employed Aristotle's logical method to establish a transition from Greek to Christian ideas. Today, scholars have access to the Sanskrit classics, which the Jesuits did not. From them, it can be seen that any attempt at a reconciliation on a dialectical level was doomed to failure. Nevertheless, an attempt *was* made, and it remains one of the most interesting efforts at compromise—and understanding —ever made between East and West.

The person selected for this enterprise was Robert de Nobili, an Italian aristocrat who had become a Jesuit. He arrived in Goa in 1605 with instructions to make his way to Madura, then the most important centre of Hindu learning. The choice of an Italian was as much a part of the Jesuit plan as the decision to send him to Madura. The Portuguese had, since 1567, been actively hostile to Hinduism in their territories. Temples had been destroyed and their revenues diverted for the upkeep of Christian churches; Brahmins were, on Sundays, forced to listen to Christian sermons. De Nobili, as an Italian, could honestly dissociate himself from the Portuguese and their deeds. This he did, and claimed he had given up all for the life of an ascetic. On his journey, he dressed as a Brahmin.

Once at Madura, de Nobili learned Tamil, one of the most difficult of Indian languages. But he found that the holy texts were available only in Sanskrit and that no one but a true Brahmin could learn that language. Nevertheless, through a Brahmin friend, he succeeded in obtaining copies of the secret texts and studied them until finally he felt that his knowledge of them permitted him to advance his syncretic system. This he did in 1609, by publishing a book in Sanskrit, exquisitely phrased and brilliant in argument. How de Nobili managed to affix Christianity —with its essential concept of the duality of man and God, and the nature of revelation—to the Brahminic vision of the non-dual nature of reality in which all things are part of the Atman, the World Soul, indivisible, unknowable, yet real, and awareness of whose existence comes through meditation when subject and object disappear . . . how de Nobili managed this is unknown today, for his book no longer exists. Yet his ideas *did* appeal, possibly to some Hindu thinkers who were moving away from belief in absolute non-duality.

De Nobili now took the next, and most dangerous step, of moving from philosophy to ritual. He built a church. For de Nobili to establish himself as a *guru*, or teacher, was all very well. The precedent was firmly established, and a place existed for such as he within the structure of society. His actions sat comfortably within the Hindu tradition. But to establish a place of worship, to indulge in alien rituals, removed him from it and placed him in opposition to the outward expression of Hindu beliefs. To argue and speculate is one thing, but to deny, by the exercise of ritual, the existence of the manifestation of the absolute—the Trinity of Brahma, Vishnu and Siva—was atheism. De Nobili was charged with just that. He survived the accusation, only to be crushed by the unwillingness of the leaders of his own church to accept the concessions he made to caste prejudices in allowing converts to wear the Brahminical cord and other forms of social identification. De Nobili realized that these were outward appearances which could readily be accepted, just as pagan festivals had been absorbed by the early church. In this belief he was confirmed in 1623 by a decree of Pope Gregory XV:

> Brahmins are kept from the confession of Christ by difficulties about the cord and the Kudumi [the tuft of long hair worn by South Indians]. Desiring to procure the conversion of these nations, after suitable discussion we accord to the Brahmins and

other Gentiles the cord and the Kudumi, sandal paste and the purification of the body. These should not be received in idol temples but only from priests after they have blessed them.

But de Nobili's victory came too late. The echoes of controversy had reached the Brahmins. The role of *guru* no longer sat comfortably on de Nobili's shoulders. The isolation of the recluse and the respect that came with it were broken. Though de Nobili continued to teach and convert, it was outside the intellectual circles of Madura that his mission was successful. The great experiment, de Nobili's dream of converting the Brahmin hierarchy, dissolved into an argument over caste-marks and cords—in themselves, important, but in no way comparable with the grand vision of the Italian Jesuit.

Before de Nobili arrived in India, the Society of Jesus had launched the boldest enterprise in the history of Christian missions in Asia. Chinese contact with the Christian world had once been extensive. Nestorian Christianity had received the protection of emperors. With the collapse of the Mongol dynasty in 1368, however, it had been suppressed. Then, in 1601, the Jesuit Matteo Ricci arrived in Peking in the garb of a Buddhist monk, and with the Chinese name of Li Ma-tou. Noticing the contempt with which the Confucian *literati* looked upon the now decadent Buddhism, he swiftly changed his robe for the customary dress of a scholar. Ricci's first object was to gain the protection of the emperor. He did this by presenting the emperor with a harpsichord, a map of the world, and two chiming clocks. His petition was clearly expressed; the wise man from the West brought with him the science of the West: 'Your humble subject,' he wrote, 'is perfectly acquainted with the celestial sphere, geography and calculations. With the aid of instruments he observes the stars, and he understands the use of the gnomon.' Ricci received an imperial pension, and was allowed to reside in the city. He attained the high honour of giving lessons in science to one of the emperor's sons. To Ricci, it seemed that Western science would open the door to Christianity. Ricci and his successors became, as far as was possible, identified with China. Ricci even produced a map of the world in which the two hemispheres centred upon China and not upon Europe. The Jesuits wore the outward appearance of mandarins, ate Chinese food, spoke Chinese competently. They also observed that Confucianism and ancestor-worship, the beliefs of the rulers, were not so much a religion as a moral code which might be reconciled with Christianity. Ricci produced several works of Christian apologetics—and a Chinese translation of Euclid's *Elements*. He also observed the fundamental importance of the calendar in Chinese life, its occult significance in the ordering of festivals which ensured the stability of the throne as well as the prosperity of the nation. The action of a Jesuit astronomer in reforming the calendar, and revolutionizing Chinese astronomy, helped to discredit the Muslim astronomers whose errors were thought to have endangered the throne.

Secure in their scientific superiority, the Jesuits believed that the time was ripe for a fusion of Christian and Confucian ethics. They drew up a plan for what was, in fact, the establishment of an autonomous Chinese church, complete with its own rites. The first ruling, of Pope Innocent X in 1645, was unfavourable, and the subsequent controversy, famous in the history of the church, continued with great bitterness until 1742, when the Bull *Ex Illa Die* wrecked the work and the hopes of the Jesuits completely. Ironically enough, nearly two hundred years too late, in December 1939, the Vatican announced that ancestor-worship and Confucian rites were not incompatible with the Catholic faith.

Until the final blow fell, the Jesuits continued their work. In the middle of the seventeenth century both the son and the empress of the Ming ruler Yung-li were baptized, the former with the name of Constantine. Unfortunately, the hope implicit in such a name was not fulfilled, as the days of the Ming were already numbered and the reign of the Manchu was beginning. The Jesuits found the new régime still anxious for their scientific expertise; but in 1665 an imperial edict was promulgated which banned Christian proselytizing. This did not, however, remove the influence of the Jesuits. The emperor, K'ang Hsi, was initially firm:

> As to the Western doctrine which exalts the Lord of Heaven, it is opposed to our traditional teaching. It is solely because its apostles have a thorough knowledge of mathematical sciences that they are employed by the state. Be careful to keep this in mind.

NEW   177

But the services to the state of two Jesuits changed K'ang Hsi's attitude. The first, Father Verbiest, cast the cannon which ensured an imperial victory over rebels in 1674. The second, Father Gerbilian, as a member of a Chinese delegation to the Russians, helped to negotiate the Treaty of Nerchinsk in 1689. In 1692, K'ang Hsi therefore issued two edicts of toleration. The first declared:

The men of the West have rectified the calculation of the calendar. In times of war they have repaired old cannon and constructed new ones. They have devoted their energies to the good of the empire and have taken much trouble to this end. Moreover, since the Catholic religion contains nothing evil or irregular, its adherents should be able to continue to practise it freely. We order that the former memorials and resolutions against the said religion be withdrawn.

The 'Rites' controversy, however, destroyed all the advantages of the reopening of China to Christianity. When, in 1715, the 'Rites' were condemned, the emperor himself supported the Jesuits; but the intervention of a heathen in theological matters only assisted the Jesuits' enemies in Europe. In 1717, the emperor, angered by the disregard paid to his explanations, forbade the preaching of Christianity. The great experiment was over.

The Jesuits in India and China had both attempted a compromise: one with the metaphysic of Brahminism, the other with the ethical system of Confucius. Both had failed despite the success of their creators. The Jesuits saw the universality of Christ's teaching in terms of adaptation and compromise. Unfortunately, they took this view at the time of Europe's expansion, when Western traders and pirates called themselves 'Christians' and claimed uniqueness for their faith. Henceforth, the missionary effort was to impose not Christianity, as such, but a Westernized version of the teachings of Christ, an expression not of the brotherhood of man but of a superior civilization.

The first Asian nation to comprehend the difference between the teachings of Christ and the aggressiveness of Western Christianity—and to act upon the knowledge—was Japan. The

Portuguese arrived there in 1542 or 1543, and Xavier, on his journey of conversion, paid it a visit in 1549. The Portuguese found Japan in political chaos. There was no central government, and the country was divided up between warring barons. One, Nobunuga (1543–82), set out to unify the country, but Buddhist sects formed a dangerous military and political threat to his ambitions. This may have accounted for Nobunuga's cordiality towards the Jesuit missionaries who followed Xavier. His successor, Hideyoshi (1535–98), also welcomed them, and conversions ran into many hundreds of thousands, including nobles and soldiers. Some of Hideyoshi's generals displayed the Cross on their banners during the Korean campaign of 1591–8. Hideyoshi was more interested in trade than religion, but it was difficult to divorce the religion of the Portuguese from the products they came to sell. He soon began to fear, however, that foreign priests might be the vanguard of a foreign invasion, and in 1597, twenty-six Christians, including six Europeans, were executed for conspiracy. Hideyoshi died in 1598 and the Christians were left in peace until his successor, Ieyasu (1542–1616), also began to sense the danger that lay in a growing Christian population and increasing numbers of foreign priests.

When Dutch and English traders arrived—and seemed quite content to do business without proselytizing—Ieyasu began to contemplate action against Christianity, especially after the discovery of what appeared to be a plot to overthrow him using foreign troops. In 1612 and the following year edicts were issued prohibiting Christianity, but they were not very strictly enforced. In 1614, a further edict ordered that all foreign priests should concentrate in the town of Nagasaki, all churches should be demolished, and all native Christians should renounce their faith. The edict accused foreign priests of 'longing to disseminate an evil law . . . so that they may change the government of the country and obtain possession of the land'. Ieyasu died in 1616, and his successors embarked on rigorous persecution. Christians were tortured to make them renounce their faith, and thousands were martyred. The government was determined to root out what it firmly believed to be a subversive faith. By the middle of the seventeenth century, it had virtually succeeded.

Unlike the Catholic Portuguese, the Dutch and the English did not carry with them any concept of a Christian world-state. Their aim was trade, not conversion. Until 1813, in fact, the English East India Company prohibited missionary activity in its territories, as it believed that Christian propaganda might well incite the people to rebellion. The British in India were anxious not to disturb the traditional pattern of Indian life in case it exploded in their faces. But by the early part of the nineteenth century, the success of the Industrial Revolution was beginning to bring about a significant change in Britain's attitude to Asia. The East had formerly been a source of luxury goods; now, it was a vast potential market for the new products of the machine. This change brought new political and moral attitudes, an entirely new concept of colonial responsibility, and a belief that the 'benefits' of a superior civilization must be made available to all. The new British middle-class saw, in the products of their looms and iron-works, the materials of a new Jerusalem. The new industrialists believed that Progress and Christianity were inseparable, and they succeeded in forcing the East India Company to open the door to Christian missionaries.

By the 1820s, a new generation of British officials and soldiers had arrived in India, inspired with evangelical fervour, looking with horror at widow-burning, infanticide and other such expressions of popular Hinduism. They forced the government to act. In the army, Christian officers often terrified their men by beseeching them to desert their faith and embrace Christianity. Unlike Christianity, Hinduism is indivisibly part of the social order. Man's place in society is carefully ordered by the mechanism of caste. If a man's caste is broken, his place in society is destroyed. More than that, he stands on the threshold of damnation—for the Hindu believes in continuing reincarnation; only after he attains the highest level of caste may his soul enter oblivion, the heaven of the Hindus. Attempts at conversion led to a number of mutinies until, in 1857, the Bengal army broke into revolt. Christians, both European and Indian, were murdered, churches destroyed. Though the Mutiny was finally suppressed, the Protestant Crusade was over. In one sense, the Indian Mutiny was a war between the gods and it was the Christian God who retired from the field.

Throughout the nineteenth century, the militant and essentially colonial nature of Western Christianity was obvious. The contempt of so many Christians for the civilization of those they hoped to convert seemed to supply an ideology for aggression. To many Asians, it appeared that the missionary was almost inevitably followed by guns and gunboats. In Indo-China in 1788, a French missionary bishop, with the aid of a French military expedition, had raised an army to place his own candidate on the throne of Annam. When, in the following century, missionaries were forced upon Asians by treaty, they appeared as part of the package of aggression. If Christians were attacked, the Western powers usually retaliated. It was hardly surprising that Asians still outside the net of Western imperialism should fear the coming of the missionaries.

In China, missionary activity had been restricted by the Chinese themselves. *Merchants* were tolerated—if only at arm's length—and confined to a ghetto at Canton, where they were allowed to set up residence during the trading season which lasted from October to March. The Chinese did not hide their dislike for foreigners and continually reminded them of their inferior status. Efforts, made primarily by the British, to put trade on a treaty basis were repulsed; any treaty between China and another country would have implied equality of status—which was quite unacceptable to the Chinese.

There were missionaries anxious and waiting to convert the heathen Chinese. They learned the Chinese language, acted as interpreters for the merchants, translated texts, and waited for the gates to be forced. This was accomplished by the British who, on 3 November 1839, began what is known as the Opium War.

Basically, the campaign was fought in order to force China to trade in opium produced by India. The root causes were, of course, more complex than this, but Britain acted to protect and support the smuggling of a deleterious drug into China in direct contravention of the laws of that country. When the treaty ending the war was signed in 1842, the terms included the opening up of China to Christian missionaries. The Chinese not unnaturally came to associate the importation of missionaries with that of opium. They wanted neither, but were compelled by defeat to accept both.

Other Western nations profited from Britain's action. The

Americans signed a treaty in 1844. The French, in 1846, were granted an edict tolerating Roman Catholicism and promising the restoration of churches confiscated during past persecutions.

Soon afterwards, Christian missionaries were penetrating into the interior of China. One of these, a Baptist, passed on the message of Christianity to a man named Hung, who thereafter proclaimed that he was 'the younger brother of Christ' and that his mission was to create the kingdom of God on earth. This kingdom he called T'ai P'ing, 'Supreme Peace', and he set about establishing it, attracting to his banner an oppressed peasantry as well as those who hated the ruling dynasty. The progress of his rebellion was startling. Hankow fell to him in 1852 and Nanking in the following year. In 1854, Tientsin and the imperial capital, Peking, were threatened by his troops. Hung saw Christianity as a universal faith, but in a particularly Chinese form, and he wedded the Chinese concept of kingship with Christian ideas. Thus he offended the Western Christians who had initially approved of him, as well as the missionaries, who reacted as the enemies of the Jesuits had done over the Jesuit attempt to reconcile Confucius and Christ. Hung's temporal successes frightened the Western powers, who preferred to deal with the weak and pliable Manchus. They supported them against Hung and in the end defeated him in a bloody civil war. The only mass movement in the history of Asia directly inspired by the teachings of Christianity received the dustiest of answers from the Christian powers of the West.

These same powers forced more treaties on the Chinese, giving themselves extraterritorial rights, and classifying their missionaries as 'protected persons'. Even Chinese converts were entitled to call on the aid of a foreign power against their own government. Some, obviously, were converted more by the visible advantages of protection than by the spiritual blessings of Christ's teaching. The missionaries and their churches—built in pseudo-Gothic style and known as Yang-tang, or 'Europe-temples'—were just as much a symbol of the West as any gunboat or flag. From merely disliking Christians and their places of worship, the Chinese came to hate them. The so-called 'Boxer' rebellion of 1899–1901 was basically anti-Christian, and its first acts were to massacre Christians and destroy their churches. Its suppression by the Western powers increased China's humiliation—and her hatred of the West.

Christian missions continued to work amongst the crumbling ruins of Chinese civilization. On the lowest levels, they did make conversions. Famine, and the relief organization of the missionaries, made it possible to buy faith for a bowl of rice. Many of the converted came to be known derisively as 'rice Christians'.

The failure of Christianity in Asia was inevitable, for its guilt was established by association. The universality of Christ's teachings was never apparent, since the religion of the foreigners was always tagged as a *foreign* religion, a symbol of alien exploitation and aggression. Such good works as the missionaries performed—and there were many—lay outside the context of proselytism. They were humanitarian acts rather than religious ones. It is unlikely that Christianity in Asia will ever recover from its association with Western imperialism. In any case, the antithesis is no longer between Christ and Muhammad, Christ and Siva, or Christ and Confucius, but between democracy and communism, the two great secular religions of our time.

The Empire of Learning

Though European Christianity lost the battle for the soul of Asia, certain other manifestations of Western civilization were to conquer the minds and direct the hands of Asians. The Portuguese arrived at a time when Asian societies were undergoing profound and mysterious changes. The great civilizations of India and China were developing a kind of creeping paralysis. Chinese maritime activity, which had seemed the precursor of a new imperialism, suddenly ceased. India's ships, after many centuries of active seaborne trade, left the seas to the Arabs. It was as if the fuel of commerce had run out and its motors lay idle and rusting. The Portuguese—and the Dutch, English and French who followed them—did not realize that the Mughal or the Chinese emperors represented stagnant societies. On the contrary, they saw them as immensely powerful, much more powerful than the Europeans, who were at first only maritime adventurers seeking no greater conquest than trading-posts and repair stations for their ships. But the Europeans brought with them new and dynamic skills such as superior navigation and knowledge of the technology of war. Gunnery and seamanship had saved da Gama's little fleet on its first probe into Asia; later, Portugal's military science was to sustain her forts and trading-centres. Its quality impressed local rulers.

A powerful indication of the limited aims of the Europeans was their willingness to deal in arms with the rulers of Asia. The arquebuses carried by the first Portuguese to arrive in Japan were much admired there, so much so that for years afterwards firearms were known as *tanageshima*, from the name of the island on which the Portuguese had landed. The Japanese soon learned to make smooth-bore muskets for themselves and the campaigns of Nobunuga gave an early demonstration of the full use of the musket's fire-power. In China, Jesuit priests became armourers. The guns cast by Father Verbiest ensured an imperial victory over rebels in 1674; his reward was an edict of toleration for

Christians. In India, Europe's superiority in the field of weapons was fully recognized, and a growing number of Europeans were employed by the Mughal emperors as well as by other Indian rulers. Not only the casting of cannon fell under the supervision of European armourers. Artillery units manned and officered by Europeans soon became an essential part of native armies.

As Britain and France manoeuvred for dominion in eighteenth-century India, native rulers learned another lesson from European military science. The French empire-builder Dupleix (1697–1763), was the first to train Indian troops in the European style. Two Englishmen, Stringer Lawrence and Robert Clive (1725–74), carried Dupleix's lead further, and discovered that small numbers of native soldiers, properly led and disciplined, could defeat the vast, disordered rabble that constituted the army of a native prince. Native rulers soon employed European military adventurers to train their men and lead their armies. In the Indian Mutiny of 1857, part of the army of the English East India Company turned against the Company not only its own military science but its marching tunes as well. The rebels moved into battle to the sound of fife and drums, or the skirl of the bagpipes.

The Japanese, though quick to adopt Western weapons, were slow to take over Western military organization. But after the opening of Japan by the American Commodore Perry in 1853 and the rapid modernization of the country, Western military and naval organization became necessary if the rulers of Japan were to succeed in their aim of preserving the country from Western imperialism. The government discovered—in the course of suppressing an armed rebellion in 1877—that soldiers conscripted from among the common people could, if properly trained and disciplined in the European fashion, defeat the *samurai*, the old warrior class which in the past had exercised a dangerous monopoly in the arts of war. From 1900 until the end of the Second World War, the Japanese armed forces were to play a decisive role in Japanese policy-making. Japanese naval forces defeated those of Tsarist Russia in 1904–5, and gave the first concrete demonstration that the West's own weapons could be used to defeat the West. Later, in 1941–2, the Japanese paid the West back in the coinage of its own conquest.

The West, of course, also gave more peaceful gifts, although in the end these, too, were to diminish and finally destroy Western rule in Asia. Their effect was more subtle than that of military science, though far less superficial. The Europeans brought not only their guns but their belief in the power of the printed word. They saw the value—at least to themselves—of expanding literacy amongst those they hoped, on one level, to convert to their religion, and, on another, to incorporate into the great edifice of their rule.

The extended use in Asia of movable type and of the printing-press was a product of missionary activity both Catholic and Protestant. The Jesuits set up a press in Japan very soon after their arrival. In China, Fathers Ricci and Ruggieri were responsible for printing two tracts and a map of the world from wood-blocks. Metal type was brought from Europe to Macao, the Portuguese enclave on the south China coast, in 1588, but it was to be left to Protestant missionaries to be the real pioneers of printing with metal type. The first fount was prepared at Macao in 1815 under the direction of the English missionary Robert Morrison, but it was only towards the middle of the nineteenth century that press, as distinct from block, printing came into vogue in China. In 1869, the Chinese government borrowed metal type from the foundry of the Presbyterian mission press in Shanghai to use for official publications. In India, too, missionaries were responsible for cutting a number of linguistic scripts in metal type. The Baptist William Carey translated the Bible and printed it in thirty-six languages, including Chinese and Burmese.

It was also missionary endeavour that first led to the introduction of Western ideas of education in Asia. In Britain, the upsurge of religious feeling which marked the early years of the nineteenth century was to have great effect on the administration of India. The evangelicals believed that the relation of God and man was entirely personal and that access to this relationship could only be achieved through His revealed word. Education, they maintained, was the key to conversion; the ability to read, a passport to Heaven. The missionaries had been prepared to translate the Bible into Indian vernaculars, but the anglicizers amongst them believed, in effect, that *English* was the language of God.

Nothing was actually done until the East India Company Charter Act of 1813, when the evangelicals managed to have a clause inserted in the charter to the effect that 'it shall be lawful for the governor-general-in-council to direct that . . . a sum of not less than one lakh [100,000] of rupees in each year shall be set apart and applied to the revival and improvement of literature and the encouragement of the learned natives of India, and for the introduction and promotion of a knowledge of the sciences among the inhabitants of the British territories in India'. The sum allocated was extremely small and no one seemed to have much idea about how it should be used. The instructions issued by the directors of the East India Company to their representatives in India were, perhaps deliberately, vague and it was 1815 before Lord Moira (later Marquess of Hastings), who was governor-general from 1813 until 1823, was able to consider what action might be taken. Hastings's opinion was that there must be improvements in the education of the masses. 'The remedy,' he said, 'is to furnish the village schoolmasters with little manuals of religious sentiments and ethic maxims conveyed in such a shape as may be attractive to the scholars, taking care that while awe and adoration of the Supreme Being are earnestly instilled, no jealousy be excited by pointing out any particular creed.' There were other equally woolly suggestions for helping institutions of higher learning. The Company ignored them all, and for some years the education allocation was not disbursed.

Though the government appeared incapable of formulating any educational policy, private individuals and organizations were anxious to establish schools. They, unlike the government, wanted to provide Western education in the English language—which, though not explicitly stated, had been the intention behind the clause in the Charter Act of 1813. In 1817, a number of Indians and British established the Calcutta School Book Society and the Hindu College. Their example was followed by others, and more schools teaching English were established, some sponsored by missionaries, others by Indians. Their motives differed. Most Indians saw English education as a passport to official appointments and as a tool of commerce. The missionaries, on the other hand, saw it as a means to conversion through which Indians 'now engaged in the degrading and polluting worship of idols shall be brought to the knowledge of the true God and Jesus Christ whom He has sent'.

There were other, perhaps more cogent, reasons for establishing Western-style educational institutions with English as the medium of instruction. One was that it made the best use of limited funds. Translations into many languages cost money, and the vernaculars were, for the most part, undeveloped, without adequate equivalents for English words and phrases. In 1835, the government finally decided to put all its funds to work to promote 'European literature and science among the natives of India'—a decision which would satisfy both God and the economy. This enterprise was far-reaching, for it opened India's door to a vast new range of Western ideas.

The British government's view—arrived at only under great pressure—of the benefits of Western education was reinforced by the attitude of educated Indians, particularly of those in Bengal, which was still—in the first decades of the nineteenth century—the epicentre of British rule and experience. Indian Bengal, in fact, represented a society in decay. The sacred Hindu texts were almost completely unknown, and contemporary vernacular literature was languishing. One of the first to react to Western ideas was Ram Mohun Roy (1772–1833), a Brahmin who, in order to read the Bible, added English, Greek and Hebrew to his repertoire of Sanskrit, Persian and Arabic. But he could not wholly accept Western beliefs; instead, in 1828, he helped to found the *Brahmo Samaj*, an organization whose aim was to purge Hinduism of idolatry and evil practices. Ram Mohun was, however, a strong supporter of English education and believed that Western liberal political ideas could be wedded to traditional Hindu practice. His impact on Bengali intellectuals was profound, and the *Brahmos* who followed him helped to awaken the Hindu conscience and prepare it for the struggle against the West by refusing to accept that Indian thought was in any way inferior. Ram Mohun also founded the first Indian newspaper.

A very different reaction can be seen in the work of Henry Derozio (1809–31) who was much influenced by Rousseau, Shelley and Byron. The movement he began despised religion and attacked superstition and orthodoxy; its main contribution was its radical belief in intellectual freedom.

Your hand is on the helm—guide on, young men,
The bark that's freighted with your country's doom.
Your glories are but budding; they shall bloom
Like fabled amaranths Elysian, when
The shore is won, even now within your ken,
And when your torch shall dissipate the gloom
That long has made your country but a tomb,
Or worse than tomb, the priest's, the tyrant's den.
Guide on, young men; your course is well begun;
Hearts that are tuned to holiest harmony
With all that e'en in thought is good, must be
Best formed for deeds like those which shall be done
By you hereafter till your guerdon's won
And that which now is hope becomes reality.

(Sonnet to the Pupils of the Hindu College)

The two strands, that of the *Brahmo Samaj* and that of Derozio, produced what has been called the 'Bengali renaissance'—a flowering of vernacular poetry and ideas, deeply influenced by Western literary forms. There were poets like Michael Datta, and novelists like Bankimchandra Chatterji, above all the towering figure of Rabindranath Tagore, who was awarded the Nobel Prize for Literature in 1913. These writers, working in English and in Bengali, were examples of the fruitful impact of the West. Others still continue their tradition today.

Elsewhere in Asia, the impact of Western attitudes was more superficial, though French rule in Indo-China produced many writers deeply influenced by French thought, who expressed themselves with considerable elegance in the French language. In Japan, its doors wide open to winds from the West, compulsory education was established in 1872, with the result that Japan is the most highly literate nation in Asia. But much of Japan's Westernization was donned, like European clothes, to prove to the world that she had become a civilized, modern state. Technology and science were warmly welcomed; they carried with them no particular ideological commitments. But Western political and social ideas were resisted. In fact, every increase in outward Westernization called into being an increased inward Japanization.

Even under the impact of the Western powers in the nineteenth century, China, like Japan, regarded the West as superior only in technology. But the Chinese attempt to reconcile traditional patterns of society with Western industrial and economic techniques failed, and at the end of the century they began a scrutiny of Western philosophy and literature for clues to the power of the West. Writers such as Lu Hsun (1881–1926) took Russian authors like Gogol, Chekhov and Gorky as their models. Translators produced elegant versions of such lesser English writers as Rider Haggard and Conan Doyle. In much the same way Asian élites assumed Western styles of behaviour, drank whisky, brandy and champagne in great quantities. It was a conscious search for explanations of the collapse of Chinese society, for the secrets of the dynamism of the West, for an identity in the terms of that Western world whose machines had conquered not only Asia but apparently the forces of Nature itself.

Everywhere in Asia Western example was being carefully observed. Whenever the West penetrated some new country, it brought with it the seeds of revolutionary change. Napoleon, when only a short distance along the road of his ambition, had taken with him to Egypt in 1798 a printing-press and Arabic type which he had plundered from the Vatican. Napoleon's campaign, though a failure, laid the foundation of French cultural influence in the Near East. Mehmed Ali (?1769–1849), who became Turkish governor of Egypt in 1805, established schools of engineering and medicine under professors from France. He sent students to study in Europe, preference being given to military and naval subjects, engineering, medicine and pharmacy, arts and crafts. Missions from France established schools there, and made French the language of the Egyptian intelligentsia. A French soldier reorganized and modernized the Egyptian army, and a French naval engineer created the Egyptian navy. Mehmed Ali's two immediate successors were anti-Western, but Ismail (reigned 1863–79) employed American officers in his military academy. Catholic and Protestant missionaries moved into Syria and the Lebanon. An American mission press was established in Beirut in 1835, and the Imprimerie Catholique by the Jesuits in 1853. An American college, now the American University, was established in Beirut in 1866. Schools, presses, newspapers and magazines all spread Western influences. Muslim reformers sought to reconcile Islam with Western science—which was not so much a new departure as an echo of the days when Islam had been the great transmitter of technology to the West. But Westernization was late in coming to the Muslim East. The twentieth century, with its system of rapid communications, increased intellectual influences. The pattern, however, was much the same as in the farther lands of Asia.

In the realm of the visual arts, European influence in Asia during the age of expansion was extensive but superficial. Asia's principal source for European styles was the engravings carried by ambassadors and missionaries, anxious to show the faces of their kings or tell the story of their Saviour. The Mughal emperor Jahangir (1605–27), a connoisseur of art, was always anxious to see and possess examples of European work. The emissaries of Britain and Holland supplied him with large numbers. The Jesuits, too, presented him—as they had his father, the emperor Akbar—with a Bible illustrated with the works of Flemish artists of the school of Quentin Matsys (1466–1530), as well as many other specimens of European sacred art. Copies were made by Mughal artists, sometimes of whole paintings, sometimes of details. Both the Court and the artists themselves became enthusiastic about European art and it became fashionable to treat European painting as an ideal for Indian artists to aim at.

Mughal painters were quick to assimilate Western pictorial science, and Western subjects were popular. Jahangir had one of his palaces at Lahore decorated with portraits of the Madonna and Christ. Details from European paintings were incorporated into Mughal work so that a typical Mughal foreground was often set against a background which had been faithfully copied from a Western engraving—the incongruity of the parts producing that quality of make-believe which is an essential part of exoticism.

Under Jahangir's successor, Shah Jahan (1627–58), panels of Florentine *pietra dura* work were imported and used in the decoration of interiors. Some of this inlay of semi-precious stones in marble may possibly have been created on the spot by Tuscan and French mosaic workers. But such technical innovations had no effect on indigenous styles, although it seems likely that the use of the nimbus or halo around the heads of the Mughal emperors, in portraits designed for propaganda purposes, was in fact copied from European religious pictures.

The vogue for European art in India was not paralleled in China. Though there were a number of painters amongst the Jesuits—the most important being Castiglione (1688–1766), who created a synthetic style welding Chinese technique to Western naturalism—they had little effect on the Chinese tradition. A number of artists admired Western perspective and shading, but they considered these as technical tricks to be treated with reserve. One Chinese who attended a Jesuit school in the Summer Palace at Peking explained the Chinese outlook on Western painting when he pointed out that: 'The Westerners take advantage of theoretical rules in their pictures, which gives them a vivid representation of depth and distance. They always add shadows to human beings, houses or objects painted on the canvas . . . shadows which end in a triangular point. Their frescoes depicting real buildings are so real that one is tempted to walk right in. Our students could use with benefit a small part of these techniques.' But, he added, the same techniques were 'totally devoid of personality . . . such works cannot be termed real painting'. Such copies of European paintings as were produced by Chinese artists were usually on porcelain or mirror-glass and were designed exclusively for export to Europe, where the mingling of the familiar and the exotic was much admired.

In Japan, under Portuguese influence, a good deal of copying and painting in semi-European style took place. Even after the expulsion of foreigners the interest in European art and European subjects persisted. At Nagasaki, a school of painters—the most important of whom was Shiba Kokan (1738–1818)—displayed considerable Dutch influence, presumably derived from prints supplied by the traders living at Deshima. But the real effect was not to come until the middle of the nineteenth century.

As the British expanded their dominion over India in the latter part of the eighteenth century, they discovered that the Indian scene was 'picturesque'. Some of the results of this discovery have been recounted in a previous chapter. But they found Indian artists were 'completely ignoramus' with 'respect to design, taste, composition, perspective, consistency and harmony'! So the artists tried to adapt themselves to the demands of their new customers. Certain conventions appeared, blue and white skies with jagged clouds, backgrounds of buildings and trees, receding foregrounds —all unmistakably European. This 'Indo–British' painting flourished at various centres until the middle of the nineteenth century, when it went into decline partly because of Victorian concepts of the superiority of Western civilization. Photography, too, soon made the painted picture-postcard unfashionable. But the early period did have some effect upon later Indian paintings; for example, water colour replaced the usual Indian medium of tempera. Perhaps the most important effect, however, was the break with traditional subject matter. From a preoccupation with aristocratic subjects, artists turned to the everyday, which was what the British wanted and which eventually became commonplace.

From the 1860s onwards, the predominant European influence on Asian painters was that of the 'School of Art'. Many banal copies of equally banal Victorian subjects were produced. Before Indian art could move on again, this dead weight had to be shrugged off. Though there are a number of interesting Indian artists today, many are still slaves to the fashionable theories of Europe and America.

The opening of Japan to the Western world naturally increased artistic interest in Western forms and techniques. Kuniyoshi (1798–1861) imitated Western prints. The illustrations in books translated from Western languages were usually imitative of Western styles. In 1881, two Italian professors of painting arrived in Tokyo and the practice of painting in oils in the Western manner soon became popular.

In China, after the revolution of 1911, the Westernization of art came into full flow and the French concession in Shanghai became a little Montmartre. But under the pressures of civil war and Japanese aggression, painting became realist and propagandist. Today, while China embraces 'socialist realism', Western art has become increasingly abstract. East and West have changed places.

The Portuguese made of Goa the most sumptuous European city in Asia. Its churches and public buildings have a baroque elegance which even today presents a peculiarly Iberian appearance. These buildings did not influence Indian rulers, except in the use of some decorative details, but in China Jesuit architects were to create for the emperor a fantastic parallel to European chinoiserie. One day in 1747, the emperor Ch'ien Lung (1735–96) came across an engraving of a fountain in the garden of a French château. Consulting the Jesuits, he had one of them construct a similar fountain. But it needed a suitable setting, and Ch'ien Lung decided to build a miniature Versailles within the grounds of the Yuan Ming Yuan, his summer palace in the western hills near Peking. Castiglione was appointed architect. At the very time when Europe was welcoming 'Chinese' landscape gardening, a set of European buildings surrounded by European formal gardens was being created in China. The buildings were mainly of white marble, ornate and rather Italian in style, with exterior horseshoe staircases, rococo ornamentation, Doric columns and Classic peristyles—a pleasure palace like that of Augustus the Strong or of Coleridge's *Kubla Khan*. They were destroyed in 1860 on the instructions of the British commander Lord Elgin, whose father, forty years before, had stolen from the Parthenon the marbles which today still bear his name.

In India, as the British settled down in their growing cities and felt less threatened by the country's native rulers, they began to build themselves churches and houses in the Palladian and Classical styles. By the end of the eighteenth century, Calcutta was known as 'the city of palaces'. The actual style of building became rather mixed, however, in the attempt to reconcile polite English architecture with concessions to the rigours of a hot climate. Lofty Classical piazzas, with their pillars rising the full height of the house, let in the sun's rays in the early afternoon, so the windows had to be filled with Venetian blinds. Then *tatties*, made of fine strips of bamboo threaded together, were fitted into the spaces between the columns. But the architectural obstinacy of the British produced some pleasant buildings, private, public and religious. The style even became fashionable with Indians. By 1823, Bishop Heber noticed that the houses of wealthy Bengalis were 'adorned with verandahs and Corinthian pillars'. At Lucknow, the capital of the Nawabs (and, later, kings) of Oudh, European fashion was particularly appreciated. Painters such as Zoffany received the rulers' patronage; palaces in a mixture of Mughal and Classical styles were erected—one, according to a surviving picture, being decorated with both Indian paintings and British sporting prints! Many of the buildings in this peculiarly Eurasian city were destroyed in the Indian Mutiny of 1857, but enough remain to show that they were as much monuments to the interchange of East and West as the pavilion at Brighton.

As the century wore on, the British became less and less interested in India. Civil servants no longer considered it their home. A decline in English sensibility condemned elegance to decay, and the norms of architecture decreed that government offices and railway stations—the principal buildings erected by the British—should resemble either Renaissance palaces or Gothic cathedrals. Palladian architecture had fitted quite happily into the landscape. Copies of Flemish *hôtels de ville* did not. Some concessions were made to India's Mughal past. A cupola, a dome or two, were often arbitrarily added. In Bombay, that Asian monument to the Victorian dream of the Middle Ages, the Municipal Building—thick with European motifs—has been extended since independence in the same style and at very considerable cost. Naturally there were other imitations. Indian princes built themselves Italianate palaces—at Gwalior, Indore and Baroda. Rich merchants erected pseudo-Gothic mansions of the true Victorian horror type and filled them with the most representative examples of Victorian 'art'. In all these buildings there was always something of the oriental, either overtly in the form of an added dome or two, or subtly in the treatment of details by Indian craftsmen unsure of their sources. The last examples of the Eurasian style, under British rule, were the principal buildings of New Delhi, designed by Sir Edwin Lutyens and Sir Herbert Baker, and completed only a short time before Indian independence.

The Westernization of Japanese architecture during the Meiji era (1868–1912) had a distinct political purpose. Most buildings in the Western style were erected or sponsored by the government to demonstrate, in Western terms, the country's growing maturity. As in China, the Western powers had forced on Japan what were known as 'unequal treaties'—designed primarily to protect Western citizens from the operation of traditional legal codes which did not appeal to their own standards of justice. The Japanese government believed that an apparently wholehearted acceptance of Westernization would help them make out a case for the revision of the treaties. Buildings—and especially public buildings—would offer visible proof of their commitment. The British built a Western-style embassy in Tokyo as early as 1862, but it was burnt down by anti-foreign rioters before it could even be occupied. The majority of Western buildings first appeared at the ports which had been opened to foreign trade. Foreign architects soon arrived, and Japanese architects and craftsmen were quick to imitate their methods. The most important of these was Shimuzu Yoshisuke, who built the first Western-style hotel for foreigners in Tokyo in 1867. Very soon, foreign experts were invited to act as special advisers on government projects for building the offices for its new Western-style administration. The first major government building was a new mint. When the railway system was begun in 1872, the stations were Western in style, built of wood but with a stone exterior. Most of the architects were foreigners and the buildings they designed usually reflected current taste in their own country. All were totally unrelated to the Japanese climate and urban scene. During the second half of the nineteenth century, the Japanese people got into the habit of working in Western-style buildings but living in Japanese-style houses. This situation still exists today, even though Tokyo, for example, has been twice rebuilt—after the fire of 1872 and the earthquake of 1923. In the 1880s, as there emerged the first generation of students who had studied under Western architects, a few members of the upper classes commissioned brick and stucco houses with glass windows and shutters, in a sort of Renaissance style. But inside, it was usually only the room set aside for receiving foreign visitors which was furnished in Western style. The remainder of the rooms conformed to Japanese tradition.

By the end of the nineteenth century the principal streets of Japanese cities had begun to take on a distinctly Western look. The buildings were Western in style, the streets were paved and lit by gas and electricity. Telegraph and telephone wires demonstrated technical sophistication. Japan presented a modern face, and the 'unequal treaties' finally went, after much negotiation, in 1899.

The impact of Western science and, later, of industrial capitalism, was to have a deep and disturbing effect on the peasant-based societies of Asia. This impact was felt at its most shattering in the second half of the nineteenth century and at the beginning of the twentieth. Earlier—before Europe's Industrial Revolution—the technology of war had been avidly adopted by many Asian rulers. But European *merchants* usually knew very little of Western science and, in any case, were there to trade not to teach. The Jesuits, however, were concerned with what was, at least in theory, an exchange of ideas. They believed that in European science they possessed a gift of incalculable value—to themselves, as well as to the Chinese for whom it was destined. Ricci and his followers had been trained in mathematics and astronomy before they left for China. They knew the latest astronomical views of Galileo, of Tycho Brahe and of Kepler, though they were forbidden by Rome to teach this new astronomy in public. The Jesuits reformed the Chinese calendar, which was of tremendous importance for regulating the agricultural seasons. But their principal contribution was probably the preparation of adequate maps of China.

After the fall of the Jesuits, China remained virtually closed to European science and technology until the Opium War of 1839–42. The Chinese made efforts to copy cannon and gunboats, but their traditional thinking was not flexible enough to encourage scientific curiosity. Westernization was mainly confined to Hong Kong and the new treaty ports until, in the 1860s, China made her attempt at modernization. Translations of Western scientific works were begun, and arsenals and technical schools were established. But modernization was considered almost exclusively as a political weapon against the West and against internal revolution. Little proper exploration of Western science was attempted until after the fall of the Chinese monarchy in 1911.

Though there was a political motive in the desire of Japan's leaders to promote Westernization, Japan's social structure, unlike China's, was amenable to change. In fact, the basic preparation for Japanese modernization had been made long before the coming of Commodore Perry and his black ships. One important factor was Japan's acceptance of the fact that useful things *could* be learned from abroad. Indeed, much of her own civilization had originally been borrowed from China. Unlike the Chinese, too, the rulers of Japan did not regard their country as the centre of the world and the sole repository of universal truth. Japan's discovery of Western science came via the Dutch at Deshima and was made by a number of intellectuals, of whom Honda Toshiaki (1774–1821) was the most important. It was these men who, between 1720 and 1798, prepared the way for the modernization of Japan which is usually associated with the coming of the Americans. During the Meiji period, many foreign scholars were invited to Japan. After 1871, a series of German doctors injected a strong German bias into Japanese medicine, while Americans dominated the field in zoology, anthropology and social studies. Education was closely modelled on Western systems.

But perhaps the most significant effect of the impact of the West on Asia is to be found in the field of economics. Industrial capitalism, with its web of factories and banks, and its problems of capital and labour, soon began to affect the outlook of Asians as well as introducing new social forces into traditional societies. In India in the second half of the nineteenth century, the development of the cotton and jute industries and of coal-mines in Bengal, and the establishment of engineering and other works, were not solely a product of foreign (that is, British) investment. Indian capitalists soon appeared and dominated the cotton and steel industries. Indian industrial magnates were to play an important role in the struggle for freedom from British rule, some of them financing nationalist activities. The British government, though it did not encourage Indian industrialists, did not discourage them either. Indians were not quick to adopt Western banking and investment techniques and the essential principle of the joint-stock company, but in the twentieth century Indian-owned finance houses expanded considerably.

In China, indigenous capitalism was slow to get under way. This was almost entirely the fault of the government and the lack of interest amongst conservative civil servants in Western science and capitalist techniques. But the great Chinese official Li Hung-chung (1823–1901) did build up an industrial empire. Li sponsored a cotton mill in 1878; by 1894, he had five in operation. But the modernizers had continually to fight against entrenched conservatism. There was no favourable response to the total appeal of Western ideas, whether in their technical form or in their social implications. As a result, the expansion of industry in China was extremely slow.

Not so in Japan. There, the government provided not only political stability but also initiative. Strategic industries—those dealing with the necessities of Western weaponry—were the first to be established. Railways followed. The government set up a Ministry of Industry in 1870, one of whose tasks was to create amongst the people a climate of opinion favourable to *industrial* expansion. In 1878 a popular children's song, known as the 'Civilization Ball Song', was composed; as the ball bounced, the children enumerated the ten most desirable Western objects— gas lamps, steam engines, horse carriages, cameras, telegrams, lightning-conductors, newspapers, schools, letter post, and the steamship. The government gave strong leadership in the process of modernization, but this would have meant little if the people themselves had not been willing to follow and respond to the new opportunities.

But whatever the depth and nature of the response, Asia's discovery of the Western empire of learning was to have far-reaching consequences, especially upon the politics of the twentieth century.

The Republic of Man

Towards the end of the nineteenth century, Asian intellectuals made one great discovery. This was that the success of the West, its domination of the forces of nature and its political domination of the world, were not as esoteric as the first shattering impact had made them seem. In Asia, the power of the ruler was assumed to stem from occult sources, and society was but a reflection of some divine order. From an Asian point of view, the European possessed magical weapons in the steamship, the railway and the electric telegraph; because he possessed these, he must logically possess superior occult power. At first, Asians believed that the European's religion might explain his superiority, but this was soon proved to be untrue. As Western education spread and the works of Western historians and political philosophers became available to Asians, intellectuals began to think that the key might lie in Western political processes. This assumption was reinforced by the West's own valuation of its political institutions and, more powerfully, by its refusal to grant them to its colonial subjects.

The example presented by the West was not, of course, confined to the processes of parliamentary democracy. Libertarian and egalitarian ideas, stemming from the French Revolution and its successors, also had considerable influence upon Asians. So too had authoritarian political philosophies.

Such discoveries were not made overnight, nor simultaneously throughout Asia. It was in British India, with its freedom of speech and of the Press, that the first appreciation of Western political ideas emerged. It was encouraged by the new principles laid down in the Charter Act of 1833 which, in theory at least, acknowledged that Indians should not be excluded from a share in the government of their country merely because they *were* Indians. There was, of course, no question of granting representative institutions, but the Act acknowledged that Indians could be employed in the higher reaches of the civil service which actually ruled India. After 1833, educated Indians began to give more and more attention to political ideas and to their expression. In 1858, the British Crown took over effective rule in India from the English East India Company. Politics soon became a popular theme, especially in Bengal. Intellectuals began to compare the British House of Commons—which at least represented a variety of interests—with the viceroy's Executive Council, which embodied only those of the British conquerors.

Moderate Indians retained their belief in the evolutionary processes of parliamentary democracy. Some professed a Gladstonian liberalism. One organization, the Indian Association, established in 1878, derived much of its inspiration from Italian political thought—from Garibaldi, Mazzini and Cavour. A life of Mazzini was even translated into Bengali. But whatever the models, all the moderates believed in equality of political rights. But there were others who rejected the revolutionary concept of equality, so alien to the structure of Hindu society which is based on the acknowledged inequality between castes. This reaction produced extremist movements, but curiously enough these were more than just an atavistic reaction to Western ideas. The history of the West had shown that the most important political unit was the nation-state and the strength of the nation lay in its sense of folk, community and history. Before the coming of European cultural historians, most Asians had known little of their own past. They were unable to observe the historical process, because they were unaware of its existence. European curiosity dug up Asia's past, its literature, its religions and its heroes, and in doing so gave to Asians a living sense of historical reality.

In India, extremists looked to the Hindu past which had been revealed to them by European scholars. Young men, partly educated in the Western manner yet finding themselves without the status they believed their education entitled them to, also saw that under the impact of the West the traditional order of Indian society was changing. Their reaction was a strange blending of Western ideas of nationalism with enthusiasm for the old religion, of Western techniques of political agitation with *revenants* from the Hindu past. Revolution was their aim, not slow progress towards the Western democratic ideal. The vocabulary of their revolution was purely Western. The precedent of the French Revolution was widely quoted. So, too, was Garibaldi.

The violent doctrines of the Hungarian revolutionary Louis Kossuth (1802–94) were eagerly received. The concept of a war of independence was taken from the United States; from Ireland, the weapon of the boycott; from Russia, the secret organization of the Nihilists.

But the ideology was strictly Hindu. The *Bhagavad-gita* became a devotional manual and its teaching was perverted to give sanction to assassination. The goddess Kali, the destroyer of demons, became the Joan of Arc of Bengali nationalists. They rearmed her with the bomb and the pistol—the classic weapons of European rebellion. This aspect of Indian nationalism had its heyday from 1905 to 1914. After the end of the First World War, the Indian National Congress—which had been founded by an Englishman in 1885—remained essentially evolutionary under the leadership of Mahatma Gandhi and Jawaharlal Nehru, accepting the steady grant of representative institutions. Its leaders sometimes *talked* revolution, but in practice they waited for the *gift* of independence —a surprising tribute to British ideals. But the European revolutionary tradition still had its appeal. The European example of rebellion against tyranny drove the Bengali nationalist Subhas Chandra Bose into alliance with the Japanese in the Second World War, in a futile endeavour to win India's independence by violent means.

The Japanese, borrowing feverishly from the West, thought that they could weld Eastern ethics to Western science. The rulers of Japan were ready to adopt anything from the West that seemed useful, but they tried to keep a Japanese body inside a Western uniform, to maintain the individuality of Japanese tradition within the garment of Western civilization. They were basically pragmatic in their approach. Utility was their criterion, and it is not surprising that English utilitarian philosophers like Jeremy Bentham and John Stuart Mill exerted great influence on Japanese intellectuals.

The Japanese were quick to realize that, as the West considered the trappings of democracy as a sign of maturity, it might prove some defence against domination by the Western powers to adopt democratic institutions. They had also learned from their examination of European history that popular revolution was a natural consequence of the denial of democracy. The Japanese government began with advantages that were not shared by those other countries in Asia which attempted to establish constitutional governments. There existed in Japan at the time of the opening of the country to Western ideas a fairly broad stratum of society that was not only well educated but politically conscious. Because of this, agitation for representative government began early, and a number of political clubs were founded in the 1870s. One, the *Risshisha*, or 'Society to Establish One's Moral Will', was named after the Japanese translation of a Victorian best-seller, Samuel Smiles's *Self Help*. The government experimented with representative institutions and, in 1881, the emperor announced that a national assembly would be constituted in 1890. Until that date, Japan was in the unique position of having three political parties— one government and two opposition—but no parliament. The constitution, when it was promulgated in 1889, turned out to be based not on Westminster but on Berlin. Ito Hirobumi (1841– 1909), one of the most influential of Meiji statesmen, had visited Germany and Austria and found the conservatism of Bismarck much to his taste. The new constitution, sponsored by Ito, followed German precedent. The cabinet, for example, was responsible not to parliament but to the emperor, and all popular rights were securely hedged by such phrases as 'within limits not prejudicial to peace and order'. The constitution satisfied minimal demands for representative government while providing maximum authority for the cabinet. In the twentieth century, this circumscribed democracy led to a search for alternatives—for some, socialism and other radical Western ideas, for others, military dictatorship.

Several non-European countries which had escaped becoming colonies of the Western empires attempted in the late nineteenth and early twentieth centuries to set up constitutional governments in imitation of the West. In the Turkish empire, Western-style reforms were first instituted by the Sultan in the strictly military field in order to create a 'modern' army. But modernization, in the second half of the nineteenth century, could not be taken piecemeal. The desire for modern (that is, Western-style) political institutions usually found expression within a short time after the acceptance of purely technical innovations. Many Turkish liberals viewed the establishment of representative institutions as a means of saving the Turkish empire from collapse in the face of rising nationalism in the provinces of the empire.

In 1879, liberal pressures did lead to the granting of a constitution, which was greeted with great enthusiasm. But the Sultan Abdul Hamid (1876–1908) suspended the constitution only one and a half months after it had been promulgated, and it remained suspended for thirty years. In the Turkish empire, Islam, with its traditional antagonism towards Christianity, inhibited the adoption of Western ideas. Many modernizers thought it would be possible to take techniques from the West while remaining loyal to Islamic ethics. It was not until after the First World War that thoroughgoing Westernization was attempted.

The rest of the Islamic world had also been cut off from Europe by the nature of its religion. It was left to Arab political exiles who had found refuge in Britain and in France before 1914 to absorb European political ideals. After 1918 and the division of the Turkish empire into spheres of European influence, political action was fundamentally anti-colonialist. This produced a growing alienation from the West and its ideals, and a widespread feeling of cultural and political disenchantment, even amongst Western-educated intellectuals.

This period coincided with the decay of the Western empires and with the rise of non-democratic political systems in Europe. In face of totalitarian fascism and Russian communism, Western liberal institutions ceased to be a talisman to Arab nationalists; they appeared to have lost their power, their magic authority and purpose. In fact, democracy had lost the glamour of success.

The Westernization of China's political system was at once more subtle and more natural than in other Asian countries. At the beginning, Chinese leaders had only accepted technical innovations from the West for the advancement of personal and political aims within the existing structure of power. Until 1894, the court remained firmly under the control of the empress dowager, Tz'u-hsi. Her forceful personality was directed towards preserving the dynasty by balancing the central power against new regional interests which had been growing in strength since the penetration of the West. Regional governors, who had achieved power while engaged in suppressing rebellions, naturally refused to give it up, and buttressed it by building arsenals and industries in their provinces. But with the defeat of China by Japan in 1895, the pressure for central reform as a political necessity grew rapidly. Even the emperor was converted. But when he issued a series of reforming—and modernizing—edicts, the empress-dowager took over the government again by a *coup d'état*. Reform from the top being apparently out of the question, progressive Chinese were forced to turn to revolution.

The father of the Chinese revolution, Sun Yat-sen (1866–1925), gave 'people's rights' an important place in his programme. But the processes of democracy were never tried in China, partly because of the continuing revolutionary situation after the monarchy was overthrown in 1911, partly because of their lack of appeal. There were, however, other Western political ideas which seemed attractive to the Chinese mind. A number of Chinese thinkers, both conservative and radical, sought from the West a modernizing philosophy. The American writer John Dewey and the Englishman Bertrand Russell both visited China in 1919–20, although neither understood the Chinese need for an all-embracing philosophy of history to replace the all-embracing, but now ineffective, philosophy of Confucianism. The outbreak of the Russian revolution in 1917, however, not only offered a new philosophy but showed that it could actually work in practice.

In one sense, it is not too far-fetched to say that China's adoption of communism—the most important single event of the twentieth century—had one of its remote sources in China's own philosophy. The explanation of this is to be found in the ideas of the German scholar G. W. F. Hegel (1770–1831). Hegel's philosophy was complex and difficult, but in his dialectical pantheism there was a direct line to the Chinese-influenced concepts of Leibniz. Hegel had considerable appeal for Japanese intellectuals, and it was probably through them that his ideas first reached China. One of the founders of the Chinese communist party, Li Ta-chao (1888–1927), was profoundly influenced by Hegel and, in particular, by his anti-individualism and belief in the existence of vast, impersonal forces shaping historical evolution. As a preparation for Marxist–Leninism, the interest of Chinese intellectuals in Hegel's ideas could not have been improved on. The historical–psychological urge of the Chinese to reduce any belief to one all-embracing formula—a formula expressed by Confucius in his statement that 'one single principle suffices to understand all'—was satisfied by the Leninist interpretation of the philosophy of history first propounded by Karl Marx (1818–83), who was himself deeply influenced by Hegel. In Marx's explanation, the implications of the forces of science were simply stated in the perspective of history. The new universal formula was that of dialectical materialism, for it took into account all the contemporary phenomena of Western imperialism and technical superiority. Its sense of authority and of destiny has struck a repeating chord in the Chinese soul. Marx, through the new and dynamic interpretation given to his philosophy by Lenin, has become the Confucius of the new China. In 1949, when the People's Republic of China was established, a new and pregnant synthesis of East and West appeared upon the stage of the world, with consequences few would care to prophesy.

Postscript

If we look into the future, is it not a heritage that we have to leave to posterity, that all different races commingle and produce a civilization that perhaps the world has not yet seen? There are difficulties and misunderstandings, but I do believe . . . 'we shall know each other better when the mists have rolled away'.

MOHANDAS KARAMCHAND GANDHI

A Common Heritage

This book has tried to reveal something of the nature of the dialogue that has been going on between East and West for some three thousand years. It is a record of the mutual refreshment of cultures, of the exchange of ideas and techniques which have produced often profound changes, both material and spiritual. It is not, unfortunately, a record of mutual understanding between East and West, for much of the story of the interchange of ideas is one of avid but ignorant acceptance. The past, indeed, had its excuses—though some of them may not be to our taste today. The modern world, the world we all live in, has none. Ignorance not only still exists; it is reinforced by those very instruments peculiar to our age which could replace it with understanding. Motion pictures, television, jet planes, and glossy art books do not automatically extend the range of the mind. In a very real sense, they more often confuse it with slick rationalizations and misleading images. The nineteenth century, in which were formed so many of the stereotypes which still dominate our view of the world, spread its shibboleths over a comparatively narrow stratum of society. Today, the area of misinformation—and the number of the misinformed—has been enormously extended. With increasing affluence in the West and a desire for at least the appearance of culture, a sort of formless dilettantism has appeared. There is a disc of an Indian *raga* on the stereophonic record-player; the latest expensive book on Chinese art lies open at its most exotic colour plate. But the art book on every coffee-table frequently clutters the mind as well as the coffee-table. Mass communications may produce an *awareness* of other cultures, but it is an awareness too flimsy to break through the iron curtain of long-established—and often unrecognized—prejudice.

Much of this prejudice is the product of the dominant role the West played in Asia throughout the nineteenth century and the first half of the twentieth. All conquerors are supported by a confident belief in their own superiority. The Europeans, as they consolidated their rule in Asia, found reason and justification for their dominance in what they saw as the superiority of European civilization. This, of course, implied criticism of indigenous Asian civilizations—as expressed, for example, in the contrast between the 'dynamic' West and the 'unchanging' East. When European rule ended in Asia and new, independent nations emerged, it might have been supposed that this contrast would assume only historical interest. Unfortunately, this has not happened. The dynamism of the West still seems to be expressed in its apparently illimitable control over the forces of nature, in its burgeoning technology, and the social structure which contains it. The immobilism of the East seems to show itself in Asia's inability to recreate itself in the 'modern'—that is, Western—image. Even the West's fear of aggression by communist China is in keeping with the past, for co-existent with the myth of the unchanging East there loomed that of the Yellow Peril, of Asiatic Hordes, and Cunning Orientals. Added together, they make what might be called the 'Fu Manchu syndrome'.

In case Westerners should feel that their superiority includes a monopoly of myths, it should be emphasized that Asians cling to many which are no less absurd. Their struggle for independence led Asians to the assumption that all their ills emerged from the intrusion of the West. In their search for traditional dignity, Asians have idealized their religions, their cultures, even in some cases their political systems. They have attacked Western 'materialism' and smugly contrasted it with Eastern 'wisdom'. In this they have had strong support from such Westerners as are in revolt against the rigidities of their own social order. But fanaticism, cultural arrogance, and individual despair are no man's monopoly. The hermit's cell and the laboratory are essentially avenues of the same escape.

Myths, hardened into almost unconscious convictions, deeply affect understanding between cultures. Nowhere is this more obviously expressed than in the West's appreciation of the superiority of its own technology and science. Science has created a new universal culture, but, though *modern* science is solely a product of Western endeavour, its foundations owed much—as this book has shown—to sources outside Europe. Before 1500, Europe's debt to Asian science and technology was almost total, yet many apparently responsible Western writers still give the impression that pure and applied science emerged spectacularly, and apparently without antecedents, from the furnace of the European Renaissance. There is a similar absolutist view of art. European painting and sculpture are in some special way *alive*—and all other art is really archaeology.

The political problems of our time, the infrastructure of racial fear which seems an essential component of contemporary anguish, perpetuates old myths as well as creating new ones. Yet we are fortunate in living at a time when the means of satisfying curiosity have never been more widely accessible. Knowledge of our world, and of all the worlds preceding it, is immense. We can, if we wish, objectively observe any particular culture in the past as part of the march of history. When we do so, it becomes clear that East and West share a common heritage, that we are divided not by race or religion or language, but only by ignorance of our interdependence.

'Modern' science and technology are neither cultural monopolies nor enemies of cultural identity. To accept them does not automatically entail acceptance of Christianity, or democracy, or Roman law, or anything else characteristically 'Western'. Technology is neutral, and because it is so it permits the creation of plural societies, the blending of international science with national cultures. Between such societies, there can only be a dialogue of equality.

The understanding of different cultures is a matter of perspective, and it is the historians, the social scientists, the art historians, and the writers on comparative religion who control its width. The parochiality and lack of imagination displayed by so many of them sustains intellectual imperialism and cultural arrogance. Yet the condition of our time, with its need for—at the very least—mutual toleration in order to ensure mutual survival, is favourable to understanding. For all its over-publicized failures, the United Nations Organization is a symbol not just of the difficulties of international understanding but of the necessity of its pursuit upon every level of human activity. A knowledge of the way in which greatly differing cultures have contributed to the common property of man can only help us on the way towards realizing that world community which, in embryo, already exists.

Bibliography

The titles given below are a selection from the most valuable used in the preparation of this book. No general histories are included, nor are any of the vast number of highly relevant—though necessarily specialized—articles from learned journals.

INTRODUCTION: *The Meeting of East and West*

ALLCHIN, B. and R. *The Birth of Indian Civilization.* London 1968; Baltimore 1969

ANDERSSON, J. G. *Children of the Yellow Earth.* London 1934

BEAZLEY, C. R. *The Dawn of Modern Geography.* 3 vols. London 1897, 1901, 1906; Gloucester, Mass.

BLACHE, P. VIDAL DE LA. *Principes de Géographie Humaine.* Paris 1948

BRAIDWOOD, R. J. *The Near East and the Foundations of Civilization.* London 1952

BREASTED, J. H. *The Conquest of Civilization.* New York 1926

CHATLEY, H. *The Origin and Diffusion of Chinese Culture.* London 1947

CHILDE, V. GORDON. *What Happened in History.* New edn. London 1964; Baltimore 1954

—— *New Light on the Most Ancient East.* London 1934; New York 1968

CREEL, H. G. *Sinism: A Study of the Evolution of the Chinese World View.* Chicago 1929

DAVIES, N. M. *Picture Writing in Ancient Egypt.* London 1959; New York 1958

DIRINGER, D. *Writing.* London 1962; New York 1962

DIXON, R. B. *The Building of Cultures.* London 1928

FURON, R. *Manuel de Préhistoire Générale.* Paris 1943; Paris Pubns 1966

213

GRANET, M. *La Civilisation chinoise*. 2nd edn. Paris 1948; Paris Pubns 1968

HOPKINS, L. C. *The Development of Chinese Writing*. London n.d.

KROEBER, A. L. *Configurations of Culture Growth*. Berkeley 1944

LAUFER, B. 'The Bird Chariot in China and Europe' in Anthropological Papers written in honour of Franz Boas, ed. LAUFER. New York 1926

LEROI-GOURAN, A. *Évolution et Techniques*. Vol. I, *L'Homme et la Matière*. Paris 1943. Vol. II, *Milieu et Techniques*. Paris 1945

MENZIES, J. M. *Oracle Records from the Waste of Yin*. Shanghai 1917

MUMFORD, L. *Technics and Civilization*. London 1934; New York

PIGGOTT, S. *Prehistoric India*. New edn. London 1962; New York 1942

ROSTOVTZEFF, M. I. *The Animal Style in South Russia and China*. Princeton 1929

—— and others. *Independence, Convergence and Borrowing, in Institutions, Thought and Art*. Cambridge, Mass. 1937

WOOLLEY, L. *Ur of the Chaldees*. London 1938

REALMS OF GOLD

From Distant Ophir

CARY, M. and WARMINGTON, E. H. *The Ancient Explorers*. New edn. London 1963; Baltimore 1963

FILLIOZAT, J. *La Doctrine classique de la médécine indienne*. Paris 1949

GRENFELL, B. P. and HUNT, A. S. *The Oxyrhynchus Papyri*. London 1903

HERZFELD, E. *Iran in the Ancient East*. Oxford 1936

HYDE, W. W. *Ancient Greek Mariners*. New York 1947

LEEMANS, W. F. *Foreign Trade in the Old Babylonian Period*. Leiden 1960; New York 1960

MCCRINDLE, J. W. *Ancient India as Described in Classical Literature*. London 1901; Chicago 1901

POWELL, J. E. *The History of Herodotus*. London 1930

RAWLINSON, H. G. *Intercourse between India and the Western World from the Earliest Times to the Fall of Rome*. 2nd edn. Cambridge 1926

SCHEFOLD, K. *Orient, Hellas und Rom in der archäologischen Forschung seit 1939*. Berne 1949

THOMPSON, J. O. *History of Ancient Geography*. Cambridge 1948

In the Shadow of Olympus

FERGUSSON, J. and BURGESS, J. *The Cave Temples of India*. London 1880

FOUCHER, A. *L'Art Gréco-Bouddhique de Gandhara*. Paris 1905–22
—— *La Vieille Route de l'Inde de Bactras à Taxila*. Paris 1940–7

GHIRSHMAN, R. *Bégram*. Cairo 1946

GROUSSET, R. *De la Grèce à la Chine*. Monaco 1948
—— *Sur les Traces du Bouddha*. Paris 1929

MCCRINDLE, J. W. *Ancient India as Described by Megasthenes . . .* Bombay 1877; Chicago
—— *Ancient India as Described by Ptolemy*. Calcutta 1885; Chicago
—— *The Invasion of India by Alexander the Great as Described by Arrian*. London 1896

MARSHALL, SIR JOHN. *Taxila*. 3 vols. Cambridge 1951; New York 1959

NARAYAN, A. K. *The Indo-Greeks*. London 1957

TARN, W. W. *Alexander the Great*. 2 vols. Cambridge 1948; Boston 1956
—— *The Greeks in Bactria and India*. Cambridge 1951; New York 1951

VALLEE POUSSIN, L. DE LA *L'Inde aux temps des Mauryas*. Paris 1930

The Silk Road and the Monsoon Wind

BERTHELOT, A. *L'Asie ancienne centrale et sud-orientale d'après Ptolémée*. Paris 1930

BOSTOCK, J. and RILEY, H. T. (trs). *The Natural History of Pliny*. London 1890

BOULNOIS, L. *The Silk Road*. London 1966; New York 1966

BREITSCHNEIDER, E. *Botanicum Sinicum: Notes on Chinese Botany from Native and Western Sources*. London 1882

COEDES, G. (trs). *Textes d'auteurs grecs et latins relatifs à l'Extrême Orient depuis le 4e siècle avant JC jusqu'au 14e après JC*. Paris 1910

FRANK, T. *An Economic History of Rome.* New York 1923

HADI HASAN. *A History of Persian Navigation.* London 1928

HERRMANN, A. *Die alten Seidenstrassen zw. China v. Syrien.* Berlin 1910

HIRTH, F. *China and the Roman Orient.* Shanghai 1939; New York 1962

HOURANI, G. F. *Arab Seafaring in the Indian Ocean in Ancient and Mediaeval Times.* Princeton 1951

HUDSON, G. F. *Europe and China.* London 1931

HUSSEY, J. M. *The Byzantine World.* London 1957; New York

HUZZAYIN, S. A. *Arabia and the Far East: Their Commercial and Cultural Relations in Graeco-Roman and Irano-Arabian Times.* Cairo 1943

LEE, H. *The Vegetable Lamb of Tartary: A Curious Fable of the Cotton Plant.* London 1887

LOUDET, S. M. *Les Rapports de l'Inde avec l'Occident d'Alexandre à l'Empire romain.* Paris 1948

MCCRINDLE, J. W. *The Commerce and Navigation of the Erythraean Sea.* Calcutta 1879

NOUGIER, L. R. and others. *Histoire universelle des explorations.* Paris 1955

POUJADE, J. *La Route des Indes et ses navires.* Paris 1946

REINAUD, J. T. *Rélations politiques et commerciales de l'Empire romain avec l'Asie orientale.* Paris 1863

SCHOFF, W. H. *Early Communication between China and the Mediterranean.* Philadelphia 1921

—— *Parthian Stations of Isadore of Cherax: an account of the overland Trade Routes between the Levant and India in the 1st century B.C.* Philadelphia 1914

—— (trs). *The Periplus of the Erythraean Sea.* New York 1912

STEIN, SIR AUREL. *Serindia.* 2 vols. Oxford 1921

WARMINGTON, E. H. *The Commerce between the Roman Empire and India.* Cambridge 1928

THE FERTILE CENTURIES

The Funeral of the World

BURKITT, F. C. *The Religion of the Manichees*. Cambridge 1925

BURY, J. B. *The Invasion of Europe by the Barbarians*. London 1928; New York 1967

CUMONT, F. *Textes et monuments figurés relatifs aux mystères de Mithras*. Paris 1896–9; New York

DODDS, E. R. *Pagan and Christian in an Age of Anxiety*. Cambridge 1965

DORESSE, J. *The Sacred Books of the Egyptian Gnostics*. London 1960

GIBBON, E. *The History of the Decline and Fall of the Roman Empire*. 1st edn. London 1776–88; New York

GRANT, M. *The Climax of Rome*. London and New York 1969; Boston 1968

LATTE, K. *Römische Religionsgeschichte*. Munich 1960

MESSINA, G. *Christianesimo, Buddhismo, Manicheismo nell'Asia antica*. Rome 1947

LUBAC, H. DE. *La Rencontre du Bouddhisme et de l'Occident*. Paris 1952

PEROWNE, S. *Caesars and Saints*. London 1962; New York, 1963

TEGGART, F. J. *Rome and China: A Study of Correlations in Historical Events*. Berkeley 1939

THOMPSON, E. A. *A History of Attila and the Huns*. Oxford 1948

TOUTAIN, J. *Cités romaines de la Tunisie*. Paris 1896

VERMASEREN, M. J. *Mithras: The Secret God*. London 1965; New York 1963

WILDEGREN, K. *Mani and Manichaeanism*. London 1965

The Triumph of the Son of God

ABERG, N. *The Occident and the Orient in the Art of the Seventh Century*. Stockholm 1945

BREASTED, J. *Oriental Forerunners of Byzantine Painting*. Chicago 1924

DEMUS, O. *Byzantine Mosaic Decoration*. London 1947

DOUGLAS, D. C. *The Norman Achievement 1050–1100*. London 1969; New York 1969

EVANS, J. *Art in Mediaeval France*. Oxford 1948
HAMILTON, J. A. *Byzantine Architecture and Decoration*. London 1956
HINKS, R. *Carolingian Art*. London 1935; New York 1962
MALE, E. *L'Art réligieux du XIIe siècle en France*. Paris 1928
MALRAUX, A. *The Metamorphosis of the Gods*. London 1954; New York 1964
MOREY, C. R. *Early Christian Art*. Princeton 1942
RICE, D. TALBOT. *The Art of Byzantium*. London 1959; New York 1963
SEZNEC, J. *The Survival of the Pagan Gods*. New York 1953
SOUTHERN, R. W. *The Making of the Middle Ages*. London 1959; New York, 1953
STRZYGOWSKI, J. *Origin of Christian Church Art*. Oxford 1923
SWARZENSKI, H. *Early Mediaeval Illumination*. London 1951
SWIFT, E. H. *The Roman Sources of Christian Art*. New York 1951
WEISBACH, W. *Religiöse Reform und mittelalterliche Kunst*. Zurich 1945
WHITE, L. *Mediaeval Technology and Social Change*. Oxford 1962

Ancient Wisdom and Foreign Riches

ARNOLD, T. W. (ed.) *The Legacy of Islam*. Oxford 1931
ATIYA, A. S. *Crusade, Commerce and Culture*. Beirut 1962
BONCAMPAGNI, B. *Della vita e delle opere di Leonardo Pisano*. Rome 1852
BROCKELMANN, C. *History of the Islamic Peoples*. New York 1947
BROWNE, E. G. *Arabian Medicine*. Cambridge 1921
BROWNE, J. W. *An Inquiry into the Life and Legend of Michael Scot*. Edinburgh 1897
CAMPBELL, D. *Arabian Medicine and its Influence on the Middle Ages*. 2 vols. London 1926
COTT, P. B. *Siculo-Arabic Ivories*. Princeton 1939
CURTIS, E. *Roger of Sicily and the Normans in Lower Italy*. New York 1912
EBERSOLT, J. *Orient et Occident: Recherches sur les influences byzantines et orientales en France pendant les Croisades*. 2 vols. Paris 1928–29
ERDMANN, K. *Der orientalische Knüpfteppich*. Tübingen 1955

EVANS, J. *Pattern*. Oxford 1931
FARCY, L. DE. *La Broderie du XIe siècle jusqu'à nos jours*. Paris 1890
FARIS, N. A. *The Arab Heritage*. Princeton 1946
FEDDEN, R. *Crusader Castles*. London 1957
FILLERY, A. *L'Art roman de Puy et les influences islamiques*. Paris 1934
HASKINS, C. H. *The Renaissance of the 12th Century*. New edn. New York 1957
HEYD, W. *Histoire du commerce du Levant au moyen-âge*. 2 vols. New edn. Amsterdam 1959
HILL, G. F. *Development of Arabic Numerals in Europe*. London 1915
HITTI, P. K. *History of the Arabs*. London 1949; New York 1963
HUSSEY, J. M. *The Byzantine World*. London 1957; New York
KARPINSKY, L. K. (trs). *Robert of Chester's Latin Translation of the Algebra of al-Khowarizmi*. New York 1915
KAYE, G. R. *Indian Mathematics*. Calcutta 1915
LATTIN, H. P. *The Letters of Gerbert with his Papal Privileges as Sylvester II*. New York 1961
LOPEZ, R. S. and RAYMOND, I. W. *Medieval Trade in the Mediterranean World*. London 1955; New York 1955
LOT, F. *L'Art militaire et les armées au moyen-âge*. Paris 1946
MASSON, G. *Frederick II Hohenstaufen*. London 1957
MAYER, L. A. *Saracenic Heraldry*. Oxford 1933
MIELI, A. *La Science arabe et son rôle dans l'évolution scientifique mondiale*. Leiden 1938
MONNERET DE VILLARD, U. *Le Pitture Musulmane al soffitto della Capella Palatina in Palermo*. Rome 1950
MURRAY, H. J. *A History of Chess*. Oxford 1913
L'Occidente e l'Islam nell'alto medioevo. Spoleto 1965
O'LEARY, DE L. *How Greek Science Passed to the Arabs*. London 1948
REY, G. *Les Croisés et son architecture militaire en Syrie*. Paris 1871
RUNCIMAN, S. *A History of the Crusades*. 3 vols. Cambridge 1954
SARTON, G. *Introduction to the History of Science*. Vol. 1. Baltimore 1927
SIGERIST, H. *A History of Medicine*. New York 1951
SMITH, D. E. and KARPINSKI, L. K. *The Hindu–Arabic Numerals*. Boston 1911
TANNAHILL, REAY. *The Fine Art of Food*. London 1968

TATON, R. *A General History of the Sciences.* Vol. 1, *Arabic and Mediaeval Science.* London 1964

THORNDIKE, L. *A History of Magic and Experimental Science.* 6 vols. New York 1923, 1934, 1941

THE AUGMENTATION OF THE INDIES

The Opening Door

BAR SAUMA. *The History of the Yaballaha III, Nestorian Patriarch, and his Vicar, Bar Sauma, Mongol Ambassador to the Frankish Courts at the end of the Thirteenth Century.* Trs. J. A. Montgomery. New York 1925

BEAZLEY, C. R. (ed.). *The Texts and Versions of John of Plano Carpini and William de Rubruquis.* London 1903

BOXER, C. R. *South China in the Sixteenth Century.* London 1953

BUDGE, SIR E. A. WALLIS (ed.). *The Monks of Kublai Khan.* London 1928

DAWSON, C. *The Mongol Mission.* London 1955

FOSTER, SIR W. *England's Quest of Eastern Trade.* London 1933; New York 1967

GAMA, VASCO DA. *A Journal of the First Voyage of Vasco da Gama 1497–1499.* Trs. and ed. E. G. RAVENSTEIN. London 1898

GROUSSET, R. *L'Empire des steppes.* Paris 1939

—— *Bilan de l'histoire.* Paris 1946

HART, H. *Sea Road to the Indies.* New York 1950

LETTS, M. *Sir John Mandeville, the Man and his Book.* London 1949

LINSCHOTEN, J. H. VAN. *The Voyage to the East Indies,* from the English translation of 1598. Eds. A. C. BURNELL and P. A. TIELE. 2 vols. London 1885

MELY, F. DE. *De Périgueux au Fleuve jaune.* Paris 1927

NEWTON, A. P. (ed.) *Travel and Travellers of the Middle Ages.* London 1926; New York 1967

ODORIC DE PORDENONE. *Les Voyages en Asie du bienheureux Frère Odoric de Pordenone.* Ed. H. CORDIER. Paris 1891

OLSCHKI, L. *Guillaume Boucher, A French Artist at the Court of the Khans.* Baltimore 1946.

—— *Marco Polo's Asia.* Berkeley 1962

—— *Marco Polo's Precursors.* Baltimore 1943

PELLIOT, P. *Les Mongoles et la Papauté.* Paris 1923

POLO, MARCO. *The Description of the World.* Ed. A. C. MOULE and P. PELLIOT. London 1938

PRAWDIN, M. *The Mongol Empire.* London 1955; New York 1967

PRESTAGE, E. *The Portuguese Pioneers.* London 1933; New York 1967

ROGERS, F. M. *The Quest for Eastern Christians: Travel and Rumor in the Age of Discovery.* Minneapolis 1962

SLESSAREV, V. *Prester John: The Letter and the Legend.* Minneapolis 1959

SYKES, SIR P. *The Quest for Cathay.* London 1936

TREVOR-ROPER, H. R. *The Rise of Christian Europe.* London 1966

VAUGHAN, D. M. *Europe and the Turk.* Liverpool 1954

WITTFOGEL, K. and FENG CHIA-SHENG *History of Chinese Society.* New York 1949

YULE, SIR H. and CORDIER, H. (eds.). *Cathay and the Way thither, being a collection of mediaeval notices of China.* 4 vols. London 1913–16; New York 1966

The Face and State of Things

ARNOLD, T. W. and GROHMANN, A. *The Islamic Book.* London 1929

BACON, FRANCIS. *Philosophical Works.* Eds. ELLIS and SPEDDING. London 1905

BENNETT, J. W. *The Rediscovery of Sir John Mandeville.* New York 1959

BERENSON, B. *A Sienese Painter of the Franciscan Legend.* London 1909

BETTEX, A. *The Discovery of the World.* London 1960; New York 1960

BUTLER, P. *The Origin of Printing in Europe.* Chicago 1940

CARTER, T. F. and GOODRICH, L. C. *The Invention of Printing in China and its Spread Westward.* New York 1955

CORDIER, H. *L'Extrême-Orient dans l'Atlas Catalane de Charles V, roi de France.* Paris 1894

DAWSON, R. (ed.). *The Legacy of China.* Oxford 1964

GEIJER, A. *Oriental Textiles in Sweden.* Copenhagen 1951

HALLBERG, I. *L'Extrême-Orient dans la littérature et la cartographie de l'occident des XIIIe, XIVe, et XVe siècles.* Gothenberg 1906

HARGRAVE, C. P. *A History of Playing-Cards.* Cambridge, Mass. 1930

HOLL, K. *The Cultural Significance of the Reformation.* New York 1959

KAMMERER, A. *La Découverte de la Chine par les Portugais au XVème siècle et la cartographie des portolans.* Leiden 1944

KENDRICK, A. F. *Italian Silk Fabrics of the fourteenth century.* London 1905–6

MOIS, R. *Introduction à la démographie des villes d'Europe du XIVe au XVIIIe siècles.* 2 vols. Gemblaux 1954–6

MUNDY, PETER *The Travels of Peter Mundy.* Ed. SIR R. TEMPLE. 2 vols. London 1919

NEEDHAM, J. *Science and Civilisation in China.* 4 vols, continuing. Cambridge 1954–

PARTINGTON, J. R. *A History of Greek Fire and Gunpowder.* Cambridge 1960

PELLEGRIN, FRANCESQUE. *La Fleur de la science de pourtraicture* (1530). Facsimile ed. G. MIDGEON. Paris 1908

POUZYNA, F. V. *La Chine, l'Italie, et les débuts de la Renaissance.* Paris 1935

ROBINSON, E. F. *Early History of Coffee Houses in England.* London 1892

SCHUCK, A. *Der Kompass.* 2 vols. Hamburg 1911–15

SINGER, C. (ed.). *History of Technology.* Vol. Oxford 1956

SOULIER, G. *Les Influences orientales dans la peinture toscane.* Paris 1924

SOWERBY, A. DE C. *Nature in Chinese Art.* New York 1940

STRZYGOWSKI, J. *Influences of Indian Art.* London 1925

TAYLOR, E. G. R. *The Haven-Finding Art.* London 1956

ZANELLI, A. *Le Schiave orientali in Firenze nei secolo 14 e 15.* Florence 1885

THE DREAM OF CATHAY

Confucius Conquers Europe

ANSON, G. *A Voyage Round the World in the Years 1740–44.* London 1748

APPLETON, W. A. *A Cycle of Cathay: The China Vogue in England during the Seventeenth and Eighteenth Centuries.* New York 1951

COUTURAT, L. *La Logique de Leibniz.* Paris 1901

FUNCKE, O. *Zum Weltsprachen Problem in England im 17 Jahrhundert.* Heidelberg 1929

LACH, D. F. *The Preface to Leibniz' Novissima Sinica.* Honolulu 1957

MARTINO, P. *L'Orient dans la littérature française au XVIIe et au XVIIIe siècle.* Paris 1906

MAVERICK, L. A. *China: A Model for Europe.* San Antonio 1946

MERKEL, F. R. *G. W. von Leibniz und die China-Mission.* Leipzig 1920

DE PAUW, C. *Recherches philosophiques sur les Egyptiens et les Chinois.* Paris 1774

PINOT, V. *La Chine et la formation de l'esprit philosophique en France (1640–1740).* Paris 1932

PRITCHARD, E. H. *Anglo–Chinese Relations during the Seventeenth and Eighteenth Centuries.* Chicago 1929

VOLTAIRE, F. M. A. DE. *L'Orphelin de la Chine,* in *Œuvres Complètes,* Vol. V. Paris 1877–85

WEBB, J. *An Historical Essay Endeavouring a Probability That the Language of the Empire of China is the Primitive Language.* London 1669

The Chinese Madness

ALLEN, B. SPRAGUE. *Tides in English Taste.* Cambridge, Mass. 1937

BEAUMONT, C. *Ballet Design Past and Present.* London 1946

BINGHAM, H. *Elihu Yale.* New York 1939

BRACKETT, O. *Thomas Chippendale.* London 1924

CAWLEY, R. R. *The Voyagers and Elizabethan Drama.* Boston 1938

CLARK, T. BLAKE. *Oriental England.* Shanghai 1939

CORDIER, H. *La Chine en France au XVIIIe siècle.* Paris 1910

DANTON, G. H. *The Culture Contacts of the United States and China.* New York 1936

EDWARDS, A. TRYSTAN. *Sir William Chambers.* London 1924

ERDBERG, E. VON. *Chinese Influences on European Garden Structures.* Cambridge, Mass. 1936

GUERIN, J. *La Chinoiserie en Europe au XVIIIe siècle.* Paris 1911

GUILMARD, D. *Les Maîtres ornemanistes.* Paris 1880

HONOUR, H. *Chinoiserie: The Vision of Cathay.* London 1961; New York 1962

JOURDAIN, M. and JENYNS, R. S. *Chinese Export Art.* London 1950; New York 1968

LASKE, F. *Der ostasiatische Einfluss auf die Baukunst des Abendlandes.* Berlin 1909

PELKE, O. *Ostasiatische Reisebilder im Kunstgewerbe des 18 Jahrhunderts.* Leipzig 1924

SCHONBERGER, A. and SOEHNER, H. *The Age of Rococo.* London 1960

SIREN, O. *China and the Gardens of Europe.* London 1950

STEEGMAN, J. *The Rule of Taste.* London 1936; New York 1936

TSCHARNER, E. H. VON. *China in der deutschen Dichtung.* Munich 1939

A Floating World

BEZOMBES, R. *L'Exoticisme dans l'art et la pensée.* Paris 1956

CHISHOLM, L. W. *Fenollosa: The Far East and American Culture.* New Haven, Conn. 1963

CHRISTY, A. E. (ed). *The Asian Legacy and American Life.* New York 1942

EISENSTEIN, S. M. *Film Form.* New York 1947

—— *Film Sense.* New York 1942

GOULD, G. M. *Concerning Lafcadio Hearn.* Philadelphia 1908

LEYMARIE, J. *Impressionism.* Lausanne n.d.

MCKINNON, R. N. and others. *Indiana Conference on Oriental-Western Literary Relations.* Chapel Hill 1955

MADSEN, S. T. *Sources of Art Nouveau.* Oslo 1956; New York 1967

MINER, E. *The Japanese Tradition in British and American Literature.* Princeton 1958

REWALD, J. *The History of Impressionism.* New York 1946

RODITI, E. *Oscar Wilde.* Norfolk, Conn. 1947

SCHWARTZ, W. L. *The Imaginative Interpretation of the Far East in Modern French Literature, 1800–1925.* Paris 1927

SCOTT, A. C. *The Kabuki Theatre of Japan.* London 1955; New York 1955

VAN GOGH, V. *The Complete Letters of Vincent van Gogh.* 3 vols. London 1963; New York 1958.

WALEY, A. *The Nō Plays of Japan.* London 1921
WALWORTH, A. *Black Ships Off Japan.* New York 1966
WAY, T. R. and DENNIS, G. R. *The Art of J. McNeill Whistler.* London 1903

THE CRESCENT AND THE LOTUS

Out of the Arabian Nights

BERGOS, J. *Antoni Gaudí, l'hombre i l'obra.* Barcelona 1958
BRION, M. *Romantic Art.* London 1961
CASTEX *Le Conte fantastique en France de Nodier à Maupassant.* Paris 1951
CERULLI, E. *Il Libro della Scala, e la Questione delle fonti arabo-spagnole della Divina Commedia.* Rome 1949
CHAPLYN, M. A. *Le Roman Mauresque en France.* Paris 1928
CHEW, S. *The Crescent and the Rose.* London 1937; New York 1965
CONANT, M. P. *The Oriental Tale in England in the 18th Century.* New York 1908
DANIEL, N. *Islam and the West.* Edinburgh 1960
DENON, D. V. *Voyage dans la Basse et la Haute Egypte pendant les campagnes du général Bonaparte.* 2 vols. Paris 1802
GROHMANN, W. *Paul Klee.* London 1968; New York 1969
HUYGHE, R. *Delacroix.* London 1963
JOURDAIN, M. *Regency Furniture.* London 1948.
LAYARD, A. H. *Discoveries in the Ruins of Nineveh and Babylon.* London 1853
REMY, A. F. J. *The Influence of India and Persia on the Poetry of Germany.* London 1901; New York 1901
RIDGEWAY, W. *Origin and Influence of the Thoroughbred Horse.* London 1905
ROUILLARD, C. D. *The Turk in French History, Thought and Literature.* Paris 1938
SCHWAB, R. *La Renaissance Orientale.* Paris 1950
—— *Vie de Galland.* Paris 1964
WILSON, W. J. E. *Turkish Baths.* London 1861

The Fatal Ring

ARBERRY, A. J. *Asiatic Jones: the life and influence of Sir William Jones.* London 1946

BELL, A. F. G. *Portuguese Literature.* Oxford 1922

BESANT, A. *Kharma Dharma, The Wisdom of the Upanishads and Esoteric Christianity.* Madras 1901

BLAVATSKY, H. P. *The Secret Doctrine.* London 1888

CHRISTY, A. K. *The Orient in American Transcendentalism.* New York 1932

DATTA, B. *Swami Vivekananda. Patriot-Prophet. A Study.* Calcutta 1954

DUBOIS, J. A. *Hindu Manners, Customs and Ceremonies.* 3rd edn. ed. H. K. Beauchamp. Oxford 1928

HART, H. H. *Luis de Camoëns and the Epic of the Lusiads.* Norman Okl. 1962

HARDIE, M. and CLAYTON, M. *The Daniells.* London 1932

IRWIN, J. *Shawls.* London 1955

JACOBS, J. *Barlaam and Josaphat.* London 1896

KEITH-FALCONER, J. G. N. *Kalilah and Dimnah: or The Fables of Bidpai; being an account of their literary history, with an English translation of the later Syriac version of the same.* Cambridge 1885

LANGE, M. *Le Comte de Gobineau.* Paris 1924

LEVECQUE, E. *Les Mythes et les légendes de l'Inde et de la Perse dans Aristophane, Platon, Aristote, Virgile, Ovide, Tite Live, Dante, Boccace, Ariote, Rabelais, Perrault et La Fontaine.* Paris 1880

MEESTER, M. E. DE. *Oriental Influences in the English Literature of the 19th Century.* Heidelberg 1915

MONTAGUE, M. ASHLEY. *Man's Most Dangerous Myth, the Fallacy of Race.* New York 1965

NEWMAN, E. *The Life of Richard Wagner.* 4 vols. London 1933–47; New York 1933–1946

POPE, E. A. *India in Portuguese Literature.* Bastora 1937

RICHARDSON, J. *Théophile Gautier and his Time.* London 1954

ROLLAND, R. *Prophets of the New India.* London 1930

SANDSTROM, S. *Le Monde imaginaire d'Odilon Redon.* New York 1955

SCHWAB, R. *Vie d'Anquetil-Duperron.* Paris 1934

SCOTT, G. *The Architecture of Humanism*. London 1947
SENCOURT, R. *India in English Literature*. London 1923
SINOR, D. *Orientalism and History*. Cambridge 1957
SITWELL, O. and BARTON, M. *Brighton*. London 1935
WILLSON, A. L. *A Mythical Image: the ideal of India in German Romanticism*. Durham, N. C. 1964

THE DISCOVERY OF THE WEST

The Kingdom of Christ

BERNARD, H. *Le Père Matthieu Ricci et la societé chinoise de son temps* (1552–1610). 2 vols. Tientsin 1937
BOXER, C. R. *The Christian Century in Japan, 1549–1650*. Berkeley 1951
BRODRICK, J. *Saint Francis Xavier, 1506–1552*. New York 1952
BROWN, L. W. *The Indian Christians of St Thomas. An account of the ancient Syrian church of Malabar*. Cambridge 1956
CHAPPAULIE, H. *Aux Origines d'une église. Rome et les missions d'Indochine au XVIIe siècle*. 2 vols. Paris 1943–7
CRONIN, V. *A Pearl to India*. London 1958
—— *The Wise Men from the West*. London 1960
DUNNE, G. H., S.J. *Generation of Giants: The Story of the Jesuits in China in the Last Days of the Ming Dynasty*. Notre Dame, Indiana 1962
FERROLI, D. *The Jesuits in Malabar*. 2 vols. Bangalore 1939–51
HAAS, H. *Geschichte des Christentums in Japan*. 2 vols. Tokyo 1902–4
HSIANG, P. S. *The Catholic Missions in China during the Middle Ages 1294–1368*. Washington, D.C. 1949
HUC, E. R. *Le Christianisme en Chine, en Tatarie, et au Thibet*. 4 vols. Paris 1857–8
MACLAGAN, E. *The Jesuits and the Great Mogul*. London 1932
MONSTERLEET, J. *L'Église du Japon des temps féodaux à nos jours*. Toulouse 1958.
ROWBOTTAM, A. H. *Missionary and Mandarin*. Berkeley 1942
SALDANHA, M. J. G. DE *História de Goa*. 2 vols. New Goa 1925–6
TACCHI-VENTURA, P., S.J. *Opera storiche de P. Matteo Ricci*. Macerata 1911

WELLESZ, E. *Akbar's Religious Thoughts reflected in Mogul Painting.* London 1952

The Empire of Learning

ABU LUGHOD, I. *The Arab Rediscovery of Europe, 1798–1870.* Princeton 1963

ARCHER, M. and W. G. *Indian Painting for the British, 1770–1880.* Oxford 1956

ARCHER, W. G. *India and Modern Art.* London 1959; New York 1959

BERNARD, H. *Matteo Ricci's Scientific Contribution to China.* Peiping 1935

CHOPRA, P. N. *Some Aspects of Society and Culture during the Mughal Age, 1527–1707.* Agra 1955

DAHLMANN, J. *Missionary Pioneers and Indian Languages.* Trichinopoly 1940

EDWARDES, M. *British India: a survey of the nature and effects of alien rule.* London 1967; New York 1969

KEENE, D. *The Japanese Discovery of Europe.* New edn. Stanford, Cal. 1969

MALOWNE, C. B. *History of the Peking Summer Palaces under the Ch'ing Dynasty.* Chicago 1934

MODY, N. A. *A Collection of Nagasaki colour-prints and paintings showing the influence of Chinese and European Art on that Art.* Kobé and London 1939

NILSSON, S. *European Architecture in India, 1750–1850.* London 1968, New York 1969

OKAMOTO YOSHITOMO. *Jūrokuseiki Nichi-o kotsushi no kenkyu* (The story of the intercourse between Japan and Europe during the 16th century). Tokyo 1944

PASKE-SMITH, M. *Western Barbarians in Japan and Formosa in Tokugawa times.* Kobé 1930

PELLIOT, P. *Les Influences européennes sur l'art Chinois au 17e et au 18e siècle.* Paris 1948

PROLKAR, A. K. *The Printing Press in India.* Bombay 1958

SANSOM, G. B. *The Western World and Japan.* London 1950; New York 1950

SCHWARTZ, B. *In Search of Wealth and Power: Yen-fu and the West.* Cambridge, Mass. 1964

The Republic of Man

AHMAD, J. M. *The Intellectual Origins of Egyptian Nationalism.* Oxford 1960

BLACKER, C. *The Japanese Enlightenment.* Cambridge 1964

EDWARDES, M. *Asia in the European Age.* London and New York 1962

FITZGERALD, C. P. *Revolution in China.* London 1952

GIBB, H. A. R. and BOWEN, H. *Islamic Society and the West.* 2 vols. Oxford 1950–7

GOKALP, Z. *Turkish Nationalism and Western Civilization.* London 1959

HOOK, S. *From Hegel to Marx.* London 1936; New York 1950, 1958

HOURANI, A. *Arabic Thought in the Liberal Age (1798–1939).* Oxford 1962

LEVENSON, J. *Confucian China and its Modern Fate.* London 1958; New York, 1968

MCCULLY, B. T. *English Education and the Origins of Indian Nationalism.* New York 1940

MAJUMDAR, B. B. *History of Political Thought in Bengal, 1821–84.* Calcutta 1934

—— *Indian Political Associations and Reform of the Legislature, 1818–1917.* Calcutta 1965

MALIK, M. *Moslem Nationalism in India and Pakistan.* Washington D.C. 1963

NITOBE, I. and others. *Western Influences in Modern Japan.* Chicago 1931

RIENCOURT, A. DE. *The Soul of China.* London 1959

SINGH, I. *Rammohun Roy.* Bombay 1961

SSU-YU TENG and FAIRBANK, J. K. *China's Response to the West.* Cambridge, Mass. 1954

WANG YU-T'ING *Chinese Intellectuals and the West, 1872–1949.* Durham, N.C. 1966

Index